SOME CORNER OF A FOREIGN FIELD

Also by Roger Williamson

IMAGES OF THE END AND CHRISTIAN THEOLOGY (*editor*)

JUST WAR IN THE GULF?

NOAH'S ARK AND THE NUCLEAR INFERNO

OVERCOMING THE INSTITUTION OF WAR (*editor*)

PROFIT WITHOUT HONOUR? Ethics and the Arms Trade (*for CCADD*)

SELLING WEAPONS: A Deadly Business, Seminar Report for Swedish Red Cross (*editor with Börje Sjöqvist and Peter Nobel*)

THE ARMS TRADE TODAY: 'Arms Transfers and Proliferation', Conference Report for World Council of Churches (*editor*)

THE END IN SIGHT? Images of the End and Threats to Human Survival (*editor*)

THE HOLY LAND IN THE MONOTHEISTIC FAITHS (*editor*)

THE ROLE OF RELIGION IN CONFLICT SITUATIONS, Consultation Report for Middle East Council of Churches (*editor*)

TRUE TO THIS EARTH: Global Challenges and Transforming Faith (*editor with Alan Race*)

Some Corner of a Foreign Field

Intervention and World Order

Edited by

Roger Williamson

for
The Council on Christian Approaches
to Defence and Disarmament (CCADD)

 First published in Great Britain 1998 by
MACMILLAN PRESS LTD
Houndmills, Basingstoke, Hampshire RG21 6XS and London
Companies and representatives throughout the world

A catalogue record for this book is available from the British Library.

ISBN 0–333–69200–4

 First published in the United States of America 1998 by
ST. MARTIN'S PRESS, INC.,
Scholarly and Reference Division,
175 Fifth Avenue, New York, N.Y. 10010

ISBN 0–333–69200–4

Library of Congress Cataloging-in-Publication Data
Some corner of a foreign field : intervention and world order / edited
by Roger Williamson.
p.   cm.
Includes bibliographical references and index.
ISBN 0–333–69200–4
1. Intervention (International law)   2. United Nations—Armed
Forces.   3. International relations.   I. Williamson, Roger, Dr.
KZ6369.S67 1998
641.5'84—dc21   97–47058
                                                                      CIP

This book is printed on paper suitable for recycling and made from fully managed and
sustained forest sources.

10   9   8   7   6   5   4   3   2   1
07   06   05   04   03   02   01   00   99   98

Printed and bound in Great Britain by
Antony Rowe Ltd, Chippenham, Wiltshire

Contents

Acknowledgements

This book is the result of a collaborative effort between many people. The project was initiated when I was working as Director of the Council for Arms Control, based at King's College, London, in 1994. This provided a framework within which earlier drafts of a number of the papers could be discussed in seminars both at King's College, London and also at the International Institute for Strategic Studies. My successor as Director of the Council for Arms Control, Ken Aldred, OBE, continued to support the project. The CCADD International Conferences also provided a testing ground for the project and some of the papers (Langan, Roper). Other authors contacted by colleagues within CCADD readily made available and updated manuscripts related to the topic. It is a matter of some regret that we were unable, in spite of efforts in that direction, to get a fully representative group of authors. Contributors from countries of the South and women are severely under-represented. It is to be hoped that others will be able to correct this balance more successfully.

I am grateful to the following for their help: Annabelle Buckley at Macmillan and Sheila Chatten for ensuring the smooth publication of the book; Sir Arthur Hockaday, David Summerhayes and Sir Hugh Beach for additional proofreading and editorial advice; Louise Williamson for encouragement, advice and proofreading; Sue McKinney and Iris Teichman for assistance with typing of manuscripts. I am grateful to my late brother Peter Williamson and my sister-in-law Mandy for providing the computer on which much of the preparatory work for this volume was done.

The production of this collection has been almost entirely a voluntary effort relying on the cooperation and goodwill of busy people, many of whom have gone a second mile by waiving fees which they could normally expect to command, working out-of-hours on their manuscripts, responding to questions about their texts and exhibiting a willingness to accept proposed changes. It has to be underlined that the authors wrote in a personal capacity and that it is very much the ethos of CCADD that no one is bound by conclusions or formulations emanating from other authors. CCADD exists to stimulate open and frank discussion on issues of defence and disarmament, not to formulate a 'party line'.

In this spirit, the following collection is offered in the awareness that it is a contribution to ongoing debate, and certainly not the last word.

Dr Roger Williamson
London, 1997

Notes on Contributors

Correlli Barnett CBE is an eminent military historian. After working in public relations from 1952 to 1963, he was historical consultant and scriptwriter for the BBC TV series *The Great War* (1963–4). From 1973 to 1985 he was a member of the Council of the Royal United Services Institute for Defence Studies. He was Keeper of the Churchill Archive (1977–95) and Defence Lecturer, Cambridge University (1980–3). He was awarded an Honorary DSc (Cranfield University, 1993). Main publications include: *The Desert Generals* (1963), *The Swordbearers: Studies in Supreme Command in the First World War* (1963), *Britain and Her Army* (1970), *The Collapse of British Power* (1972), *Marlborough* (1974), *Bonaparte* (1976), *The Audit of War* (1986), *Engage the Enemy More Closely: The Royal Navy in the Second World War* (1991), *The Lost Victory: British Dreams, British Realities, 1945–1950* (1995).

Hugh Beach* spent 40 years in the British army, seeing active service in the Second World War in France and Java. He commanded the Army Staff College from 1974 and was Master General of the Ordnance (Army Board for procurement of weapon systems) from 1977 to 1981. He was the Warden of St George's House in Windsor Castle from 1981 to 1986 and the Director of the Council for Arms Control (1986–9). He is at present chairman of the Society for Promoting Christian Knowledge (SPCK). General Sir Hugh Beach has published numerous articles, reviews, lectures and chapters in books, mainly on defence, arms control and Christian subjects.

Brian Beedham* is Associate Editor of *The Economist*, and was its Washington correspondent from 1958 to 1961 and Foreign Editor from 1964 to 1989. The subjects of his recent writings include the future of the Atlantic alliance, relations between Islam and the West and the balance of power in East Asia.

Comfort Ero* is Research Assistant for the *UN and Conflict Programme* at the United Nations Association-UK. She has written extensively on the dilemmas of humanitarian intervention and has produced the following papers on the Liberian conflict: *Ecowas and Subregional Peacekeeping in Liberia* and *Subregional Peacekeeping and Conflict Management: The Liberian Civil War* (1995). She is currently undertaking a PhD on the *Evolution of the Idea and Practice of Intervention in Sub-Saharan Africa* in the Department of International Relations at the London School of Economics.

Richard Falk is Albert G. Milbank Professor of International Law and Practice at Princeton University. He is a prolific author who has published well over 20 books including *Indefensible Weapons* (1982, with Robert Jay Lifton), *The Promise of World Order* (1987), and, more recently *Explorations at the Edge of Time: The Prospects for World Order* (1992) and *On Humane Governance: Toward a New Global Politics* (1995). The last named work was a report to the international World Order Models Project (WOMP) one of the many networks of scholars, lawyers and campaigners for international justice and peace to which Professor Falk has contributed.

David Fisher* is the Deputy Head of the Defence and Overseas Affairs Secretariat in the Cabinet Office. Prior to that he was the Under Secretary of State in the Ministry of Defence responsible for defence equipment. From 1988 to 1992 he was Defence Counsellor in the United Kingdom Delegation to NATO where he helped revise Alliance defence policies and strategy following the end of the Cold War. He contributes regularly to books and journals on defence and ethical issues and is the author of *Morality and the Bomb*, a study of the ethics of nuclear deterrence written while he was a Research Fellow of Nuffield College, Oxford. He underlines that he writes here in a personal capacity.

Richard Harries* is Bishop of Oxford and President of the Council on Christian Approaches to Defence and Disarmament. Among other offices which he holds, he is Chairman of the Church of England's Board for Social Responsibility, a member of the Board of Christian Aid and Chairman of the Council of Christians and Jews. He is also a member of the House of Lords. He chaired the Church of England's Working Party on *Peacemaking in a Nuclear Age* (1988). He has written 18 books on a range of subjects, including spirituality, and the ethics of war and peace. His books include: *Christianity and War in a Nuclear Age* (1986), *Art and the Beauty of God* (1993) and *Questioning Belief* (1995). The last named book contains a range of his essays on issues of war and peace, power and ethics.

Anthony Harvey* was formerly a Lecturer in Theology, Fellow of Wolfson College and Chaplain of The Queen's College, Oxford. In 1982, he became a Canon of Westminster, where he is now Sub-Dean. His publications include: *Companion to the New Testament* (1979), *Jesus and the Constraints of History* (Bampton Lectures, 1982) and *Strenuous Commands: The Ethic of Jesus* (1990). He was the author (with others) of a previous CCADD study on *Retaliation* (1992).

Michael Howard* served with the British Army in Italy during the Second World War. He has held successively the Chair of War Studies at King's College, London, the Chichele Chair of History of War at Oxford, the Regius Chair of Modern History at Oxford, and the Robert A. Lovett Chair of Military and Naval History at Yale. He is Life President of the International Institute for Strategic Studies and a Vice-President of CCADD. He is an international authority on Clausewitz and has written widely on warfare and restraints on war in the nineteenth and twentieth centuries. His books include: *The Franco-Prussian War* (1961), *War in European History* (1976), *War and the Liberal Conscience* (1981) and *The Causes of Wars* (1983).

John Langan, SJ[†] is the Rose Kennedy Professor of Christian Ethics at Georgetown University. From 1995 to 1997, he served as Wirtenberger Chair in Social Ethics at Loyola University, Chicago. He edited *The Nuclear Dilemma and the Just War Tradition* and participated actively in the debate over the US Catholic Bishops' pastoral letter *The Challenge of Peace*. He has written extensively on human rights, just war theory, and Catholic social teaching. He holds a PhD from the University of Michigan. He was ordained to the priesthood in 1972.

Suzanne Long* is a graduate of King's College, London and Union Theological Seminary, New York. Following a career in teaching, she became Executive Secretary (Peace and Human Rights) of the British Council of Churches. Since 1990, she has been Policy and Information Officer of the United Nations Association (UNA-UK) with particular responsibility for refugees and human rights issues. She was a peace monitor in 1993 in the Johannesburg townships and an international election observer for the South African election in 1994; she also monitored the Russian presidential election in 1995. She was a contributor to *Dimensions Universelles des Droits de l'Homme* published in conjunction with UNESCO in 1990.

Oliver O'Donovan is Regius Professor of Moral & Pastoral Theology and Canon of Christ Church, Oxford. He was educated in classics at Oxford before turning to theology, which he studied there and at Princeton University, where he was taught by the leading Protestant exponent of just war theory, Paul Ramsey. He taught in Oxford and Toronto before taking up his present post in 1982. His work, which has been devoted to recovering the classical Christian tradition of moral thought, includes books on Augustine, on artificial reproduction, and on nuclear deterrence (*Peace and Certainty*, 1988), as well as on ethical theory (*Resurrection and Moral Order*, 1986) and political theology (*The Desire of the Nations*, 1996). He has been active in ecumenical discussion, especially between the Anglican and Roman Catholic churches.

Anthony Parsons (1922–1996) served in Italy and the Middle East during the Second World War. He was awarded the Military Cross. He was Ambassador to Iran during the last five years of the Shah's reign and British Ambassador to the United Nations at the time of the Falklands War. After retirement, he served as Margaret Thatcher's special adviser on foreign affairs. Subsequently he taught and researched politics at Exeter University. His publications include *The Pride and the Fall* (1984) on the last years of the Shah's rule, *They Say the Lion* (1986) a personal memoir and *From Cold War to Hot Peace* (1995) an evaluation of armed interventions by the United Nations. He died in 1996, shortly after completing his contribution to this volume.

Barrie Paskins* has been a member of the Department of War Studies, King's College, London, since 1971. By training and inclination a philosopher, he specialises in philosophies of war, ethics of war and the literature of war. The author of numerous writings on the ethics of military affairs, he was a member of the Working Party which produced *The Church and the Bomb: Nuclear Weapons and Christian Conscience* (1982) and co-author (with M.L. Dockrill) of *The Ethics of War* (1979). His current research interests range from the foundations of ethics, through Tolstoy's philosophy of history, to the idea of the just war.

Oliver Ramsbotham* is Senior Lecturer in the Department of Peace Studies, University of Bradford and Director of Research at the Centre for Conflict Resolution. His publications include: *Choices: Nuclear and Non-Nuclear Defence Options* (1987), *Modernising NATO's Nuclear Weapons* (1989), *Beyond Deterrence: The New European Security Debate* (with Hugh Miall, 1991) and *Humanitarian Intervention in Contemporary Conflict* (with Tom Woodhouse, 1996).

John Roper† was educated at the Universities of Oxford and Chicago after military service in the Royal Navy. From 1961 to 1970, he taught economics at the University of Manchester. He was a Member of Parliament from 1970 to 1983, a shadow spokesperson on Defence from 1979 to 1981 and Chief Whip of the Social Democratic Party from 1981 to 1983. From 1983 to 1990, he was a senior member of staff at the Royal Institute of International Affairs, London and in 1990 was appointed the founding director of the Institute for Security Studies of the Western European Union in Paris. He held this post until September 1995, when he returned to the Royal Institute of International Affairs as an Associate Fellow.

Brian Wicker* has spent much of his professional life as a teacher of literature and philosophy, first in the Extramural Department of Birmingham University, later as Principal of Fircroft College of Adult Education. Soon after becoming a Catholic in the 1950s, he became active in the peace movement, joining PAX (later Pax Christi). On retirement, he took an MA in the Department of War Studies at King's College,- London. His publications include *Culture and Liturgy* (1963), *Culture and Theology* (1966), *First the Political Kingdom* (1967), *The Story-Shaped World* (1975) and *Nuclear Deterrence: What Does the Church Teach?* (1985). He is Honorary Secretary of CCADD.

Roger Williamson* studied at Oxford (BA in Philosophy, Politics & Economics 1974), Hamburg (1974–6) and Birmingham Universities (1976–80; PhD Theology in 1980). He worked for the British Council of Churches (1978–86), was Director, then Research Director with Life & Peace Institute, Uppsala, Sweden (1986–92). Following freelance work as a peace researcher (1992–4), he joined the Church of England's Board for Social Responsibility. He has edited and written numerous books and articles on peace, human rights, social ethics and ecumenical theology, including *Profit without Honour: Ethics and the Arms Trade* (1992) for CCADD. He is actively involved in committees of the Conference of European Churches and the World Council of Churches.

Dedication and Introductory Essay

Richard Harries, Bishop of Oxford and President of CCADD, introduces the volume with a **personal dedication in memory of Sydney D. Bailey**, the Quaker expert on the United Nations.

Professor Sir Michael Howard, one of the Vice-Presidents of CCADD, provides an **Introduction** to the theme, highlighting key issues.

Sydney D. Bailey (1916–1995): In Memoriam

Richard Harries

Sydney Bailey, the great Quaker expert on the United Nations, was a central figure in the life of the Council on Christian Approaches to Defence and Disarmament (CCADD) from its beginning in 1963. I got to know Sydney best as a member of a working party under his chairmanship which eventually produced *Human Rights and Responsibilities in Britain and Ireland: A Christian Perspective* (published by Macmillan in 1988). This working party was set up at the highest level, politically and ecumenically (including within its membership Mary Robinson, who subsequently became President of the Irish Republic). The project was, in fact, very much Sydney's initiative and he worked behind the scenes to bring the group into existence. It was his conviction that, whatever the political outcome in Northern Ireland, there were certain fundamental rights and obligations that needed to be recognised by all parties, and that spelling these out in advance could help ease the way towards a political solution. It was a typical expression of Sydney's practical, constructive approach to apparently insoluble political dilemmas.

It would also be right, at the outset of this book dedicated to Sydney, to pay tribute to Brenda his wife, without whom he would hardly have been able to operate. Sydney was partially paralysed as a result of illness contracted during his Quaker ambulance service in China in the Second World War and as we met in Dublin, Belfast or London there was always Brenda standing by with a wheelchair and helping hand.

Mention of China enables me to share one incident in Sydney's life which remains vividly with me. At our meetings it was customary to celebrate Holy Communion together informally in a room and all, including Roman Catholics, were glad to partake. After one such service Sydney told me that, when in China, he had come across a dying Chinese. The man turned out to be a Christian and he asked for a priest from whom he could receive the sacrament. There was no priest available and, indeed, no bread or wine. So Sydney read the institution narrative from the Gospels and gave the man Holy Communion with the only elements available, rice and water. 'Was I wrong, Richard?' he asked. 'Of course not', I replied. It was a wonderful expression of the Quaker sacramental view of life.

In our attitudes to the use of armed force, Sydney and I were polar opposites. He was a Quaker, I am a Niebuhrian. I believed that during the Cold War a nuclear stalemate was the safest of the options available. He could not, of course, countenance this from a moral point of view. But although we were so different in our approaches, Sydney was always good to talk with because he was less concerned about ideological stances than with how, in the real world, things could be moved forward in the direction of peace and justice. He was also refreshingly undogmatic and honest, being willing to concede weaknesses in a pacifist or nuclear pacifist approach, when he recognised them. Then, of course, he knew so much more than most of us about the details of peacemaking and peacekeeping. For all these reasons and others it was indeed fitting that Lord Runcie, when Archbishop of Canterbury, should have awarded Sydney a Lambeth doctorate.

According to his own account, Sydney was converted to pacifism by a senior Anglican figure who preached at his school – expounding Jesus' injunction to 'render to Caesar the things that are Caesar's' as a mandate to defend and extend the British Empire. Even at the age of 14, Sydney's analytical mind was sufficiently developed to distinguish between the 'defending' for which he could see the arguments and the 'extending' which he rejected. Thereafter he was the only boy in his school not in the Officers' Training Corps.

For Sydney Bailey pacifism was not an excuse for lazy thinking or posturing from the 'moral high ground'. If anything, it led him to be more exacting and determined to engage with the views of others of different persuasions. His concern was not to disapprove, but to improve the response to complex moral challenges through rigorous discussion with a wide range of diplomats, civil servants, ethicists and policymakers.

Even in the last months of his 79-year life, book after book emerged as he distilled his experience for coming generations. This last fruitful period is an immense testimony both to his wisdom and to the disciplined use of the limited time when he was not prevented by pain from writing. The results were *Peace is a Process* (1993), *The UN Security Council and Human Rights* (1994), and updated versions of *The United Nations: A Concise Political Guide* (1995) and

Procedures of the UN Security Council (1997) – both revised in cooperation with Sam Daws. It is hard to choose individual works from Sydney's writings for particular mention, but *Four Arab–Israeli Wars and the Peace Process* and his two-volume epic *How Wars End* stand out as exceptional.

With his longstanding interest in the debate on the ethics of nuclear deterrence, to which a working group of CCADD has made its own diverse contributions (cf. G. Goodwin ed., *Ethics and Nuclear Deterrence*, Croom Helm, London and Canberra 1983), Sydney was a member of the Anglican Working Party which produced *The Church and the Bomb* (published 1982). I had the privilege of chairing the subsequent working party which produced *Peacemaking in a Nuclear Age* (1988). The churches at official level have not yet engaged in a significant reconsideration of security policy in the post-Cold War era. Sydney's voice in such a re-evaluation will be sorely missed, but his indirect influence through those who have discussed with him and learned from him will continue.

Sydney Bailey took a keen interest in this project on 'The Ethics of Intervention', which emerged from cooperation between CCADD and the Council for Arms Control, based at the Centre for Defence Studies at King's College. He spoke actively in favour of the project at a CCADD annual general meeting. In dedicating this volume to his memory, we are conscious that the debate on the issues is the poorer because Sydney is not able to join in the continuing discussions about the proper role of the United Nations, the responsibilities and possibilities of armed forces, non-governmental organisations (NGOs) and churches in this complex field.

CCADD has instituted a memorial fund in honour of Sydney Bailey. It is a measure of the high regard in which Sydney was held in the Middle East that His Royal Highness Crown Prince El Hassan Bin Talal of the Hashemite Kingdom of Jordan readily agreed to give the first 'Sydney Bailey Memorial Lecture' in Westminster Abbey on 10 March 1997. The fund is intended to provide for an annual lecture and to make Sydney's books available to suitable research institutions and scholars.

Finally, it is also necessary to note with sadness the passing of Sir Anthony Parsons, a contributor to this volume. The essay published here is one of the last published works by Sir Anthony. It continues the analysis provided in his book *From Cold War to Hot Peace: UN Interventions 1947–1995*. It is rare to have the opportunity to pay tribute to a Quaker pacifist and an official British representative to the United Nations in the same short piece. In this case the concern for an effective UN, desire for a just peace in the Middle East and a deep study of the prerequisites of international order is inextricably linked with the lives of both.

BIBLIOGRAPHY

Bailey, S.D., *Four Arab–Israeli Wars and the Peace Process*, Basingstoke and London: Macmillan, 1990 (1st edn 1982).

Bailey, S.D., *How Wars End: The United Nations and the Termination of Armed Conflict 1946–64*, Oxford: Clarendon Press (2 Vols), 1982.

Bailey, S.D., *Human Rights and Responsibilities in Britain and Ireland: A Christian Perspective*, Basingstoke and London: Macmillan, 1988.

Bailey, S.D., *Peace is a Process: Swarthmore Lectures 1993*, London: Quaker Home Service, 1993.

Bailey, S.D., *Procedures of the UN Security Council*, Basingstoke and London: Macmillan, 1997.

Bailey, S.D. and Daws, S., *The United Nations: A Concise Political Guide*, Basingstoke and London: Macmillan; Langham MD: Barnes and Noble, 1995.

Bailey, S.D., *The UN Security Council and Human Rights*, London and Basingstoke: Macmillan; New York: St Martin's Press, 1994.

Church of England, *The Church and the Bomb: Nuclear Weapons and Christian Conscience: The Report of Working Party under the Chairmanship of the Bishop of Salisbury*, London: Hodder and Stoughton; London: CIO Publishing, 1982.

Church of England, *Peacemaking in a Nuclear Age: A Report of a Working Party of the Board for Social Responsibility of the General Synod of the Church of England*, London: Church House Publishing, 1988.

Goodwin G., (ed.), *Ethics and Nuclear Deterrence*, London and Canberra: Croom Helm, 1983.

Parsons, A., *From Cold War to Hot Peace: UN Interventions 1947–1995*, London: Penguin, 1995.

Introduction
Michael Howard

In his contribution to this volume Brian Beedham asserts that 'wars of intervention' will 'probably [be] the most common sort of war in the next 20 or 30 years'. Whether we believe this prophecy or not, such wars are certainly likely to be far from unusual, and all governments and armed forces in the Western World are working out doctrines and methods for dealing with them. No longer is the question of intervention in the affairs of troubled states to be determined by 'Cold War' criteria ('They are intervening, therefore we must; if we don't, they will'). So what excuse do we now have for interfering in the affairs of other peoples, and thereby placing the lives of our own forces at risk?

There is nothing new about wars of intervention. During the era of European imperial expansion intervention by colonial powers in indigenous quarrels, with or without the consent of the participants, was a normal means for acquiring influence and ultimately establishing hegemony. It is still often seen as such, rightly or wrongly, by those in whose affairs more powerful states take it upon themselves to intervene. However well meant, intervention, or at least military intervention, is exercised only by the strong against the weak. In the history of Europe those states too weak to prevent it – Poland, Venice, to say nothing of dozens of German and Italian principalities – simply did not survive. Those that did established between themselves written, or more often unwritten, agreements on the basis of *cujus regio, ejus religio*. The rights of state-sovereignty were established at the Peace of Westphalia and confirmed in the Charter of the United Nations. As Barrie Paskins puts it in Chapter 8, 'We all [still] tend to believe that Westphalia was a positive achievement and that it is desirable for each state to have a recognised sphere of internal affairs in which other states are required not to interfere'. The advent of democratic self-government in all its forms during the nineteenth and twentieth centuries has powerfully reinforced these taboos.

Nonetheless, although the old dynastic and religious wars of intervention that had wracked Europe from the fifteenth to the seventeenth centuries gradually died out, wars of secular ideology were to take their place. Revolutionary France intervened in the affairs of its neighbours to uphold the Rights of Man. The Holy Alliance intervened 30 years later to suppress them. Shortly afterwards powerful pressure groups were urging the British government to intervene on behalf of self-determination in Greece (which it did) and in Italy (which it did not). History was to repeat itself, in the 1930s, in the Spanish Civil War. But it was the conflicts, both of religion and of self-determination, that raged in the Balkan peninsula throughout the nineteenth century that were to be of greatest significance for the future. First, the ferocity of Turkish repression evoked a demand from 'public opinion', at least in Britain, for intervention on purely humanitarian grounds; and secondly the Powers of Europe were for nearly half a century to act in concert to deal with the issue, cooperating in what we would now call 'peacemaking' and if necessary 'peace enforcement'. In doing so they laid the foundations for comparable activity by first the League of Nations and ultimately the United Nations, and created the framework, however vestigial and geographically limited, for what we now term 'the international community'.

There was another aspect of Great Power intervention in the Balkans that was to be of relevance to our own times. It was possible only because the Ottoman Empire was too weak, either to preserve order within its European territories, or to prevent its stronger neighbours from intervening to do so. When it committed far worse atrocities against its Armenian subjects in distant Anatolia, 'the international community' was properly shocked but could do nothing to prevent it. Intervention becomes an issue, not when governments are persecuting their subjects, but when the government in question is so weak, or so divided, or so impotent, that intervention becomes not simply desirable but feasible. Some contributors to this volume ask whether Hitler's persecution of the Jews in the 1930s, or, more to the point, whether the Holocaust if begun five years sooner, should have provoked military intervention. The answer, alas, has to be no. Whatever other sanctions the rest of the world might have imposed on Germany to satisfy their consciences, it is virtually inconceivable that any other nation would have declared war on the most powerful state in Europe to prevent it from maltreating its own subjects.

It has been the rapid dissolution of political power at the end of the twentieth century that has once again brought us up against the problems faced by our Victorian forebears. The dissolution of colonial power in Africa and of Soviet power in Eastern Europe (or, in the former Yugoslavia, the discipline imposed by resistance to Soviet power) has destroyed the authorities who effectively 'kept order'; and if they sometimes did so by horrendous means, they were sufficiently powerful to make external intervention out of the question. The traditional dichotomy defined by Anthony Harvey in Chapter 4, between concern for justice and respect for 'properly constituted authority', was always there; but whereas the 'proper constitution' of that authority was a matter of opinion, its strength was a matter of fact, and rendered any question of intervention to protect 'human rights' purely academic. But what happens when that authority disintegrates to the point of being brutal internally but weak externally, like post-Gulf War Iraq; or cannot prevent mutual massacres among its subjects, as in the former Yugoslavia or Rwanda and Burundi? Or dissolves into mere anarchy, as in Liberia, Somalia, and probably Sierra Leone? And when the consequent plight of the indigenous populations is displayed nightly on the television screens of the rest of the world? The capacity for intervention is no longer in question, but is there a right? Above all, is there a duty?

The contributions to this volume provide an entire spectrum of responses. At one extreme we have that of Correlli Barnett. In his view there is no such thing as an 'international community' or a 'world order'; only a 'world arena for rivalry between myriad human groups'. In this arena the responsibility of governments is simply to protect the 'vital interests' of the groups that they represent. The record shows that intervention has often been counter-productive and only prolonged the agony; so do not, Dr Barnett advises his audience, 'commit a single soldier, aircraft or warship anywhere except to protect your own truly vital interests'.

For Brian Wicker, on the other hand, there does exist a true world community, with global responsibility for the preservation of a just order. The violence that has erupted in Bosnia or Rwanda and Burundi, he considers, should be seen as 'acts of public disorder, or affrays on a massive scale'. The world community must therefore create a world police force under the United Nations to deal with them; not only restoring order, but bringing the perpetrators to justice. He proposes a UN Police Staff Committee, under a more truly representative Security Council, and the creation of a global police structure and culture: 'a massive task', he comments, as well he may.

Few of the other contributors go to quite such lengths. Most of them accept the United Nations as the proper authority at least to legitimise intervention, although the late Sir Anthony Parsons points out, from his own vast experience, the problems that this involves. 'Security Council authorisation, yes' is his succinct conclusion: 'Security Council command and control, no'. Barrie Paskins is even more cautious in his recommendations: 'if force is to be used ... against the perpetrators of crimes against humanity' he asserts, 'then the possibility of action by individual states or coalitions of states needs to be recognised as not subject to veto by any member of the Security Council or General Assembly who happens to find the action impolitic'. For sovereign states he claims, *pace* Correlli Barnett, exist for the common good, and not just that of their own members. 'If people are being killed or otherwise tormented by their proper protector then the universal political order is being violated, and every state needs to consider how to respond.'

Such response, of course, need not necessarily be military. There is an entire spectrum of intervention, from quiet diplomatic hints to area-bombing by B52s; a spectrum outlined by David Fisher and, in greater detail, by Oliver O'Donovan. The latter, however, makes the excellent point that it is not only acts of force that constitute 'war'. War he sees as an entirely legitimate activity, 'an act of judgement, serving the need of the international community for just order'. But economic sanctions, he points out, are also acts of war, since they 'strike directly at the ordinary, life-sustaining functions of the community', and may thus be even more inhumane than the use of force. The same view is expressed by Hugh Beach and David Fisher, both of whom take issue with the accepted 'just war' teaching that the use of force should always be a last resort. The rapid and timely use of force, they suggest, might resolve problems far more economically and humanely than the gradual application of more 'humane' means that only allowed disorder to fester and grow worse.

Most of our contributors agree that the appropriate criteria for 'just intervention' are those for 'just war'; legitimate authority, just cause, right intent, probability of success, proportionality, non-combatant immunity and (for some) last resort. There is also something of a consensus, summed up by Comfort Ero and Suzanne Long, that the traditional rights of sovereignty have been overridden by the Genocide Convention of 1948, and that the United

Nations provided a precedent, taking it well beyond its accepted role of peacemaking and even peace enforcement, by Security Council Resolution 688 of April 1991 authorising intervention in Iraq to protect the Kurdish minorities against Saddam Hussein. This opened the door for the UN, as Anthony Parsons points out, to 'a zone previously alien to it...namely intervention in civil wars, and the reconstruction of collapsed states'. So the right of intervention is now recognised in international law. The capacity, at least for the present, is hardly in doubt. Is there a duty? Even more important, is there a will?

It is here that the scepticism voiced by Correlli Barnett becomes significant. The states with the greatest capacity to intervene in the affairs of their neighbours, and most likely to be influenced by considerations of humanity and justice, are for the most part democracies, and however urgent the perception of 'duty' may be among their educated elites, the will to intervene must be that of their electorates. Those electorates may be moved by the terrible scenes shown nightly on their television screens – moved perhaps to subscribe generously to non-government organisations involved in famine relief – but they are not necessarily prepared to sacrifice the lives of their own countrymen in restoring justice and order in 'far away countries of which they know nothing' – and about which, as Brian Beedham points out in his essay on the media (Chapter 19), it is increasingly unlikely that they will know anything. In an unpublished piece on intervention and Bosnia, contributor John Langan very properly reminds those preachers and publicists who are foremost in urging intervention that: 'It is very important for those who live by the word...to bear in mind the reluctance of the majority to prefer principles and theory to persons and present needs'. Television can show not only starving children but humiliated or massacred European and American soldiers. Within five years, experience in Bosnia and Somalia has moved a public opinion that enthusiastically supported intervention in the Gulf in 1991 a long way towards Barnett's end of the spectrum.

Just how far can be seen by the conditions for intervention laid down by President Clinton's *Presidential Directive* of 1994 and the British government's *Statement on the Defence Estimates* of 1995, both of which emphasised the criteria of the national interest and the safety of their national forces as prime criteria for intervention. These criteria are not incompatible with those for a 'just war', not least that which demands 'probability of success'. But concern for the lives of one's own troops – the 'body-bag factor' that bulks so large, particularly in American calculations – does not come cost-free. In the article referred to, John Langan quite properly observes, 'While a low casualty rate is a very welcome result, . . . to build this outcome into the notion of success is to opt for a form of morality on the cheap'. It makes it particularly difficult to observe also the requirements of discrimination and proportionality. Often, as the Gulf War showed, one's own troops can best be protected by a ruthless lack of concern for the lives of their opponents.

The most difficult problems that now confront us are thus not so much ethical or even military as political. Even if we accept that there is a duty to intervene, how do we, in democracies, generate a will to do so? 'This', as Ero and Long remind us, 'is the most crucial and complex issue confronting the UN. If it cannot devise ways in which to influence domestic policy, then the prognosis is not very good for the future of UN humanitarian operations'. For humanitarian operations increasingly involve assuming political responsibilities in the region concerned; political responsibilities usually require the backing of military force; and military force, however discriminatingly used, means ordering one's forces to kill and risk being killed. Wars of intervention, however just, are still wars.

The international community is slowly learning, by trial and error, what to do and what not to do; but it is hardly surprising if governments now tend to approach the problem in the state of mind described by Stanley Hoffmann, as quoted by Ero and Long: 'There is little good that we can do, and some good we try to do produces more harm than good – so let us above all not do harm, even if it means caring less about doing good'. Responsible officials are as impatient with the well-meaning cry, 'Something must be done' as humanitarians are with officials who seem reluctant to do anything. It is a dilemma recognised by all the contributors to this volume, and that alone should make their work command attention, from officials and non-officials alike.

Part I
Intervention – The New Face of War?

Following the introductory overview by Michael Howard, the theme *'State Sovereignty, Human Rights and Intervention'* is addressed by *Roger Williamson*, who poses a central dilemma relating to the state in different circumstances as protector of, or threat to, human rights.

In *'Some Corner of a Foreign Field'* *David Fisher* applies the just war theory to the issue of the right or even duty of states to intervene in the internal affairs of other states.

The conundrum posed by *Brian Wicker* *'When Is a War Not a War?'* explores the distinction between war and police action, which he develops further in his later contribution (Chapter 9).

1 State Sovereignty, Human Rights and Intervention[1]

Roger Williamson

We live in a world of nation states in which there are efforts to create an international community. There are peoples without a state for whom the achieving of full statehood would be a great advance, including the Palestinians, the Kurds, and the people of East Timor – as we were reminded by the award of the Nobel Peace Prize to Catholic Bishop Belo in December 1996 (CIIR, 1996; Linden, 1996). For such peoples, the existence of their own nation state would perhaps be the single most effective step in the protection of their people – as, for example, the achieving of liberation was for the people of Namibia who had previously suffered under occupation by South Africa. There are others who see the possibility and danger of war as the strongest argument against the system of nation states, since nation states can and do resort to war. The critics of the system of nation states feel that it is a system built upon the permanent possibility of war. They therefore think that this system must be transcended. In both cases the question of the ethical responsibility of the 'international community' is raised; or if that is too exalted a phrase, there is an insistence that the question of the responsibilities of other nation states or concerned groups of people is addressed. It is important to understand that the nation state itself, depending on the specific circumstances, may be a good *defender* of human rights (as one might argue in the case of Namibia) or a serious, even the main, *threat* to human rights, as, for example in the case of Hitler's Germany, Stalin's Soviet Union, or, in the history of the last few decades, Pol Pot's Kampuchea, some of the military dictatorships of Central and Latin America in the 1970s and 1980s, or the government of Sudan today for the Southern Sudanese. In such cases, the state becomes exactly what St Paul said it was not – a 'terror to good behaviour' (cf. Romans 13:3).

Even in the particular case of military intervention in sovereign states by the UN, there is still a multitude of questions to be addressed as the studies in this volume show. The immediate post-Cold

War expectations directed towards the UN seem, in retrospect, to have been excessive. The enthusiasm for peacekeeping has now been curbed by greater realism. Rather than seeing the UN as the avant-garde or architect of a New World Order – a phrase invoked to help in the justification of the Gulf War – it is more realistic to see the UN as 'an insurance policy and a fire-brigade' (Brian Urquhart in Steele, 1996:5). Even if this more sober role is considered, the questions still remain. What kind of intervention? What is the UN? Who does the intervening if the UN intervenes? Will the intervention be in the name of the UN and sanctioned by the UN, or actually under UN military command? Will such interventions in the future be peace enforcement (use of force without the consent of one or more of the conflict parties) or a reversion to traditional peacekeeping, between the fronts?[2]

The moral authority of the nation state is clearly related to ethical questions about the legitimate means of self-defence, the limits to obedience to the state, and the dangers both of arms in a world marred by evil and of evil in a world full of arms. Key concepts in the discussion are sovereignty and the state's monopoly of legitimate use of armed force or violence. In addition, since the breakdown of medieval attempts to control the state by moral (Church or Papal) authority – an attempt which has interesting echoes in efforts to provide an Islamic framework for the ethics of international affairs – the more recent movement has been to emphasise human rights and international law. The person must be defended against the state and an attempt must be made to introduce some element of restriction on naked power as the means of determining what happens in relations between powerful and less powerful states. Both movements can be characterised as serious efforts to limit the extent to which 'might is right'.

THE STATE[3]

Issues related to the legitimacy of nation states, how this legitimacy is lost and what external actors then can and should do, are clearly important. What is a state? The Inter-American Convention on Rights and Duties of States, 1933, succinctly defines:

> Art.1. The state as a person of International Law should possess the following qualifications: (a) a permanent population; (b) a

defined territory; (c) government; and (d) capacity to enter into relations with other States.

(Osmanczyk, 1985:777)

Anthony Giddens offers a definition of the nation state as follows:

> A nation-state refers to a political apparatus, recognized to have sovereign rights within the borders of a demarcated territorial area, able to back its claims by control of military power, many of whose citizens have positive feelings of commitment to its national identity.

(Giddens, 1989:303)

The point concerning the monopoly over the use of military and police force is of particular importance in the Weberian (Max Weber) understanding of the state:

> The definition of 'state' that Weber offers involves three main elements: (i) the existence of a regularized administrative staff able (ii) to sustain the claim to the legitimate monopoly of the means of violence and (iii) to uphold that monopoly within a given territorial area.

(Giddens, 1985:18)[4]

The state's monopoly of legitimate force or violence and the issue of sovereignty belong together. The territory of a state is the area, defined by internationally accepted boundaries, over which that state can plausibly be said to have sovereignty. The monopoly of armed force possessed by the state is accepted by its citizens for two principal purposes – preservation of law and order within the state, and defence from external aggression for the state's citizens. The German theologian Helmut Gollwitzer called the monopoly of legitimate violence by the state a 'precious step of progress in civilisation'.[5] In his ethical framework, he also develops an ethic for resistance to the state (citing Bonhoeffer) if the state becomes dictatorial or totalitarian – and thus ceases to be a 'Rechtstaat' or state based on the rule of law. Gollwitzer insists on the right of resistance under such circumstances. In theological terms, this kind of approach has been advocated most powerfully in recent times in the *Kairos Document* from South Africa.[6]

In order to counterbalance the concept of sovereignty, and the consequent right of any state to legislate for its own people, the developing acceptance and understanding of human rights has been essential. In the Middle Ages, natural law played a similar role, backed by the authority of the church. One can, however, question how effective the principles derived from natural law ever were in defending those who got on the wrong side of the 'powers-that-were'. Finally, one must underline how far away nice theoretical liberal descriptions of 'rational allocation of resources' and so on are from the reality of the many 'failed states' in today's world. It is revealing that one leading specialist on Africa has written an entire book on the 'curse of the nation-state' because of the burden it imposes on the populations and the legacy of inappropriate forms of government and boundaries from the colonial period (Davidson, 1992; cf. Ki-Zerbo, 1995). Part of the curse is that it is virtually impossible to see how it can be lifted, since the most likely means of rearranging boundaries would be a further spate of wars, whether internal or regional.

THE 'JUST WAR' TRADITION, LEGITIMATE USES OF FORCE AND THE DANGERS OF 'INTERVENTION'

The ambivalence of the state was well brought out in the thinking of Augustine. On the one hand, in *De Civitate Dei*, he stressed that the state must be based on good law: 'Take away justice, and what are governments but brigandage on a grand scale' (Augustine, *De Civitate Dei/City of God* 4.4, quoted in: Chadwick, 1986:99). In the Judaeo-Christian tradition, from the warnings of 1 Samuel 8 onwards, we have seen a history in which the double face of the state is apparent. One face of the state is the promise of protection – the other face is the need for taxation, military service, and often violation of the integrity of its own citizens in various ways. The story of Nathan the prophet confronting David over his abuse of God-given state power by taking Bathsheba, the wife of Uriah the Hittite while he was doing military service, exemplifies the warnings of Samuel about the dangers of having a king (2 Samuel 11–12). What is at first sight a story about the power of lust proves to be at least as much about the effects of the lust for power.

The warnings of Augustine are relevant for our own times. Augustine was a conservative, but ambivalent, figure – and a brilliant theorist – for better or worse. Part of his effort in *The City of God* was an attempt to separate the claims of Rome from those of the Kingdom of God. The 'two kingdoms' teaching' –

which Luther developed from Augustine's basic approach – can be used, like much else, in a conservative or a radical way. Augustine tried to ensure that there was no over-identification between the claims of the Roman Empire and the claims of God's rule in human affairs.

But in the Middle Ages, the Christian Gospel was used as legitimation for a fatal kind of intervention, which still has its consequences. A full history is not possible, but one should recall the way in which 'Christian' theology was coupled to the Crusades in a socio-economic, political and military enterprise of intervention, which was legitimised by the 'Christian' goal of 'liberating' the Holy Land from the Muslim 'infidel' – even against the wishes of the indigenous Christian population.[7] That kind of anti-Islamic and anti-Arab sentiment has still not been expunged completely from Western culture. There is a danger that views such as Samuel Huntington's 'Clash of Civilisations' (perhaps one should say 'clash of generalisations' because of his tragically fatalist view of the inevitable confrontation between cultural blocs) will be used as the rationale for treating Islam as the new 'enemy' now that the threat of communism no longer serves that function for legitimising Western military power.[8]

The end of the Middle Ages saw the beginning of another interventionist project – the colonial period. The politico-religious mix here is also of considerable interest. Just war argumentation was used by a brave minority voice (for example, Bartolomé de las Casas) in an attempt to defend the indigenous people of Latin America – but the mainstream just war theology was uncritical towards the colonising enterprise or even provided Christian theological legitimation for it, because of the perceived benefits of 'evangelisation' and the 'civilising' imperative vis-à-vis the indigenous peoples of the Americas (Bainton, 1982:166–7). This, too, was a project of 'intervention' for which Christian legitimation was provided (cf. Galeano, 1973; Boff and Elizondo, 1990).

In our own day, there is always the danger that any Christian statements *in favour* of intervention will be co-opted by the most powerful forces. This has happened before – over centuries, prompting comment on the linkage between trade, Christian mission, colonialism and the attendant economic and military penetration. The perspective from the other side was given eloquent expression by Ethiopian Emperor Tewodros II in the early 1860s: 'I know their game. First traders and missionaries, then ambassadors, then the cannon. It's better to get straight to the cannon.' (Cited in Davidson, 1994:13).

Today, the prime candidate for the interventionist paradigm in the military sphere is the project of the *Pax Americana* (the security interests of the North-West of the world) and in the economic sphere, the interests of the rich countries of the North (Barnet, 1972; Klare, 1992). Certainly no global interventionist project is thinkable without US involvement, whether this is a national (US), NATO or UN approach. Given past misuse of the Christian just war tradition in the interests of the most powerful forces for intervention, we should be very careful not to provide the 'sheep's clothing' of Christian ethical reasoning to the 'wolf' of intervention and unjust patterns of domination.

At least two developments beyond the system of nation states (with the last resort of war) are required before one could speak convincingly of the 'international community'. The first would be the provision of effective security and human rights for individuals, ethnic groups and those at risk of government repression. The second requirement would be development of a system of international responsibility for securing peace and the arbitration of conflicts, which would make the 'last resort' to war unnecessary for the nation state, thus undercutting the logic of Article 51 of the UN Charter.

One should be cautious of being over-optimistic. There are many problems which beset such a prescription. The first is obviously the need for an effective international policing function – as Brian Wicker argues in Chapter 9. As *The Economist* (1993) put it: 'Who will fight for the world?' Clearly something between major power isolationism and interventionism is required. Kuwait may feel that the 'world community' responded adequately in the case of the Kuwait War, but even this instance of the international community responding to aggression against a UN member state raises many questions. Could such a response be relied upon by all other countries suffering similar aggression, whether or not they had vital resources? To what extent was this a *UN* response? Would a similar response be forthcoming if the issue was of less obvious interest to the USA and other industrial nations? (As a Palestinian schoolgirl is said to have remarked, 'We have oil, too, but it is olive oil'.)

For all its shortcomings, national sovereignty has also been a means of limiting the possibilities for intervention by outside powers. If now, under the guise of concern for human rights, the 'world community' (which may in practice mean 'powerful nations' or alliances involving powerful nations) has an accepted reason for intervention in the internal affairs of other nations, this could lead to protracted wars of a new kind.

There is a case for arguing that what we should strive for is *non-intervention* (something most Central Americans regard as a vital part of an acceptable international policy), rather than the provision of new reasons for more powerful nations to intervene in the internal affairs of less powerful states. A classic modern text against intervention (in the spirit of Las Casas) is the letter by Archbishop Romero to President Carter, shortly before Romero was murdered:

> Therefore, since I as a Salvadorean and archbishop of the San Salvador archdiocese have an obligation to work for the reign of faith and justice in my country, I urge you, if you really want to defend human rights
>
> - to prohibit the giving of military assistance to the Salvadoran government.
> - to guarantee that your government will not intervene directly or indirectly with military, economic, diplomatic or other pressure to determine the fate of the Salvadoran people.
>
> (Romero, cited in Pearce, 1981:230–1)

Rather than direct military intervention under the guise of protection of human rights, one can argue that human rights protection should be addressed through the UN's human rights machinery (suitably strengthened – see Bailey, 1994), trade embargoes and sanctions, and should not be used as a cause for new policies of military intervention in the new millennium. The indiscriminate effects of sanctions are pointed out by Oliver O'Donovan in Chapter 7 – and one need look no further than Saddam Hussein's Iraq for an illustration that the unintended consequences of sanctions may well be the double punishment of a people already suffering under a repressive government – without necessarily harming their persecutors unduly. This example also raises questions concerning criteria for success and failure – how does one tell whether a sanctions policy has failed or whether it has not yet succeeded? Does the 'last resort' criterion require one to wait until it is clear that sanctions have failed before resort to military action? Indeed, in certain circumstances sanctions may strengthen the 'us against the world' syndrome and provide further legitimation for a repressive government to cling to power and repress its own people.

Advocates of intervention in the 1990s seemed to forget that much of the world experienced more than enough of intervention in the proxy wars of recent decades with the superpowers fighting out their mutual rivalry in somebody else's 'backyard' and providing high-sounding legitimations for their intervention – whether it was the right of self-determination, support for peace-loving forces, protection of human rights, an 'invitation' from within the country in question (for example, Czechoslovakia or Afghanistan in cases of Soviet interventionism), or rejection of the other side's expansionism. War can always be clothed in high-sounding rhetoric from right or left, North or South, nationalist or internationalist. Less glorious ways of talking about the 'necessity' of intervention are 'interference in the internal affairs of other countries' and 'fighting wars on other people's territories'.

PROBLEMS OF BOTH INTERVENTION AND NON-INTERVENTION

Both basic positions – the plea for *non*-intervention and the argument in favour of responsible intervention – are problematic. The position which argues that internal affairs are internal affairs and that human rights violations are not a reason for supplying arms or getting involved in the civil wars of other countries can lead to cynicism in the face of the massive and protracted suffering of others. On the other hand, the seemingly righteous position that human rights are a universal concern could lead to intervention and escalation of local wars. This danger is perhaps less acute than during the days of the East–West conflict, when the wars fought with direct or indirect (for example, arms transfers) involvement of one or both blocs condemned countries such as El Salvador, Nicaragua, Guatemala, Mozambique, Angola, Afghanistan, and much of South-East Asia to seemingly endless bloodshed. Had those conflicts been treated as the 'internal affairs' of the country in question, many would have been killed, but the countries might have been spared war of such a destructive kind, with dramatic levels of suffering – the long years of deaths of civilians (the 'people in between'), destruction of crops, dislocation of population, destruction of the infrastructure and the other results of modern war run on technology from the industrialised nations, including the continued scourge of huge numbers of landmines making return to the land and agricultural production dangerous and unpredictable (ICRC, 1996; UNICEF, 1994). The debate about military intervention must be held in a context of realism – even after the end of the Cold War when intervention is freed from the risks of escalation into East–West alliance confrontation, the calculation must still be made whether intervention is likely to increase or decrease the sum of human suffering, and, a related point, whether it is likely to prolong warfare or help to bring it to a relatively better conclusion than if the parties are left to 'fight it out'.

At the outset of a war, who can predict the 'true cost of conflict' and who has the right to decide on behalf of others that the price is worth paying – often in other people's blood and suffering? (Saferworld, 1994). If the arms had not kept flowing, fewer deaths would have resulted (Williamson/CCADD, 1992; Singh, 1995; ICRC, 1996; UNICEF, 1994). One could say, at the risk of sounding simplistic, that one help that the outside world could have provided was to promise not to 'help' – to refuse to intervene militarily except under UN auspices through traditional peacekeeping operations, to refuse to deliver arms and only to 'intervene' if asked to help in finding a negotiated settlement.

It seems to me that the question of intervention and the possible ethical justification for it has been well addressed by the principles of the Conference on Security and Cooperation in Europe (CSCE) agreement. What would need to be done, however, would be to have these (a) internationally accepted and implemented, (b) all implemented simultaneously in spite of the apparent contradictions between them (for example, between Principles VI and VII) and (c) agreed definitions of each of the relevant terms being internationally accepted and impartially determined in cases of conflict. The Principles are:

    I. Sovereign equality, respect for the rights inherent in sovereignty.
    II. Refraining from the threat or use of force.
    III. Inviolability of frontiers.
    IV. Territorial integrity of States.
    V. Peaceful settlement of disputes.
    VI. Non-intervention in internal affairs.
    VII. Respect for human rights and fundamental freedoms, including the freedom of thought, conscience, religion or belief.
    VIII. Equal rights and self-determination of peoples.

IX. Cooperation among States.
X. Fulfilment in good faith of obligations under international
law.

(cited in Weingärtner, 1994:14)

It is hard to calculate the extent to which the Helsinki Process, by encouraging the development of awareness of human rights in Eastern Europe, helped over a 15-year period to ease the relatively peaceful transition away from communism in most of Eastern Europe in the period up to 1991. Certainly a direct interventionist war to attempt to overthrow communism would have been incalculably destructive. There are serious problems in any weakening of the restriction on intervention – which is actually prohibited under the *UN Declaration on the Inadmissibility of Intervention, 1965*.

THE STATE: THE NEED FOR A POSITIVE BUT CRITICAL EVALUATION

As has been mentioned, Paul tells the Church in Rome that the State 'is not a terror to good behaviour'. But we know it can be precisely that. In his sermon at the 1994 CCADD International Conference, the former Archbishop of York reminded us of the benefits of government over anarchy (Habgood, 1996). The understanding of the mainstream Christian churches has been in line with Augustine's perception, which in the words of Henry Chadwick has been a 'positive evaluation of government as a providential instrument of order – if not getting one to heaven, at least hedging the road to hell' (Chadwick, 1986:100). Nations are human constructs, not God-given constants, so I support the right of the Eritreans or the Namibians to decide that they should be an independent nation (cf. Gellner, 1983; Anderson, 1991; Hutchinson and Smith, 1994) – although this does not mean that every ethnic group should insist that the right to self-determination equals a right to a nation state. Thus, the theology of intervention based upon a positive and critical evaluation of government. *Positive* because the 'state's monopoly of legitimate violence is a valuable step in civilisation' (Helmut Gollwitzer). *Critical* because government can become so tyrannical that *in extremis* it has to be overthrown by force. There is a right to self-defence. It is odd to think that Ugandans under Idi Amin had a moral right to overthrow Amin, but that it would have been wrong for Tanzanians a few miles away to assist them – yet one is also keen to uphold the taboo (or at least considerable, but not total, inhibition) against external intervention. But we need to think more deeply about who has the right to use force to protect others and how it should be exercised. Where there is a state which is good, or even acceptable, or perhaps even bad but not tyrannical, the *state* is usually seen as the appropriate primary body to defend its people. The critical role of the church is to remind the state of its duty to defend its citizens. But the crisis of the nation state in many parts of the contemporary world is precisely the situation in which the state can become the enemy of a section of the people or even the majority of the citizens which it should protect.

It is also necessary to heed the warnings of Helder Camara about the 'spiral of violence' (Camara, 1971). The state monopoly of legitimate violence means that the state is also usually the expert in killing and the exercise of force, as, for example, the Chinese students of Tiananmen Square discovered to their cost. Resistance is dangerous whether by non-violent or violent means. But we cannot say an absolute 'No' to resistance: against occupation – as in Namibia, or against tyranny as in Idi Amin's Uganda, or against a state when it is used as a weapon of oppression by one community against another.

NOTES

1.	See entries on: Afghanistan (p.7), Czechoslovakia (p. 189), Grenada (p.315), Helsinki Final Act (pp.333–44), Intervention (pp.418–19), Intervention, UN Declaration on the Inadmissibility of, 1965 (p.419), United Nations Charter, 1945 (pp.836–41). All in: Osmanczyk, 1985.
2.	See Bailey and Daws, 1995; Childers, 1994; Clements and Ward, 1994; Evans, 1993; United Nations, 1990.
3.	See Weber, 1991.
4.	*The Nation-State and Violence* is an important theoretical work in which Giddens goes beyond the Weberian definition.
5.	'Das staatliche Gewaltmonopol ist ein kostbarer zivilisatorischer Fortschritt, den wir sorgsam hüten müssen.' Gollwitzer, 1976:139.
6.	cf. Brown, 1990. This valuable documentation contains the texts of the Kairos, Kairos Central America and Road to Damascus Documents as well as valuable commentary and suggestions for discussion.
7.	cf. the eyewitness accounts in: Pernoud (ed.), 1971.

8.   See e.g. the works of Edward Said (see Bibliography) on this point. cf. Huntington, 1993. For an attempt to formulate other, non-competitive (or at least non-destructive) forms of relationship between the main world religions, see Küng, 1991; Küng and Kuschel, 1993.

BIBLIOGRAPHY

Anderson, B., *Imagined Communities*, London & New York: Verso, 1991 (1st edn 1983).

Bailey, S.D., *The UN Security Council and Human Rights*, Basingstoke & London: Macmillan; New York: St. Martin's Press, 1994.

Bailey, S.D. and Daws, S., *The United Nations: A Concise Political Guide*, Basingstoke & London: Macmillan, 1995 (3rd edn).

Bainton, R.H., *Christian Attitudes toward War and Peace*, Nashville: Abingdon, 1982 (12th printing, 1st edn 1960).

Barnet, R.J., *Intervention and Revolution: The United States in the Third World*, London: Paladin, 1972 (1st US edn 1968).

Boff, L. and Elizondo, V. (eds.), *1492–1992: The Voice of the Victims* (*Concilium* 1990/6), London: SCM; Philadelphia: Trinity Press International, 1990.

Brown, R. McAfee (ed.), *Kairos: Three Prophetic Challenges to the Church*, Grand Rapids: Eerdmans, 1990.

Camara, H., *Spiral of Violence*, London: Sheed & Ward, 1971.

Chadwick, H., *Augustine*, Oxford & New York: Oxford University Press, 1986.

Childers, E., *Challenges to the United Nations: Building a Safer World*, London: CIIR; New York: St. Martin's Press, 1994.

CIIR (Catholic Institute for International Relations), *East Timor: The Continuing Betrayal*, London: CIIR, 1996.

Clements, K.P. and Ward, R., *Building International Community*, St. Leonards, NSW, Australia: Allen & Unwin, 1994.

Davidson, B., *The Black Man's Burden: Africa and the Curse of the Nation State*, London: James Currey, 1992.

Davidson, B., *The Search for Africa: A History in the Making*, London: James Currey, 1994.

Economist, 'Who Will Fight for the World?' *The Economist*, 30 Jan. 1993, 15–16.

Evans, G., *Cooperating for Peace: The Global Agenda for the 1990s and Beyond*, St. Leonards, NSW, Australia: Allen & Unwin, 1993.

Galeano, E., *Open Veins of Latin America: Five Centuries of the Pillage of a Continent*, New York & London: Monthly Review Press, 1973.

Gellner, E., *Nations and Nationalism*, Oxford & Cambridge: Blackwell, 1983.

Giddens, A., *The Nation-State and Violence*, Cambridge: Polity Press; Oxford: Basil Blackwell, 1985.

Giddens, A., *Sociology*, Cambridge: Polity Press; Oxford: Basil Blackwell, 1989.

Gollwitzer, H., 'Zum Problem der Gewalt in der christlichen Ethik', in: Gollwitzer, H., *Forderungen der Umkehr: Beiträge zur Theologie der Gesellschaft*, Munich: Chr. Kaiser, 1976, 126–46.

Habgood, J., 'On War', *Theology*, July–August 1996, 258–61.

Huntington, S.P., 'The Clash of Civilisations?' *Foreign Affairs*, Vol. 72, No. 3, Summer 1993, 22–49.

Hutchinson, J., and Smith, A.D., (eds.), *Nationalism*, Oxford & New York: Oxford University Press, 1994.

ICRC (International Committee of the Red Cross), *Anti-personnel Landmines: Friend or Foe?* Geneva: ICRC, 1996.

Ki-Zerbo, J., ' "Which Way Africa?": Reflections on Basil Davidson's The Black Man's Burden', *Development Dialogue*, 1995:2, pp.99–123.

Klare, M, *The New Pax Americana: US Interventionism in the Post-Cold-War Era*, Uppsala: Life & Peace Institute, 1992.

Küng, H., *Global Responsibility: In Search of a New World Ethic*, London: SCM, 1991.

Küng, H. and Kuschel, K.-J. (eds.), *A Global Ethic: The Declaration of the Parliament of the World's Religions*, London: SCM, 1993.

Linden, I., 'A Prize Shames the World into Action', *The Independent*, 14 Oct. 1996.

Lossky, N. *et al.* (eds.), *Dictionary of the Ecumenical Movement*, Geneva: WCC; Grand Rapids: Eerdmans, 1991.

Osmanczyk, E.J., *Encyclopedia of the United Nations and International Agreements*, Philadelphia & London: Taylor & Francis, 1985.

Pearce, J., *Under the Eagle: U.S. Intervention in Central America and the Caribbean*, London: Latin America Bureau, 1981.

Pernoud, R. (ed.), *Die Kreuzzüge in Augenzeugenberichte*, Munich: DTV, 1971.

Romero, O., 'Archbishop Romero's Letter to President Carter', (17 Feb. 1980) in: Pearce 1981:230–1.

Saferworld – Cranna, M., (ed.), *The True Cost of Conflict*, London: Earthscan, 1994.

Said, E. W., *Covering Islam: How the Media and the Experts Determine How We See the Rest of the World*, London, Melbourne & Henley: Routledge & Kegan Paul, 1985 (1st edn 1981).

Said, E. W., *Orientalism: Western Conceptions of the Orient*, London: Penguin, 1991 (1st edn 1978).

Said, E.W., *The Question of Palestine*, London: Vintage, 1992 (revised edn, 1st edn 1979).

Singh, J., (ed.), *Light Weapons and International Security*, Delhi: Indian Pugwash Society and Basic, 1995.

Steele, J., 'A Peace of the Action', *The Guardian* (2), 30 Dec. 1996, 4–5.

UNICEF, *Anti-personnel Land-mines: A Scourge on Children*, New York: UNICEF, 1994.

United Nations, *The Blue Helmets: A Review of United Nations Peace-keeping*, New York: United Nations, 1990 (2nd edn).

Weber, T.R., 'State', in: Lossky 1991:953–6.

Weingärtner, E., *Protecting Human Rights: A Manual for Practitioners*, Geneva: Churches' Human Rights Programme in the CSCE, 1994.

Williamson, R. (for the Council on Christian Approaches to Defence and Disarmament), *Profit without Honour? Ethics and the Arms Trade*, London: CCADD, 1992.

2 Some Corner of a Foreign Field

David Fisher

Dulce et decorum est
Pro patria mori

In what circumstances can a state legitimately put at risk the lives of members of its armed forces? An argument frequently used against military intervention, for example in the former Yugoslavia, is that a state can legitimately put at risk the lives of its young soldiers in the defence of its own territory but it has no such right if engaged in foreign interventions. This would be particularly so if the intervention contemplated were, as in Chamberlain's infamous description of Czechoslovakia, in 'a quarrel in a far-away country between people of whom we know nothing'. It may, moreover, be argued that there are especially compelling arguments against the use of conscript forces for such foreign adventures.

In this chapter I shall assess some of the ethical issues raised by these arguments. I shall also consider two related issues: first, whether in order to minimise the casualties suffered by its own forces it is morally permissible for a state to maximise the damage wreaked on an adversary's forces, as was arguably done by the coalition forces in the Gulf War; and second, what basis there is for choosing between interventions. If it is right to intervene in the former Yugoslavia, why not in Cambodia or Somalia? But how then do we avoid placing impossible demands on our armed forces? All of these issues raise interesting questions about the mutual obligations that hold between a government and its armed forces.

Any use of military force – whether to conduct warfare in the classic sense or for intervention – can involve the threat or infliction of harm. Ethical constraints upon its use are, therefore, appropriate. The just war tradition thus provides a helpful framework for assessing when it is legitimate to use military force not only to wage war but also for intervention. The just war theory argues that it is only permissible to resort to war (the *jus ad bellum*): if war is declared by a competent authority; if no suitable peaceful means of resolving the dispute are available; for the sake of a just cause; and provided that the harm judged likely to result from the war is not disproportionate to the likely good to be achieved, taking into account the probability of success. Moreover, the war should be conducted in such a way that the harm judged likely to result from a particular military action should not be disproportionate to the likely good to be aimed at; and non-combatant casualties should be minimised (the *jus in bello*). With appropriate modifications, these conditions can, in my view, be applied to assess the ethical permissibility of military interventions (Fisher, 1994:51–9).

An important but difficult issue that has to be settled in so applying the just war theory, is what would constitute a just cause for intervention. Given the great harm that can be caused by interventions and their misuse by great powers to interfere in the affairs of smaller states – as evidenced by the events of the first half of this century – international law has until recently deemed there to be a strong presumption against any intervention. Most commentators have tended to apply the just war criteria very restrictively regarding the only just cause for resorting to war as self-defence against aggression. This might then legitimise interventions to assist a country defending itself against aggression but not otherwise.

While accepting the moral presumption against intervention, I believe this is an unduly restrictive interpretation and that there may be other grounds that constitute a just cause for intervention. These may include not only interventions that approximate to the self-defence paradigm but also operations, legitimised by a UN mandate, designed to keep apart belligerent parties (peacemaking); to enforce a peace settlement (peacekeeping); or for humanitarian purposes that may range from bringing aid to a war-ravaged people to the prevention of massive abuses of human rights or even genocide. In such cases intervention to prevent suffering may be morally permissible. Indeed, where it lies readily within our power to prevent great suffering such as genocide from taking place, it may be difficult to resist the conclusion that we have not only a right but a duty to intervene.

Recognition that there may be other just causes than self-defence against aggression does not, however, justify reckless interventions. For even if the cause is just, intervention would only be sanctioned if the harm judged likely to result is not disproportionate to the good to be achieved, taking into account the probability of success. And it may be very difficult, if not impossible, to satisfy this condition in many of the situations where there may be calls for intervention, not least the confused and messy circumstances of a civil war.

If, however, it can be ethically permissible, or even ethically required, for a state to intervene in the affairs of another, then it surely follows that a state may also employ the appropriate means, including military force, so to do. Those who will the end, will the means. Use of military force would, however, only be permitted if all the just war conditions were satisfied, including the likelihood of success without disproportionate harm being incurred. It would not, therefore, be permissible to put soldiers' lives at risk for the sake of a political gesture unlikely to achieve any worthwhile objective.

The Second World War is often hailed as a paradigm just war undertaken for the pre-eminently just cause of preventing Nazi aggression, not just against Britain but the whole of Europe and, indeed, the world. So it certainly was, and few would, therefore, entertain any doubts that the British government was justified in putting the lives of many thousands of British servicemen and women at risk in such a war. An interesting question is whether it would also have been justified, if the UK had intervened a year or two earlier, not to prevent aggression, but to prevent Hitler's genocide against the Jews, supposing reliable information had then been available about this? Such a cause would assuredly have been just. Let us suppose, furthermore, that Great Britain had had the necessary military means available and good reason to believe that such an intervention would achieve its objective without disproportionate cost. The just war tradition, as I have interpreted it, would suggest that intervention on such grounds would have been justified, as hence would putting our soldiers' lives at risk for such a cause.

It is sometimes claimed that there is an ethical distinction to be drawn between the use of conscript and volunteer forces for foreign interventions. Whether this is so depends in part on the nature of the understanding between a government and its people on what conscription is to be used for. This may vary between countries. Some countries (for example Germany) have explicitly justified conscription as providing forces solely for territorial defence of the homeland. For others that is not the case. Indeed, even Germany has recently determined that there is no constitutional bar to their forces operating outside German territory and they have thus been enabled to do so as part of the NATO Implementation Force in the former Yugoslavia. For Britain with its past worldwide imperial responsibilities, the role of its armed forces, even when they were conscript, has never been narrowly confined to home defence. Indeed, an important traditional role of the British Army has been peacemaking or peacekeeping in far-flung colonies: a point rather overlooked by some of the opponents of intervention, sometimes themselves the very people who have in the past supported imperialist ventures. Moreover, countries without an imperialist past but with a strong political tradition of supporting UN peacekeeping operations, need feel no necessary compunction against the use of conscript forces for this purpose.

There may, of course, be compelling practical arguments in favour of using volunteer forces for foreign interventions since they may, by dint of longer service, be better trained and equipped for the task. But I see no compelling ethical argument against the use of conscript forces, provided democratic consent for such use has been obtained. This would entail, *inter alia*, that the policy had been clearly proclaimed in advance and been supported through the democratic electoral process, in the same way as are a government's other key policies.

If it is ethically permissible for a government to undertake an intervention, it is also permissible for it to employ its armed forces for this purpose where military means are deemed most appropriate. This would apply both to conscript and volunteer forces, although because of the element of coercion involved in conscription, some constraints on the use of conscript forces may be appropriate. There may, for example, be a case for allowing a right of refusal to individual conscripts if their units are sent overseas on military interventions. Moreover, any government has an obligation not to put at risk the lives of its service personnel – whether conscript or volunteers – unnecessarily. The question I wish now to address is how far this duty can be taken ethically.

At the time of the Gulf War, the coalition governments and, in particular, the US government – ever mindful of its painful Vietnam experience – were very concerned to minimise their own casualties: to keep down the 'body-bag count'. Indeed, in responding to criticisms of the scale and duration of the coalition aerial offensive, the British Gulf Forces Commander, General Sir Peter De la Billière, responded: 'My answer is that if we stop early, we pay in British lives, and this is not a deal I wish to do' (De la Billière, 1992:279). Did such calculations lead the coalition partners to cause disproportionate damage to Iraqi ground forces – many themselves reluctant conscripts – who were subjected to a prolonged and devastating aerial bombardment prior to the launch of the coalition ground offensive?

It is, of course, much easier to make such criticisms with hindsight when we know how relatively little resistance was encountered by the coalition ground forces. This was hardly known in advance and, in any case, some effective resistance was offered. Is it, however, legitimate, as some suggested at the time of the Gulf War, for a government to kill, say, three of an enemy's soldiers in order to save the life of one of its own? From a moral viewpoint the answer is surely 'no' since one life cannot be thus evaluated differently from another.

This might then suggest that ethics would preclude sensible military strategy since a commander will naturally wish to maximise enemy casualties, while limiting his own: indeed, this may be the key to military success and hence to bringing a speedy end to the war, thereby minimising overall casualties. Ethics would quickly fall into disrepute among strategists if it led to such a counter-intuitive conclusion. Fortunately, I do not think that it does since the moral arithmetic implied by the question is misguided.

What the just war tradition requires is not that one side's casualties should be weighed against the other's but rather that we should assess whether the harm judged likely to result from the war – if one is assessing the overall strategy – or the harm likely to flow from a particular military operation, if that is what is being assessed, is or is not disproportionate to the likely good to be achieved. Thus in assessing the allies' strategy in the Gulf War, the enemy casualties – both civilian and military – caused would have to be weighed against not just the casualties suffered by the coalition partners, but all the suffering that would have continued and intensified if the illegal Iraqi occupation of Kuwait had not been terminated. Such an assessment would also properly include the unfortunate precedent set for the world order, if brazen aggression had been allowed to succeed. This involves a rather different calculation from the crude body-bag count from which we started and one against which the allies' actions would appear justifiable.

My conclusion is, therefore, that governments can legitimately employ their military forces in foreign interventions when these would themselves be sanctioned by the just war criteria. In so doing they have an obligation not to expose their forces to unnecessary risks. The extent to which this objective can be pursued by maximising enemy military casualties is constrained by the requirement that the harm produced overall should not be disproportionate to the likely good achieved.

If it may on occasion be ethically permissible to intervene to prevent suffering, the difficult question then arises as to how we choose on which occasion intervention is appropriate. How, in particular, do we avoid being drawn down a slippery slope towards involvement in all kinds of interventions? Indeed, how do we escape from suffering the kind of universal guilt experienced by Father Zossima's younger brother in *The Brothers Karamazov*, who was convinced that 'every one of us is responsible for everyone else in every way, and I most of all' (Dostoyevsky, 1982:339)? Such an assumption of universal responsibility may seem admirable but is assuredly impractical.

This impracticality underpins a *reductio ad absurdum* argument frequently advanced against intervention:

> If one ought to intervene in country A, one ought to intervene in country B, C, D, E... It would be impossible to intervene in A, B, C, D, E... One only ought to do what one can do. ('Ought' presupposes 'can'.) Therefore, one ought not to intervene in country A.

A similar argument is also mounted against overseas aid to the effect that since we cannot save the lives of all those suffering in the Third World, it is pointless to try to save the lives of any.

The argument set out above may be a formally valid inference but the key major premise is surely false. For it does not follow that if one should intervene in a particular country, one should *eo ipso* intervene in every country, any more than if one should send overseas aid to one country, one should, therefore, send it to all. We may not be able to save every dying child in the Third World but if we could save even one, perhaps we should.

The attempted *reductio ad absurdum* thus fails but it does, nonetheless, sharply underline the need to explain more clearly why we should help one country rather than another, what is the basis for choosing between interventions. For if this rests on no more than that the media are clamouring for intervention in that country (a country, no doubt, well endowed with good hotels and electronic communication facilities) then the basis for our intervention may well appear rather arbitrary.

One possible criterion for choosing between interventions might be based on a doctrine of spheres of moral responsibility. Just as the ripples caused by a pebble thrown into a pond fade and eventually disappear with distance, so too it may be supposed does our moral responsibility lessen, the further from us the events are unfolding. We have a clear responsibility towards a baby dying on our doorstep; not so towards the image of a dying Ethiopian child on our television screen. Our moral responsibility towards those immediately around us – our family, neighbours and friends – is clear and compelling; it becomes less compelling, although still discernible, towards those further away; and vanishes altogether well before the coasts of Africa.

Such a doctrine of spheres of moral responsibility furnishes a robustly practical ethic that places no impossible demands upon us, while correctly recognising the particularly strong claims that those closest to us may have upon us. It does, nonetheless, accord a significance to mere distance that it cannot bear. It is as wrong to kill an innocent stranger far away by an intercontinental missile as to kill someone close by with a hand gun. A mother would hardly consider her responsibilities towards a sick child to have lapsed if the child fell ill many thousands of miles away in Australia.

If distance alone cannot provide an adequate criterion of choice, for what suffering in the world can we legitimately be held responsible? Most obviously for that which we bring about by our intentional action, of which a paradigm case is that of murder. Our responsibility may, however, extend further than this towards those consequences which, even if not intended, were clearly foreseen.

In the case of *Regina v. Desmond, Barrett and others*, the accused had attempted to free two Fenians by blowing up the wall of Clerkenwell prison, causing the death of a number of people living nearby. Their defence was that they had not intended to kill them, even though they may have foreseen their deaths as a consequence of their actions. Their plea was rejected, with Lord Coleridge concluding that it was murder, 'if a man did an act not with the purpose of taking life but with the knowledge or belief that life was likely to be sacrificed by it' (Hart, 1968:120). The Fenians may not have intended the deaths but they did at least consent to them, as evidenced by their readiness to persist in blowing up the wall, despite having foreseen the inevitable consequences thereof.

This case thus illustrates the first element – consent – that needs to be present for a valid attribution of responsibility. It also illustrates the second – control – since the deaths were within their control: they would not have happened if they had not acted thus. A valid attribution of responsibility requires, moreover, the presence of both consent and control. Consent alone will not suffice. This is illustrated by the amputee who, unaware that he has lost a leg, wills it to move without effect; or by the poisoner who slips arsenic into his wife's bedtime cocoa only to find that she dies coincidentally of a heart attack before the fatal beverage has passed her lips. He may have consented to her death but did not control it and so – despite his malicious intent – cannot be held responsible for it.

Similarly, even if control is exercised, without consent an attribution of moral responsibility may be evaded. This was, indeed, the basis of the excuse proffered for the US bombing of the command bunker/air raid shelter at Amiriyah during the Gulf War when 314 civilians were killed. The US spokesman did not dispute that the deaths had resulted from the coalition air raid. Rather they argued that they did not know, nor could reasonably have been expected to know, that civilians were sheltering in what they believed with good reason to be a military command and control facility. If they did not know about something then a fortiori they could not have consented to it. Thus, even if there is control, without consent an attribution of responsibility may fail.

Armed with these distinctions, one can now see how distance, while morally neutral in itself, can acquire a moral significance. Reverting to our earlier example, the death of the baby on our doorstep is within our control since we could, if we chose, prevent it; it is also consented to by us, if we, nonetheless, allow it to happen. The death is thus within our responsibility, even though it is a consequence of our inaction rather than action.

The latter should not, however, surprise us since where an act or omission has identical consequences, equally within the agent's control and consented to by him or her, it may be difficult to draw a sharp moral distinction between them. The hospital ward orderly, who has inveigled an elderly, terminally ill patient to bequeath him all her money, hardly seems less culpable if he deliberately fails to switch her life support machine on (an omission) than if he deliberately switches it off (an act). It is thus with good reason that one of the confessions in the Anglican Book of Common Prayer seeks forgiveness for 'the good we have not done', as well as 'the evil we have done'; for our sins of omission as well as of commission.

The death of the Ethiopian child on the TV screen was not, however, within our control nor consented to by us: indeed, it may already have happened by the time the picture is shown. We have, therefore, no responsibility for the death, even though the image of it may properly prompt us to dig into our pockets to help prevent similar deaths. The moral relevance of distance is thus that it can explain our ignorance of events and hence, a fortiori, our lack of consent to their occurrence. This excuse is, however, becoming ever more difficult to proffer as the media explosion shrinks the world to a 'global village'. Distance can also explain our lack of control as the causal chain may become very leaky the lengthier it has to extend, as illustrated by the many mishaps that can occur between our donating to an overseas charity and the aid reaching its destination.

Applying these considerations to interventions, I conclude that a country may have a responsibility to intervene where the events taking place are, in some sense, within its control and consented to by it; conversely, it has no such responsibilities where these conditions are not met; where it may be unaware of the ills unfolding or, if aware, unable to help. On this basis, a country might perhaps have particular responsibilities towards those countries linked to it by association, whether past (for example a former colony) or present (for example an alliance) or through geographical and/or cultural proximity. In such cases our control over events and consent to their occurrence may be deemed that much greater.

One can perhaps also discern on this basis the difference in responsibilities between a regional power, whose intervention capabilities are limited, and the global reach of a superpower. The UK does, therefore, perhaps have particular responsibilities to help prevent suffering in the former Yugoslavia – a fellow European country – that it lacks in Cambodia. On the other hand, where the scale of suffering is very great and one has the capability to do something towards its alleviation, it may be very difficult to resist calls for intervention further afield in countries to which one's only link is a shared humanity. It was on such grounds that the UK declared its readiness to participate, if required, in an international intervention force to help bring humanitarian relief to Rwanda in November 1996.

None of this is, however, to suggest that an intervention should be lightly contemplated: for the presumption against intervention remains and intervention can only be justified if all the just war criteria are satisfied. However, if appalling suffering is taking place, perhaps even within our own continent and under the glare of our television cameras, and if we have the means readily available to do something about it, then the conclusion of the just war tradition, as here interpreted, is that it may be not merely permissible but even ethically required to intervene. The demands of ethics may not be impossible but they can still be very challenging.

BIBLIOGRAPHY

De la Billière, General Sir P., *Storm Command: A Personal Account of the Gulf War*, London: HarperCollins, 1992.
Dostoyevsky, F., *The Brothers Karamazov*, (trans. David Magarshack), London: Penguin Books, 1958 (reissued 1982).
Fisher, D., *Morality and the Bomb*, London: Croom Helm; New York: St.Martin's Press, 1985.
Fisher, D., 'The Ethics of Intervention', *Survival* (The IISS Quarterly), Spring 1994, Vol. 36, No. 1, London: Brassey's, pp.51–9.
Hart, H.L.A., *Punishment and Responsibility*, Oxford: Oxford University Press, 1968.

3 When Is a War Not a War?
Brian Wicker

When is a war not a war? Answer: when it is a police action. So say almost all those who have 'intervened' in recent decades, from Suez to Chechnya.[1] Not surprisingly those against whom the intervention has taken place have invariably disagreed. No, we are at war with you (they insist), for whatever you say, we constitute a separate community over which you have no jurisdiction.

Obviously both cannot be right. But they could both be wrong. For historically speaking there has been a close connection between the policemen and soldiers. In theory, of course, a police action is designed to restore law and order *within* a community, whereas a war (as Clausewitz saw) is a duel *between* communities.[2] To this extent the two concepts are incompatible. But history tells us that in reality the relationship is more complex, and that in rapidly changing societies democratic police forces emerged out of the collapse of military efforts at keeping the peace.

The Bosnian crisis illustrates my principal contention. There are, in broad terms, two ways of looking at it. The first says that the conflict is essentially a civil war, resulting from the release of pent-up tensions between different ethnic groups with the collapse of the Cold War and the disintegration of the communist Yugoslav state. As such the international community has a responsibility to intervene for humanitarian purposes, but not to take sides. But according to the second account, an internationally recognised sovereign state (Bosnia-Herzegovina) has been aggressively invaded from outside (with the collusion of the Bosnian Serbs) in order forcibly to change its character, redistribute its population by force, and create a 'Greater Serbia'. This aggression having taken place, the state of Bosnia-Herzegovina has the duty to defend itself, and to expect the international community to help it to do so, by providing the necessary weapons and equipment. Now my contention is that each of these interpretations is correct according to certain premisses. Each has good grounds in international law. But they cannot both be true. However, they could both be false. For it may be that the premisses upon which the arguments are built are themselves faulty, or obsolete. This is precisely my point. For what I am suggesting is that the Bosnian crux (among many others) reveals that we need to change our perspective on the whole situation if we are to understand the events properly. Instead of seeing the players in Bosnia-type dramas as actors on a stage called 'international relations', with all that this implies in terms of separate sovereign communities with distinct legal and political obligations, we need to see them as engaged in acts of public disorder, or 'affrays', on a massive scale. These disorders are affronts to an 'international community' which has the right and duty to deal with them by deploying suitable police forces of its own, authorised to quell the disorders and if necessary to bring the perpetrators to justice.

It is part of my argument that there is a close historical connection between the establishment of democratically accountable police forces and the emergence of unified societies in which citizens for the first time are able to think of themselves as members of a single community. Just as variegated pre-industrial Britain was forged into a single community in the late eighteenth century by the numerous factors which we have come to call 'the industrial revolution', so too at roughly the same time British citizens became conscious of the need for coherent and accountable police forces to deal with public disorders in this new, unified society. Similarly I want to argue, at the end of the second millennium, the world as a whole is coming to a similar awareness of its own essential unity, as the result of a comparable revolution in communications and other factors. Consequently it too must appreciate the need for an accountable police force to deal with the many 'affrays' which are already breaking out, or are likely to break out in future, in those parts of the globe where fault-lines between established groups are most in evidence.

In both this chapter and my subsequent one (Chapter 9), my interest focuses on the transition from soldiering to policing. For, of course, police forces emerged out of armies when the latter found themselves unable or unwilling to deal with social problems. I shall argue therefore that it is just such a transition that we are experiencing today, as we take the bumpy ride from military intervention to international police action. The very fact that military interventions, often authorised as such by the United Nations, are typically characterised by those who undertake them as 'police actions' reveals the ambiguity of the issue.[3]

To begin with it may be helpful to deal briefly with three commonly-stated but mistaken arguments about the difference between warfare and police action, as a way of introducing what I take to be a better explanation of the distinction.

WAR AND THE ABSENCE OF RULES

Clausewitz seems to have thought of war as simply the exercise of what may be called 'brute force', with the object of forcing the opponent in a duel to do our will. For 'moral force', Clausewitz insists 'has no existence save as expressed in the state and the law'. And since by definition war is outside the jurisdiction of the state, there can be no legal or moral limit to its ferocity.[4]

But is Clausewitz right? Is not war a human institution, built upon institutional facts, and thus incapable of being described wholly in terms of what G.E.M. Anscombe has called 'brute facts'?[5] Consider how the Clausewitzian war is likely to end, in 'surrender'. Now, 'I surrender' is a performative verb.[6] This implies that a successful act of surrendering requires the application of certain necessary rules. When Laertes 'surrenders' at the end of *Hamlet*, the actor who is playing the part is not himself actually surrendering: he is only 'pretending'. In contrast, the Japanese on 2 September 1945 were actually surrendering. What exactly is the difference between the genuine and the fake example? We cannot appreciate the question without understanding the rules of what Michael Walzer rightly calls the 'war convention'.[7]

Perhaps the only person who thought that war lacked all rules was General Sherman, who claimed that it was 'hell'. For hell is a 'brute fact' that lacks all rules, and thus all meaning. This is perhaps why it is so *absolutely* terrifying. But then Sherman's phrase was only a metaphor, hell being unimaginable. Even so Clausewitzian a thinker as von Moltke was unable to think of war as hell: for while he thought that it should be terminated 'by all means', he made one exception: 'save those that are absolutely objectionable'.[8] This remark points to the possibility that Clausewitz was wrong, and that there are certain natural moral limits to what people may licitly do to each other, even in war.[9]

THE QUESTION OF SOVEREIGNTY

Clausewitz seems to have assumed that what made moral limits in war impossible was the fact that law could exist only by the authority of a sovereign state. But war existed outside the reach of such law. In this respect it was distinct from police work, which by definition lay within the law as laid down by the state.

Now according to this picture, an international police force must be a contradiction in terms, notwithstanding the existence of Interpol and other similar bodies.[10] Any uninvited intervention by a police force would itself be a breach of the peace: something tantamount to illicit interference in another state's sovereignty. This was the charge placed by Argentina against Israel in the latter's pursuit of Adolf Eichmann, and by other states including the UK in the case of the Israeli kidnap of Mordechai Vanunu.

Nevertheless the UN Charter is full of holes at this point. Consider the gap between those clauses which insist upon the freedom of member states from interference from outside, for example Article 2(7), and those which authorise such interference in the name of 'threats to the peace' (for example Chapter VII). A number of possibilities can be inserted to plug the gap. As I have said, police forces emerged only slowly out of the failures of the military to keep the peace within states. Indeed, they were invented as substitutes for the military when breaches of the peace became too difficult for the latter to handle. What is interesting, then, is not so much the conceptual disjunction as the historical connection which led to it. For the transition was necessarily confused and fluid, and out of it the clear distinction between policing and soldiering only emerged relatively slowly, almost as an afterthought. We must not jump to false conclusions by looking only at the relatively stable conditions prevalent in advanced democracies today, when what matters is being able to see, within the fluidity and confusion, the seeds of a new beginning.

THE USE OF FORCE

At first glance it may appear obvious that, by comparison with the kinds and amounts of force available to an army, a police force is relatively weakly equipped, even though at times a squad of riot police looks extraordinarily like a detachment of Alexander the Great's heavy infantry. But in any case, the first glance is misleading. It is impossible to tell simply by taking a look from outside whether what is happening on the street is a military operation or a police action: for what makes the difference is not the amount or kind of force involved but the purpose for which it is being used.

The key question is this: is this action designed to restore law and order or is it to win a duel? (Of course, winning the occasional duel may well be an episode in a restoration of law and order; but in a police action, restoration of order will always trump 'winning' as the principal objective.) Upon the answer will depend the question whether what we are looking at is a police action or a war.

Yet, once again, matters are not quite so simple in practice. For in the past soldiers have often been used to restore law and order within the state. And similarly police forces can all too easily escape from the jurisdiction they are supposed to enforce and turn into thugs who only happen to wear a police uniform. Exactly how in present circumstances an international police force is to emerge out of the chaos of a military in disarray is hard to see. My point here is simply to insist that the trick must be done if we are to have much hope of providing an ethical framework for intervention.

WAR AND POLICING

The parallel between war and policing was noted by Aquinas: 'those who may lawfully use the sword to defend a commonwealth against criminals (*interiores perturbatores*) disturbing it from within may also use the sword to protect it from enemies without'.[11] But this observation pre-dated the positivist assumptions of Clausewitz' notions on law and sovereignty. For Aquinas neither warfare nor policing lay beyond the jurisdiction of law or morality, since both rested on a firm foundation of 'natural law', not on the shifting sands of international sovereignty. This is why the criteria for the '*in bello*' use of force in policing (that is, discrimination and proportionality) are broadly the same for the mediaevalist as those for warfare, even though the *ad bellum* considerations do not apply in quite the same way. For the state has no choice but to enforce the law, whereas it always has a choice whether or not to go to war. As Pope Pius XII pointed out in 1953: 'When the damages caused by war are not comparable to those of "tolerated injustice" one may have a duty to "suffer the injustice" '.[12] But this cannot be so in the case of law enforcement, for no government could possibly announce that the price for law enforcement had unfortunately become disproportionately high and that it was therefore the duty of citizens to 'suffer the injustice' of having to put up with the activities of criminals.[13] Calculating the 'just price' for a police action which we have no option but to undertake is not the same as judging the just price for a war which we are not strictly compelled to enter into.

But in any case, it is important to note that the very concept of a 'just price' (which is only another way of speaking about the criterion of proportionality) had a resonance for Aquinas which it had lost by the time of Clausewitz. For *just* prices (to be contrasted with prices influenced by private vices, like avarice) were part of the economic currency of the Middle Ages. This perhaps explains why Aquinas did not need explicitly to allude to proportionality as a criterion in his discussion of the justice of war. It was only when the concept had begun to lose its grip on people's consciousness through the encroachment of market forces, that moralists (such as Victoria) began to insist explicitly on its relevance to war. For until then a structure of just prices had been taken for granted as part of the background of economic but also of military operations. It was hardly necessary to expatiate to soldiers on something so obvious as the need to pay no more than the just price, for in mediaeval theory the concept of just price was 'structural' – that is, there was a commonly agreed theory as to the means by which to determine it. Whereas what stood in its way was a private vice: avarice in the economic sphere and what Augustine had called the 'lust to dominate' in the military.[14] However, by the time of Clausewitz the opposite was true: market forces, in the shape of avarice (the maximisation of profit) or of the lust to dominate (the winning of wars) had become structural, while ideas of what would be the just price to pay in either case had been relegated to private judgement. The result has been that arbitrary and individual judgements now masquerade as proportionality calculations. Doubtless debate over their justice will be interminable.[15]

INTERNAL AND EXTERNAL 'ENEMIES'

Today many of those who would once have been regarded as 'enemies without' (that is, aggressors from another state) need to be seen as '*interiores perturbatores* disturbing it from within' (that is, breaching the peace of the international community). This point is surely valid for situations including Somalia, Bosnia, Angola, Northern Ireland, Afghanistan, Rwanda, Chechnya where warlords with essentially private armies have been able to brawl at will, causing affrays which are intolerable to others. What is needed is police action to deal with them.

Part of the purpose of a police action will be to arrest the ringleaders and bring them to trial. If in a public disturbance the police were not engaged in law enforcement (and therefore trying to catch criminals) there would be no justification for their using force at all (except in self-defence). Similarly if the international intervenors are not engaged in law enforcement, but are solely engaged in bringing succour to the victims they are doing less than they need to be doing (and be seen to be doing) to justify their use of force. The Bosnian example has been instructive here. As long as the intervention was solely for humanitarian purposes, that is, to bring succour to victims, there was a case for the intervenors to go in unarmed. They were then clearly a disinterested group trying to help the helpless. Unfortunately the strategy failed because the conflicting parties took advantage of the intervenors' weakness, for example, by stealing their supplies and using roads that had been cleared by the intervenors to move their own military supplies. Thus it became necessary to consider using offensive force against these 'brawlers' in order to make the humanitarian effort possible. It is at points like this that the underlying purpose of law enforcement and of catching the criminals comes into view as the fundamental justification of what is being done. But this does not mean that this must necessarily be the main priority in the minds of the intervenors at every stage. First of all 'affrays' have to be put down for the sake of protecting those unwillingly caught up in them, and to remove a threat to peace and security. The priority must be coming to the rescue of those suffering by bringing them supplies, evacuating the sick and wounded and so on, sometimes even at the expense of catching the ringleaders. If the affray has underlying causes which need to be addressed by the competent authority it may (for example) be expedient that negotiations take place and criminal prosecutions be postponed or even abandoned. My point, however, is the purely logical one that the troublemaker is to be regarded as engaged in an affray rather than in a war. The implications of this distinction are far-reaching, for the purpose of intervention is not necessarily to destroy the capacity of the opponent to resist (Clausewitz) but to restore law and order within the international community and, if deemed to be for the common good, to try and punish those responsible.

Unfortunately the procedure for arresting, trying and punishing offenders at the international level does not yet exist except in a very inchoate form. Nevertheless I maintain that intervention can only be just as long as there is the possibility of a criminal process at the end of it. It follows that an *impartial international tribunal to try cases of personal or collective guilt is essential to the very concept of just intervention.* This being so, we must take all necessary steps to create the necessary legal machinery. It is not enough simply to set up a tribunal for each case as it comes along. A permanent international criminal court is a sine qua non of justice for the international community. In this connection it is interesting to note that the idea of a permanent international court of criminal justice is today not as far-fetched as it once seemed. In a recent BBC broadcast, Christopher Greenwood, Professor of International Law at the London School of Economics, said that the establishment of such a court was today being seriously considered and that a UN conference about it was likely to take place in 1998.[16] We will leave the last word to the judicious summary by Adam Roberts in his recent *Adelphi Paper.*

> Concern about implementing international humanitarian law is a driving force behind proposals for the establishment of a permanent international criminal court, which is the subject of ongoing negotiations under UN auspices. There is no disagreement that this international court would be involved in trying three 'core crimes' – war crimes, crimes against humanity and genocide. However, there are numerous issues yet to be resolved about jurisdiction over other crimes, and the extent to which the prosecutor might have an independent investigatory role. Whether or not the champions of this proposal overcome the concerns of states about independent supra-national investigations into their security activities, the demand for effective implementation of the laws of war is likely to remain very strong, and to be difficult to translate into effective policies of international enforcement against recalcitrant states.
>
> (Roberts, 1996:50)

That indeed is the challenge.

NOTES

1. For claims that these interventions were only 'police actions' cf.: 'Suez', BBC Radio 4 'Document' programme, 15 September 1994 – quoting a UK Government source. On Chechnya: see Meek (1994).
2. Clausewitz, *On War*, Book I, Ch. 1.2.
3. All the 'Peacekeeping' contributions to the Autumn 1994 issue of *Survival*, the quarterly periodical of the International Institute for Strategic Studies, reveal the difficulties of defining intervention in purely military, or 'Clausewitzian' terms.
4. Clausewitz, *On War*, Book I, Ch. 1.2 and 1.3.
5. cf. Searle (1969:50ff), drawing on Anscombe (1981:22–5).
6. cf. Austin (1962). Austin argues that some utterances, such as 'I name this ship', 'I give and bequeath my watch', etc. are neither true nor false, but rather 'happy' or 'unhappy' in the sense that sometimes the utterer successfully performs the action, sometimes not. 'I surrender' is an utterance of this kind: the saying is the doing of the action. (Of course, there are many ways of surrendering, including signing a treaty, or grovelling at the feet of the opponent. But all will have the feature of being liable to 'misfire' by failing in certain circumstances to bring off the action.)
7. cf. Walzer (1977:44–7). On some of the moral problems associated with 'surrendering' and the war convention, cf. Cook and Hamann (1994).
8. Quoted in Walzer (1977:47).
9. As Walzer (1977:47) puts it: 'The rules of war, alien as they often are to our sense of what is best, are made obligatory by the general consent of mankind'.
10. A new police security force is being discussed for the European Union. It is called 'Europol' (Orlowski, 1995).
11. cf. *Summa Theologiae* II IIae 40, 1.
12. Pius XII, *Address to the International Office of Documentation for Military Medicine*, 19 October 1953.
13. The case of the Somerset and Avon police policy is instructive here. The police had decided that they could not afford to pursue petty offenders beyond their own police territory, since catching them had become disproportionately expensive. But one policeman was reported as saying: 'I dread to think what the victims of these offences will think about it'. The government promptly stepped in and the decision was rescinded. cf. *The Daily Telegraph*, 21 and 22 June 1994.
14. cf. St Augustine, *Contra Faustus*, Lib. 22, Cap. 74, quoted by Aquinas, *loc. cit.*
15. On the interminability of modern moral debate cf. MacIntyre (1981:6). There have been a few tentative steps towards legal condemnation of particular international actions on grounds of disproportionality. Rosalyn Higgins records a UN debate in which criticism of Israeli behaviour over the 1956 war was voiced on these grounds (Higgins, 1963:203–5). More recently an official British committee criticised Iran for prolonging the Iran/Iraq war after 1987 on the grounds that its behaviour had become disproportionate. A disproportionality criticism of the American action to protect medical students in Grenada is also on record. (The latter two examples were suggested to me in conversation with Christopher Greenwood.)
16. 'Law in Action', BBC Radio 4, 6 December 1996.

BIBLIOGRAPHY

Anscombe, G.E.M., 'On Brute Facts', *Collected Philosophical Papers,* Vol. III, Oxford: Oxford University Press, 1981, 22–5.
Austin, J.L., *How To Do Things With Words,* Oxford: Oxford University Press, 1962.
Cook, M.L. and Hamann, 'The Road to Basra: A Case Study in Military Ethics', in: Society of Christian Ethics, *Annual* 1994, 207–28.
Higgins, R., *Development of International Law Through the Political Organs of the United Nations,* Oxford: Oxford University Press, 1963.
MacIntyre, A., *After Virtue,* London: Duckworth, 1981.
Meek, J., 'Chechenya', *The Guardian,* 12 Dec. 1994, 9.
Orlowski, A., *The Independent,* 16 Jan. 1995.
Roberts, A., *Humanitarian Action in War: Aid, Protection and Impartiality in a Policy Vacuum* (Adelphi Paper 305), London: IISS & Oxford University Press, 1996.
Searle, J., *Speech Acts,* Cambridge: Cambridge University Press, 1969, 50ff.
Walzer, M., *Just and Unjust Wars,* London: Allen Lane, 1977.

Part II
Intervention and the Just War Tradition

In this part of the book, the applicability of just war theory to the issue of intervention is examined in theological, historical and contemporary perspective. ***'Can an Intervention Be Just?'*** asks *Anthony Harvey*, applying this theological tradition.

'Humanitarian Intervention: the Contemporary Debate' is the theme of the chapter by *Oliver Ramsbotham*, which acts as a bridge between the tradition and the current debate.

Hugh Beach, drawing on recent examples and the thinking of the US Roman Catholic Bishops, shares his ***'Second Thoughts on First Principles'***.

4 Can an Intervention Be Just?

Anthony Harvey

The questions with which these essays are concerned are all aspects of a conflict between two basic principles that are enshrined in uneasy juxtaposition in the UN Charter of 1945. On the one hand there is the prohibition of the use of force against 'the territorial integrity or political independence of any state', and of UN intervention 'in matters which are essentially within the jurisdiction of any State' (Articles 2(4) and 2(7) respectively). On the other hand it is stated that 'All members pledge themselves to take joint and separate action' in cooperation with the UN to promote 'universal respect for, and observance of, human rights' (Articles 55, 56). These two principles, at least in their present form, are of relatively recent origin. That rights, including the right to legislate and to administer justice without interference from outside their borders, belong to 'states' as such is a notion which first emerged in the eighteenth century (for example by de Vattel, 1758); that certain rights (now called human rights) belong to every person by virtue simply of membership of the human race, and that there is a universal obligation to ensure that these rights are respected, is a principle first articulated in the seventeenth century by Hugo Grotius and John Locke. It was then made a basis of public policy by the leaders of the French and American Revolutions, and issued in the American Declaration of Independence (1776) and the French Declaration of the Rights of Man and the Citizen (1798). But the underlying motivation can be traced back much further. In particular there is a long tradition of Christian thought and practice, both in the respect due to rulers and in humanitarian concern for the oppressed, of which the roots can be found in the Scriptures themselves.

Not, of course, that there can be any easy application of scriptural texts to modern problems of intervention and humanitarian relief. So far as the Hebrew scriptures are concerned, the historic kingdoms of Judah and Israel were never (except perhaps under King Solomon) in a political or strategic position to intervene in the affairs of a neighbouring nation even had they perceived a motive to do so; and in the preceding period such parallels as may be traced (such as the penalty imposed on the Benjaminites by neighbouring tribes for a flagrant breach of the laws of hospitality and respect for aliens as recorded in Judges 19–20) are, to say the least, remote. The same is true, to a still greater degree, of the New Testament, in so far as the infant Christian community was far too small and insignificant to have any opportunity of influencing the foreign policy of any nation, and such questions cannot be expected to receive even an oblique reference in Christian sources before at least the time of the Roman Emperor Constantine in the early fourth century. Yet there were texts in the teaching of both Jesus and St Paul which from very early times were seen to bear sharply on questions which did actually impinge on the lives and reflections of Christians, such as whether there were circumstances under which they might engage in military service or retaliatory action, and the need to find ways of relieving the oppression of the poor and vulnerable in obedience to a moral tradition that reaches far back into the Hebrew scriptures. At the same time, as we shall see, there are stern words in Paul's Letter to the Romans enjoining implicit obedience to secular rulers which were to have a profound restraining influence on the will of Christians to risk any act of civil disobedience, even in the interests of humanitarian assistance to others (Romans 13.1–7). The inherent conflict between a concern for justice on the one hand and a respect for established authority on the other was made the more intractable by the existence of divinely inspired texts which could readily be quoted in support of either position.

'Do not resist evil' (Matthew 5.39); 'Love your enemies' (Matthew 5.44). Taken on their own, these commands of Jesus recorded in the Sermon on the Mount might seem to settle for ever the question of whether a Christian should take up arms or be prepared to use force to settle a dispute or remedy an injustice. Christianity, on this showing, must be a pacifist religion, and its followers must renounce the use of violence in all circumstances. Yet in practice it has only ever been a minority of Christians who have followed a policy of strict non-resistance. From the fourth century onwards Christians have generally been willing to bear arms, and their reluctance in early times to join the Roman Army was probably motivated more by the fear of being involved in idolatrous ceremonies than by any sense that the military calling was incompatible with the teaching of

Jesus (Helgeland, 1985:22–5, 50–5). When the argument turned on biblical texts, there was never any difficulty in finding some which yielded a contrary message. John the Baptist's apparent condonation of military service (Luke 3.14), Jesus' commendation of a military centurion (Luke 7.1–10), his saying about bringing not peace but a sword (Matthew 10.34) and his recommendation to his disciples to equip themselves with at any rate two swords (Luke 22.36,38) were relentlessly called in evidence by those who believed that Jesus' generalised call to non-resistance must necessarily be qualified by a reasonable prudence in warding off actual threats to life and property. Moreover the Hebrew scriptures explicitly authorised military activity and contained narratives of violent and sometimes ruthless campaigns conducted apparently with full divine approval. Jesus never repudiated these scriptures, and made no direct comment on the use of force either for policing and punishment or for defence and, if necessary, conquest.

By itself, this ambiguity of the scriptural evidence would hardly have been sufficient to cause uncertainty in the Christian response to Jesus' radical call to non-resistance, love of enemies and the renunciation of violence exemplified in his own arrest and execution. And indeed the minority of Christians who have applied this teaching literally to their own circumstances have given an impressive testimony to its practicability and its potential for reconciliation and peacemaking. But the motives of the majority who have taken the contrary view and have seen the necessity for the use of at least occasional force to secure legitimate objectives have been by no means hypocritical and have been supported by principles which, though usually presented in philosophical form, have also their roots in the Bible. The justice of God is a recurrent theme in biblical writings. This justice offers protection and vindication to the poor and the weak and results in the discomfiture of their oppressors. Its execution may involve human agents and necessarily validates such acts of coercion as may be necessary to achieve a just resolution.

Yet even here there is a strong contrary tendency. 'Vengeance is mine, I will repay, says the Lord.' (Romans 12.19; Hebrews 10.30). Admittedly this adage (which is derived from Deuteronomy 32.35) is quoted in the context of personal injury: the persecuted individual should not seek to avenge himself. But in conjunction with Paul's statement that earthly authorities are 'ordained by God', that any opposition to them is culpable and that they act as God's ministers (Romans 13.1–4), it offered a strong incentive, or in some circumstances a convenient pretext, not to take any action in defiance of an unjust ruler. So long as the conviction remained alive that however much the unrighteous may seem to flourish in this life there is certain retribution awaiting them hereafter at the hands of God, there seemed little justification for any forcible opposition to an oppressive ruler, and the question of armed intervention within the jurisdiction of another ruler for the sake of his oppressed subjects seldom arose before the modern era.

What did arise was the question of the correct personal response to the abuse of political authority. Tyrannical and oppressive rulers existed, and the Christian needed to know whether the Pauline rule of absolute obedience must be obeyed even if it involved acquiescence in atrocities. Certainly the Scriptures seemed to give clear guidance: slaves were to obey, and indeed suffer gladly under, unjust masters (1 Peter 2.18); unquestioning obedience was owed to rulers by virtue of their office (Romans 13.1). But suppose the ruler became a tyrant, and his subjects lost all personal security: was obedience to such a monster still required? Paul's ruling had been given under the relatively stable administration of the Roman Empire, and the magistrates of which he and his correspondents had experience were subject to legal restraint. But the emergence of smaller princedoms in the Middle Ages created a different situation: what assurance was there that the ruler would observe even the most basic principles of justice?

The question must often have been an agonizingly personal one for individual sufferers from tyrannical rule. But behind it lay a theoretical question of the utmost importance. The ruler could evidently make laws within his own jurisdiction; but was there any external standard of justice by which those laws could be judged or validated? If (to use the Pauline phrase) the ruler's authority was derived from God, must it not also be exercised in conformity with God's justice? Was there not some external standard against which the tyrant's laws could be measured, and, if found wanting, cease to command obedience? There was, after all, a long tradition of 'natural law', in the sense of a universal moral consensus founded upon reason and existing independently of any particular legislative authority: the principle was clearly formulated by Cicero in *De Republica* 3.22.33 and remained an important legacy of Stoic thought throughout the Middle Ages. Admittedly, from a Christian point of view, the matter was complicated by the Fall. For Augustine, 'natural law' meant the law obtaining in humanity's state of innocence; the actual laws obtaining in the Roman Empire were necessarily imperfect and provisional, and could not be relied on to reflect the justice of God; and indeed the Roman jurists were by no means agreed on the exact relationship between the *jus gentium* (the laws that actually existed among different nations) and the 'natural law' derived from enlightened reason (Tooke, 1965:78ff.). Nevertheless, from a Christian point of view, an objective point of reference existed in Scripture. In the Old Testament, the justice of God was stated in both the Law and the Prophets to demand fair treatment of all citizens, impartial administration of justice and the protection of the poor and the vulnerable. The regime of a prince which flagrantly violated these standards of justice could be described as 'not lawful' and his subjects could legitimately refuse to obey him. By the twelfth century the schoolmen were confident enough of the existence of an independent, divinely authorised, system of law to be able to propound the maxim '*lex injusta non est lex*' – an unjust law is not a law (Sieghart, 1985:21–3). It followed that no one refusing to obey such a law could be convicted of sin.

This theoretical position gave rise to two very practical questions: who would determine the precise content of this superior system, and whose responsibility was it to correct or depose a tyrannical prince? Considerable impetus towards an answer to the first question was provided by the translation into Latin of Aristotle's *Politics* (384–322 BCE) in the thirteenth century (out of the Arabic in which it had been read for some centuries by Muslim scholars) and by the brilliant synthesis worked out by Thomas Aquinas of the Aristotelian, Stoic and Christian concepts of 'law' and 'nature' which became the foundation of the entire system of 'natural law' that has lasted to this day. The definition of this 'natural law', now held to be identical with divine law, thus became the task of churchmen: through them, the Church exercised its responsibility to give moral guidance to all its members and could determine whether particular laws were 'just'. As for constraints that might be placed on a ruler who flouted these laws, the early Middle Ages had already developed a clear doctrine of the absolute supremacy of the Pope in temporal as well as in spiritual affairs. Kings and emperors derived their authority from above – from God – but mediated through the Pope. Their primary function was to bear the sword in the battle against evil and to assist the Pope in his government of the Christian world.[1] If they showed themselves unworthy of this trust, the Pope had impressive resources for imposing discipline and restoring order. He could, for example, excommunicate a disobedient ruler, with the consequence (among others) that he would be physically isolated from his own subjects, who might also find that other Christian nations had been forbidden by the Pope to trade with them – an early example of international sanctions! (Ullmann, 1961:77f.). As a last resort the Pope could depose the recalcitrant ruler and authorise other kings to march against him if he resisted.

It might appear from this account that there existed already in the Middle Ages a legal and political framework for the protection of subjects from unlawful oppression by their ruler. Certainly there was a recognition that the divinely authorised rule of a prince might become tyrannical, and that his subjects might therefore be exempted from their oath of allegiance to him and from obeying his unjust laws; but it would be something of an anachronism to assume that this would offer protection to the populace as a whole or that external force might be applied in the interests of the oppressed. It was a society, after all, in which slavery was established and in which the poor had no voice: laws were derived from a superior authority and were made by princes in their own interests. There were few champions of humanitarian treatment for the generality. Indeed by far the most common spring to set off the process of papal interference was not physical or economic misery but something regarded as much more serious (since it affected not just this life but the next), namely heresy. A prince who permitted heretical opinions to go unchecked was exposing his subjects to the danger of eternal damnation and must at all costs be disciplined.[2] But any comparable action for what would now be called humanitarian relief was extremely rare.

It was, in part at least, the disintegration of the Church as a single supreme authority at the Reformation, accompanied by the assertion of the autonomy of the human reason which we associate with the Enlightenment, which raised again the question of an objective criterion by which particular laws may be judged to be 'unjust'. If divine and natural law, as interpreted by the Church, was no longer universally recognised and obeyed, on what grounds was it possible to question the legality of an oppressive government? For an answer it was necessary to look to the philosophers; and it was in the seventeenth century, in the writings of Grotius and Locke, that there first emerged a reasoned statement of what are now called 'human rights'. There had of course been thinkers in the late Middle Ages who had articulated the principle, derived ultimately from Aristotle, that government depends upon the assent of the people and that the power of a ruler is conferred on him by his subjects.[3] But the proposition that men and women possess certain fundamental rights by virtue simply of being members of the human race was a philosophical position which provided the theoretical justification for the revolutionary movements of the late eighteenth century and has formed the basis of all thinking and legislation on human rights in the last half century.

The Christian response to this increasingly prevalent human rights language has been slow and uncertain. It is, for instance, only in the last few years that the Roman Catholic Church has been able to express approval of the principles which were proclaimed in the French Revolution.[4] It was not only that the philosophers' language was new, and made no direct reference to Christian thinking on human nature; the Bible itself seemed to give little support to it. There, the concept of 'rights' is notably absent; all the emphasis is on the obligations imposed on individuals and social classes by the divine law. The philosophers, of course, were insisting that rights and responsibilities are complementary: if legal obligations are specified in the Old Testament, it ought to be possible to infer the rights they entail. But in fact this is not always true. A farmer was obliged not to glean right up to the edge of his field: he must leave something for the alien, the fatherless and the widow (Leviticus 19.9f.). But this was no more than a moral obligation; it did not confer on the poor a right to glean enforceable by a court of law. Hence the surprisingly large number of injunctions in the Law of Moses which seem to us moral rather than legal ('Thou shalt not covet' alongside 'Thou shalt not murder'). The obligations which the strong had towards the weak, the rich towards the poor, were to be fulfilled by reason of mercy, compassion or enlightened self-interest, not out of fear of any legal redress. Hence the language of 'rights' is not easy to trace back to the Old Testament. And the New Testament seems even more recalcitrant; for there the Christian is specifically told not to press a case against an adversary (Matthew 5.25), not to resist evil (Matthew 5.39), not to seek justification (Romans 12.19), not to retaliate against oppressors (1 Peter 3.9), not even to try to win a case, it being actually better to suffer injustice (1 Corinthians 6.7). Add to all this the absolute obedience to authority enjoined by St Paul (Romans 13), which (particularly in the Lutheran tradition) has restrained some Christians from offering resistance to any form of tyranny and oppression right up to the present day, and it should cause no surprise that Christian theology has been slow to endorse the international consensus on human rights which found expression in the UN Declaration of 1948 and has been gathering momentum ever since.

Yet that, so far as Christianity is concerned, is by no means the end of the story. The philosophical basis for human rights is the absolute and equal value of every human being, regardless of race, sex or class. The same principle, expressed in terms of the inalienable dignity of every person as the object of God's love, is fundamental to Christianity. Moreover the often repeated Old Testament imperative to care and provide for the weaker and more vulnerable members of society is confirmed and deepened in the New Testament and is at the very heart of Christian charitable and social action. These principles have long been seen as part of the 'natural law' which undergirds all Christian morality. Indeed it is arguable that human rights are simply natural law in a new form, commanding as they do wide agreement and often passionate advocacy from people of many faiths or none. The legal instruments to which this consensus has given rise have simply placed a new tool in the hands of Christians, as of adherents of other religions, with which to give effect to their traditional concern for the poor, the fatherless, the widow and all their vulnerable equivalents in the sophisticated societies of today.

For here is the new factor: human rights have acquired the protection of law. The second half of the twentieth century has seen the evolution of an official code of human rights embodied in a number of international conventions by which the signatories are legally bound. For the first time since the Middle Ages it is now possible for citizens who have suffered an infringement of their rights by their own government or its agencies to appeal for redress to an international court; and a government found guilty by such a court is bound by its treaty obligations both to make restitution to the aggrieved citizen and to amend its own laws to bring them into line with the international convention.

This evolution of international legal instruments is crucial to our topic. Just as in the first half of this century the Hague and Geneva conventions and protocols outlawed certain forms of military action and created limits to acceptable conduct in war, such that any nation that was signatory to them risked reprisals if it disregarded them, so since 1945 successive human rights conventions have created legal restraints on any government that imposes on its citizens legislation that can be shown to be incompatible with them. *Lex injusta non est lex.* The medieval principle presupposed a superior authority capable of determining whether any particular law conformed to an absolute standard of justice. Today's equivalent is the judgement of an international court, set up with the consent of individual nations which are bound by treaty to respect its decisions. Whereas before the Second World War justification for penalising a state which treated its citizens barbarically was possible, if at all, only on moral grounds, since 1948 all members of the United Nations have committed themselves to the 'common standard of achievement' defined by the Universal Declaration of Human Rights (Preamble) and many have further bound themselves by treaty to regional conventions which entail bringing their own domestic legislation into line with an internationally agreed code of law. It follows that, as more and more nations accede to these conventions by treaty, infringements by any of them of the fundamental human rights of their citizens can be controlled and if necessary prevented by actions of other countries which cannot be criticised as intervention 'in matters which are essentially within the domestic jurisdiction' of the offending state (which is contrary to the UN Charter, Article 2(7)) but are in the nature of sanctions enforcing adherence to laws recognised by it as binding on its own actions. The grounds for such action are thereby raised from the level of subjective and uncertain moral judgements to that of objectively verifiable and impartially interpreted law. The conflict between the immunity of a state from interference from abroad in its own affairs and the moral necessity to intervene wherever human rights are being flagrantly infringed is resolved by institutions of international law.

Or would be resolved, if all states were signatories of international conventions on human rights. In fact, of course, the issues which are the subject of this book have arisen and in some cases are still unresolved in states which have entered into no treaty obligations with regard to human rights or in which law and order has broken down as a result of warring factions within their borders. The only legal basis for exerting more than diplomatic pressure on these states (whether through trade embargoes, sanctions or military action) is in the UN Charter; but this, as we noted at the beginning, explicitly forbids such intervention unless the state in question has committed an act of aggression. Neighbouring states, therefore, which may be affected by, for example, the genocidal policies of a government or an armed faction close to their borders creating a massive refugee problem, and the international community in general which may be shocked and alarmed by the turn of events taken by that country's 'domestic affairs', are caught on the horns of an agonizing dilemma. To take action is to breach the only legal code of international relations subscribed to by all members of the UN; not to take action is to ignore the plight of many thousand human beings whose lives might be saved by resolute opposition to the oppressor's intentions, and may be registered by public opinion as an evasion of a clear moral duty on the pretext that international law provides no authorisation for doing anything more than sending convoys of food and medicines for the relief of suffering that a determined coalition of nations might have prevented.

The sharpness of this dilemma could certainly be reduced through the development of international institutions. If a two-thirds majority could be mustered at the UN General Assembly (including all five permanent members of the UN Security Council) – an extremely unlikely event in present circumstances – in favour of revising Article 2 of the Charter so as to authorise 'such action as may be necessary by air, sea or land forces' to put a stop to grave and massive violations of human rights within the borders of any state in the world; or if regional human rights conventions were to gain the signature of all states likely to permit such violations; then concerted action on humanitarian grounds by a coalition of states, duly authorised by the relevant international institution, would cease to be illegal. But this of course, is by no means the end of the matter. What happens to be legal is not necessarily the correct moral choice. Some Christians will always take the view, for which there has been continuous support in Christian tradition down the centuries, that armed intervention, even as a last resort, is contrary to the teaching of the Gospel; and they will be supported by the prudential argument that the use of force always entails the risk of doing more harm than good. The majority, on the other hand, will be more strongly influenced by humanitarian arguments and be ready to use any practicable and proportionate form of coercion in order to save those whose lives are threatened. They will then be faced by a mass of practical questions regarding the means and scale of the force to be used and the precise objectives to be achieved; and in these matters they will be guided, as they have been for many centuries, by principles derived from natural law and governing the initiation and conduct of any 'just' (that is, compatible with the Christian conscience) war, such as lawful authority, just cause, right intention and means proportionate to the end to be achieved. Such reasoning – particularly with regard to 'lawful authority' – would be greatly strengthened if the legality of humanitarian intervention could be established either regionally or universally, and recent events have shown this to be an urgent task for the international community. But members of the Christian as of other faiths will always be conscious of the challenge inherent in their religion to set their sights higher and work for a world order in which the command to renounce the use of the sword can be obeyed without risk to the lives and well-being of their fellow men and women.

NOTES

1. This achieved classic formulation by John of Salisbury, see Ullmann, 1965:422; and Ullmann, 1961:63f.
2. This necessity eventually drove the Pope to authorise regular princes to deliver the Bohemian from the 'injustice' of the Hussite reforms, or to send Philip II's *armadas* to deliver England from an excommunicate Queen.
3. Such as Marsiglio: Ullmann, 1961:294–8.
4. The negative judgements expressed by Gregory XVI and Pius IX were first moderated by Leo XIII in the late 1880s and decisively reversed by John XXIII in the papal encyclical *Pacem in Terris* (1963). French Catholics have come to acknowledge the values proclaimed by the Revolution only recently: Woodrow, 1989:716–17.

BIBLIOGRAPHY

Helgeland, J., Daly, R.J., and Burns, J.P., *Christians and the Military*, London: SCM Press, 1985.
Sieghart, P., *The Lawful Rights of Mankind*, Oxford: Oxford University Press, 1985.
Tooke, J.D., *The Just War in Aquinas and Grotius*, London: SPCK, 1965.
Ullmann, W., *Principles of Government and Politics in the Middle Ages*, London: Methuen, 1961.
Ullmann, W., *The Growth of Papal Government in the Middle Ages*, London: Methuen, 1955, 1965.
Vattel, E. de, *Droit des Gens, ou Principes de la Loi Naturelle Appliqués à la Conduite et aux Affaires des Nations et des Souverains*, 1758 (E.T. The Law of Nations, 1769).
Woodrow, A., 'A Church Embarrassed', *The Tablet*, 24 June 1989, 716–17, referring to a document published by the French bishops in October 1988.

5 Humanitarian Intervention: the Contemporary Debate

Oliver Ramsbotham

The question of humanitarian intervention is not a new one. It can be traced back in recognisably modern form to the sixteenth and seventeenth centuries, and, in particular, to the writings of Victoria (1532), Gentili (1598) and Grotius (1625). It emerged as part of a wider process which saw the early development of modern international law at the time of the break-up of Christendom, the voyages of discovery and beginning of European overseas empires, and the evolution of the early modern state. In the centuries that followed, a number of other conceptual developments took place which have cumulatively served to define the issue in the form in which we find it today, above all, the articulation of the non-intervention norm from the eighteenth century, and the assertion of the principles of popular sovereignty and self-determination from the time of the American and French Revolutions. The debate was fully joined in the nineteenth century, particularly in relation to interventions by Western powers in the collapsing Ottoman Empire, and re-emerged unresolved in the twentieth century. Since 1945 the legal-political framework has been provided by the Charter of the United Nations. The significance of the issue today can best be brought out by setting it against this historical background. A comparison of the Cold War with the post-Cold War debate may then suggest that in the 1990s the challenge of humanitarian intervention has revived older categories. In the process it has become more complex and deeper, raising fundamental questions about the nature of international politics, international ethics and international law.

During the Cold War, in the absence of the possibility of collective action mandated by the United Nations, the issue of intervention was seen to concern forcible self-help by states in defence of indigenous human rights in other countries (Lillich, 1967). If governments abused the rights of their own citizens, should other governments intervene forcibly to remedy the situation? There was, in fact, no agreement, either about the definition of humanitarian intervention or about putative examples of it. For Verwey 'there may be few concepts in international law today which are as conceptually obscure and legally controversial' (Verwey, 1985:357), while the number of instances cited varies between four (Tesón, 1988:155–200) and 11 (Arend and Beck, 1993:112–37). Nevertheless, characteristic features listed by many of those engaged in the formal debate included: (1) that the context was one of abuse by overstrong governments; (2) that 'humanitarian' referred to the human rights of threatened populations (not the rescue of nationals); (3) that the intervention took the form of self-help by states (in strict readings collective action by the UN Security Council was not intervention); (4) that it must be without the consent, indeed expressly against the will, of target governments; and (5) that it was swift forcible military action to end the atrocities, usually by removing the offending regime. The best known examples were Indian intervention in what was then East Pakistan (now Bangladesh) in 1971, Tanzanian intervention to stop the depredations of Idi Amin in Uganda in 1978–9, and Vietnamese intervention to oust the murderous Pol Pot regime in Kampuchea (Cambodia) in 1978–9. Needless to say, in response to most of the worst atrocities of the time (including those perpetrated by Stalinist Russia and Maoist China) not only was there no forcible intervention, but even agreed collective procedures and normal diplomatic protest were muted or non-existent (Kuper, 1981).

As detailed elsewhere, despite a tendency for much of the debate to be foreclosed on formal definitional grounds, along the lines that intervention which did not violate the independence of a target state was not intervention (see Vincent, 1974:11–12), the Cold War debate was richer and more nuanced than a restrictionist approach might suggest.[1] It was simultaneously a debate in international politics, international ethics and international law. In international politics, it was conducted both at government level and at domestic political level. At government level, good accounts of official positions (albeit variously interpreted) can be found in Franck and Rodley (1973) for the Indian intervention in East Pakistan, in Hassan (1981) and Thomas (1985:92–108) for the Tanzanian intervention in Uganda, and in Ronzitti (1985) and Klintworth (1989) for the Vietnamese intervention in Kampuchea.

Turning to the situation since the end of the Cold War, how has the humanitarian intervention debate developed in response to the changed international environment of the 1990s? There is no space to attempt a general analysis of the transformed post-Cold War geopolitical situation, nor any way of knowing whether it will turn out to be a temporary aberration or a long-term watershed, but it is helpful at the outset to note how radically the five component parts of the Cold War restrictionist definition of humanitarian intervention have already been affected in the new climate. There seem to have been six main examples of humanitarian intervention between 1990 and 1996 discussed in the literature: the intervention of Economic Community of West African States' (ECOWAS) forces in Liberia from August 1990; Operations Provide Comfort and Southern Watch in Iraq from April 1991; the intervention of UNPROFOR in Bosnia mandated in August 1992 (although I would not class this as a forcible intervention); Operation Restore Hope in Somalia (including the follow-on deployment of UNO-SOM II) from December 1992; Operation Turquoise in Rwanda from June 1994; and Operation Uphold Democracy in Haiti from September 1994. The intervention in Eastern Zaire, mandated in November 1996 but subsequently abandoned, might count as a seventh. Reviewing these cases, we can take each component of the Cold War definition in turn.

(1) The context, as the UN High Commissioner for Refugees notes, is no longer characteristically one in which the suffering is caused by over-strong repressive government, but is more usually 'the product of vicious internal conflicts' associated with over-weak or contested government (Ogata, 1993:iii). This greatly complicates the task of intervenors and precludes the idea that there might be a 'quick military fix'.

(2) The 'humanitarian' component is no longer confined to protecting human rights, but now also usually includes the question of upholding international humanitarian law and providing humanitarian assistance. This firmly links the issue of forcible humanitarian intervention to the wider processes which have greatly expanded the capacity and scope for non-forcible cross-border humanitarian initiatives since the late 1960s.[2]

(3) Instead of self-help by states, every one of the six or seven examples was in some way legitimised by UN Security Council resolutions.[3] This makes a profound difference to the terms of the debate in a number of commentators' eyes, shifting attention from Article 2(4) of the UN Charter to Article 2(7) which concerns interventions by the United Nations. For some this clearly distinguishes legitimate collective action from illegitimate self-help, thus

overcoming the crucial 'argument from abuse' which has for so long been a key element in statist anti-intervention objections. Others see interventions mandated by an unreformed United Nations as equally objectionable.

(4) Nor have these interventions in general been carried out against the will of target governments, as envisaged in the classic definition, but have usually been ambiguously consensual or there has been no government to give or withold consent. In the swirling confusion of civil war, internal factions support or oppose interventions according to changeable circumstance, while in conditions of government breakdown the question is raised of the responsibility of the international community for the welfare of the citizens of collapsed states.

Finally, (5) the use of force itself has been more ambiguously related to non-forcible 'peacekeeping' and to a range of non-military cross-border enterprises than was normal in the earlier period. Although enforcement lies at one end of the scale of possibilities, the main role of military forces in these situations has been 'the establishment of a secure environment for non-military operations, such as electoral monitoring, refugee repatriation, and the distribution of humanitarian relief supplies by civilian agencies' (Berdal, 1993:11).

As argued elsewhere (Ramsbotham and Woodhouse, 1996), taken together, all of this suggests a reconceptualisation of humanitarian intervention, so that forcible action (now including collective action) is seen as one intervention option among others. Non-intervention is also thereby reconceptualised.[4] This widens and deepens the traditional debate. Confining attention to the issue of forcible intervention for the purposes of this chapter, the core of the Cold War debate remains relevant, particularly the part inherited from the nineteenth century, but fundamental questions about the nature of international law, international politics and the international community are now more urgently raised.

As noted above, the debate in international law has been transformed by the switch of emphasis from UN Charter Article 2(4) to Article 2(7). So far, forcible collective action under Chapter VII has been justified, however notionally, as a response to threats to international peace and security, thus, among other things, avoiding a Chinese veto in the Security Council. In the view of Damrosch, however, this could be expanded to include an explicitly humanitarian mandate. Under what is termed a 'teleological' interpretation of the Charter, there is no reason why the conferral of coercive powers on the Security Council with respect to threats to peace and security should not be extended to the wider purposes of the Charter. There is also the possibility under Articles 10–14 for the General Assembly to make recommendations for what Lillich has called 'uniting-against-genocide'. In short, Damrosch argues that it is not so much constitutional law as practical wisdom that gives rise to reservations about collective forcible humanitarian intervention, including the dangers for world order and the question of whether force can in the event be effective (Damrosch and Scheffer, 1991:220–2). On the question of whether international law has already become more permissive in this regard, publicists range from the scepticism of Pease and Forsythe (1993), through the cautious permissiveness of Greenwood – 'it is no longer tenable to assert that whenever a government massacres its own people or a state collapses into anarchy international law forbids military intervention altogether' (Greenwood, 1993:40) – to the forthright endorsement of a *'droit d'ingerence* [right of intervention] in international humanitarian law' by Garigue (Garigue, 1993). This raises deep questions not only *in* but *about* international law. Is it to be seen as 'a progressive instrument of change, as a means of furthering the interests of peoples rather than governments, as something antithetical to the Hobbesian world of brute force?' Or is it to be evaluated, rather, merely as 'a practical means of devising modest and limited adjustments between conflicting interests of great powers, who are the principal agents of its creation?' (Roberts, 1990:84). Two clusters of values fundamental to the UN Charter, what Damrosch calls 'human rights values' and 'state system values', are in tension here (Damrosch, 1993:93). Perhaps Farer offers a balanced overview when he argues that the task of scholars is to help expedite the evolution of international law in the direction of humanitarian protection without stripping it of its usefulness as an instrument of conservative statecraft preserving the international order, which is a necessary, but not on its own sufficient, condition for human dignity (Farer, 1991:200).

This carries the debate on to the point where it involves the question of the whole nature of international politics, and, in particular, of the 'statist paradigm' at its core. We can take Thomas' persuasive 'pragmatic case against intervention' as illustrative of the anti-intervention case (Thomas, 1993). She accepts the relativist argument that, in a state system which is more culturally heterogeneous than in the nineteenth century, intervention on 'human-itarian' grounds 'smacks of ethnocentrism', and allies to this the realist claim that, in a world where states of unequal power pursue their national interests, forcible intervention will inevitably be in the interest of the strong. The statist argument, operating at three levels, pulls the other two arguments together: (1) at systemic level the appeal is to international order threatened by a breach in the non-intervention norm, (2) at state level it is to the morality of states (states are the bearers of rights and duties in international society), and (3) at community level it is to the value of cultural diversity which underpins the non-intervention norm: non-intervention 'values and maintains the heterogeneity of an ideologically, eco-nomically, ethnically and religiously diverse world. In this sense the state has moral force to it'. The West would do well to concentrate instead on its own responsibility for many of the structural causes of poverty and instability: 'we should realise that genuine humanitar-ian assistance for those starving in the Third World would entail structural transformations in our own economies and political pro-cesses'. In short, genuine humanitarian intervention presupposes an entirely different type of international politics to the one which exists at the moment. In the meantime, the best that can be done is to try to ensure that decisions to protect human rights are taken in an increasingly democratic, transparent and accountable manner. The interventionist counter-case includes rejection of cultural rela-tivism along the lines of the papal appeal to 'the conscience of humankind' on 5 December 1992 to render humanitarian interfer-ence 'mandatory in situations which gravely compromise the survi-val of entire peoples and ethnic groups' (Coste, 1993:28), and, somewhat surprisingly, an inversion of the realist argument along the lines that 'urgent humanitarian disaster' and 'gross violation of human rights' coupled with violence is itself a threat to international order and the interests of the great powers (Delbrück, 1992:900). With regard to the statist case, we can turn to Parekh's nuanced critique, which accepts much of Thomas' argument, such as that in current conditions humanitarian intervention is bound to be arbi-trarily determined by interest and capability and subject to double standards, and that its full logic implies a radical reordering of international politics, but is in the meantime ready to endorse forcible intervention in some cases and is forthright in rejecting the assumptions and values of the statist paradigm 'in favour of a shared world and common humanity':

the concept of humanitarian intervention is logically unstable in the sense that it both presupposes and seeks to go beyond the statist manner of thinking which has dominated political life for the past three centuries... although humanitarian intervention is justified under certain circumstances, it is too limited, late and superficial to be of lasting value, and needs to be embedded in and undertaken as part of a larger project of creating a just and non-statist global order.

(Parekh, 1996:1)

So it is that current debate about humanitarian intervention in the post-Cold War world has revived medieval categories, such as 'protection of the innocent' as a just cause for the use of force, and the solidarist conception of a great community of humankind found in Victoria, Suarez and Gentili in the West, and in the concept of the *umma wahida* (the original oneness of humankind) in Islam. At the same time the forcible intervention debate has become enmeshed in more extensive discussion about non-forcible intervention within the wider humanitarian community, including the Red Cross, UN agencies and NGOs (Macrae and Zwi, 1994; Harriss, 1995). In conditions characteristic of contemporary 'complex emergencies' humanitarian action is inevitably politicised, and, more likely than not, militarised. Humanitarian agencies are well aware of the danger that intervention may prove counter-productive and are as divided on the issue of the use of force in individual cases as are governments and public opinion in general. The issue is a profoundly difficult one for outsiders of all kinds, with humanitarian need at its most intense where the international community is as yet least able to respond. The result has been manifest inconsistency, with apparent 'success' in Iraq encouraging involvement in Bosnia, but apparent 'failure' in Somalia deterring comparable action in Rwanda. Two years later, after mutual recriminations and the apparent 'success' of IFOR in Bosnia, preparations were once more made for intervention in Eastern Zaire. The fact is that the international community is not monolithic. Under one aspect it seems capable of responding to the 'humanitarian' dimension of the problem (international humanitarian law, genuine humanitarian agencies); under another aspect it is able to mount forcible 'intervention' operations (the military capabilities of the most powerful states). These two components, both necessary for forcible humanitarian intervention, are in acute tension with each other. The result has been to generate vigorous argument about the whole nature of the international collectivity itself, and about the desirability and scope for a reform of its institutions for joint decision-making and collective action. Perhaps for the first time this can be seen as a genuinely global debate. Taking the example of Islam, since the Bosnian tragedy there is now as much controversy on the issue within the Muslim world as within the West (Hashmi, 1993). Muslims and Christians have been both perpetrators and victims of unspeakable atrocities in the 1990s. In some cases Christians have persecuted Muslims (Bosnia); in others Muslims have persecuted Christians (Sudan); in others again Christians have persecuted Christians (Croatia) and Muslims have persecuted Muslims (Iraq). Impassioned argument about humanitarian intervention has gone on in predominantly Muslim as in predominantly Christian countries. Muslims have participated side-by-side with non-Muslims in all the main intervention forces. The solidarist Grotian and pre-Grotian norm is echoed in the ringing Qur'anic call for the protection of the weak, the vulnerable and the helpless:

> How should ye not fight for the cause of Allah and of the feeble among men and of the women and children who are crying: Our Lord! Bring us forth from out this town of which the people are oppressors! Oh, give us from Thy presence some protecting friend! Oh, give us from Thy presence some defender!
>
> (4:75)

It remains to be seen whether, given the conditions of contemporary international politics, this can be transmuted into a truly universal human enterprise, which is seen in all parts of the world to be both effective and legitimate.

NOTES

1. For a fuller account of the Cold War debate see Ramsbotham and Woodhouse, 1996: chapter 2, 33–66.
2. This is too large a subject to deal with adequately here, but Ramsbotham and Woodhouse, 1996 (80–5) argue that UN Security Council Resolution 688, which demanded an end to Iraqi repression and humanitarian access to the Iraqi people in April 1991, should be seen, not as a precedent for forcible humanitarian intervention (no mention was made of Chapter VII measures),

but rather as part of the evolution of non-forcible humanitarian intervention, which, accelerated by international response to the Biafran crisis in the 1960s and the Ethiopian crisis in the 1980s, culminated in a series of UN General Assembly resolutions, including GAR 43/131 (1988) and GAR 45/100 (1990), as well as GAR 46/182 (1991) which set up the new UN Department of Humanitarian Affairs.

3. The ECOWAS intervention in Liberia was retrospectively endorsed under SCR 866 of 22 September 1993; allied intervention in Iraq has been controversially linked to SCR 688 of 5 April 1991 (or, some have argued, SCR 687); UNPROFOR's mission in Bosnia was mandated by a stream of SCRs beginning with SCR 770 on 13 August 1992; UNITAF in Somalia was mandated under SCR 794 of 3 December 1992; UN intervention in Haiti was mandated under SCR 867 of 23 September 1993; Operation Turquoise in Rwanda was mandated under SCR 929 of 23 June 1994.

4. For example, among other things, the important category of 'pure non-intervention' is consequently defined for the first time, in which none of the forcible and non-forcible intervention options is taken up by the international community. This is yet another option, which can now, as a result of the reconceptualisation, be weighed up among the others.

BIBLIOGRAPHY

Akehurst, M., 'Humanitarian Intervention', in: Bull, H. (ed.), 1984, 95–118.

Arend, A. and Beck, R., *International Law and the Use of Force*, London: Routledge, 1993.

Beitz, C. *et al.*, *International Ethics*, Princeton: Princeton University Press, 1985.

Berdal, M., *Whither UN Peacekeeping?* Adelphi Paper 281, London: Brassey's for the International Institute of Strategic Studies, 1993.

Brownlie, I., *International Law and the Use of Force by States*, Oxford: Clarendon Press, 1963.

Bull, H. (ed.), *Intervention in World Politics*, Oxford: Clarendon Press, 1984.

Bull, H., Kingsbury, B. and Roberts, A. (eds.): *Hugo Grotius and International Relations*, Oxford: Clarendon Press, 1990.

Coste, R., 'The moral dimensions of intervention', *Harvard International Review*, 28–9, 67–8, Fall 1993.

Damrosch, L. (ed.), *Enforcing Restraint: Collective Intervention in Internal Conflicts*, New York: Council on Foreign Relations Press, 1993.

Damrosch, L. and Scheffer, J. (eds.), *Law and Force in the New International Order*, Boulder, CO: Westview, 1991.

Delbrück, J., 'A Fresh Look at Humanitarian Intervention under the Authority of the United Nations', *Indiana Law Journal*, 67(4), 887–901, 1992.

Falk, R., 'Intervention Revisited – Hard Choices and Tragic Dilemmas', *The Nation*, 20, 755–64, 1993.

Farer, T., 'An Enquiry into the Legality of Humanitarian Intervention', in: Damrosch, L. and Scheffer, J. 1991, 185–201.

Forbes, I. and Hoffman, M. (eds.), *Political Theory, International Relations and the Ethics of Intervention*, London: Macmillan, 1993.

Franck, T. and Rodley, N., 'After Bangladesh: The Law of Humanitarian Intervention by Military Force', *American Journal of International Law*, 67, 275–305, 1973.

Garigue, P., 'Intervention-sanction and "droit d'ingérence" in International Humanitarian Law', *International Journal*, 48(4), 668–86, 1993.

Gentili, A., *De Jure Belli Libri Tres* (trans. from 1612 edn), Washington DC: Carnegie Institute, 1598/1933.

Greenwood, C., 'Is There a Right of Humanitarian Intervention?' *World Today*, 49(2), 34–40, 1993.

Grotius, H., *De Jure Belli ac Pacis Libri Tres* (trans. from 1646 edn), Washington DC: Carnegie Institute, 1625/1925.

Harriss, J. (ed.), *The Politics of Humanitarian Intervention*, London: Pinter, 1995.

Hashmi, S., 'Is There an Islamic Ethic of Humanitarian Intervention?' *Ethics and International Affairs*, 9, 55–73, 1993.

Hassan, F., 'Realpolitik in International Law: After [the] Tanzanian-Ugandan Conflict "Humanitarian Intervention" Re-examined', *Willamette Law Review*, 17, 859–912, 1981.

Henkin, L. *et al. Right v. Might: International Law and the Use of Force*, New York: Council on Foreign Relations Press, 1991.

Hoffmann, S., *Primacy or World Order: American Foreign Policy since the Cold War*, New York: McGraw-Hill, 1978.

Jackson, R., *Quasi-States, Sovereignty, International Relations and the Third World*, Cambridge: Cambridge University Press, 1990.

Johnson, J., *Just War Tradition and the Restraint of War*, Princeton: Princeton University Press, 1981.

Johnson, J., 'Threats, Values, and Defence: Does the Defence of Values by Force Remain a Moral Possibility?' in: O'Brien, W. and Langan, J. (eds.), 1986, 31–48.

Keen, M., *The Laws of War in the Late Middle Ages*, London: Routledge and Kegan Paul, 1965.

Klintworth, G., *Vietnam's Intervention in Cambodia in International Law*, Canberra: AGPS Press, 1989.

Kuper, L., *Genocide*, Harmondsworth: Penguin, 1981.

Lillich, R., 'Forcible self-help by states to protect human rights', *Iowa Law Review*, 53, 325–51, 1967.

Lillich, R. (ed.), *Humanitarian Intervention and the United Nations*, Charlottesville: University of Virginia Press, 1973.

Macrae, J. and Zwi, A. (eds.), *War and Hunger: Rethinking International Responses to Complex Emergencies*, London: Zed Books for Save the Children Fund (UK), 1994.

Mayall, J., *Nationalism and International Security*, Cambridge: Cambridge University Press, 1990.

Meron, T., 'Common rights of mankind in Gentili, Grotius and Suarez', *American Journal of International Law*, (85), 110–16, 1991.

Mill, J.S., 'A Few Words on Non-intervention', in: *Dissertations and Discussions, Political, Philosophical and Historical*, vol. 3, 147–78, London: Longman, Green, Reader and Dyer, 1875/1959.

O'Brien, W. and Langan, J. (eds.), *The Nuclear Dilemma and the Just War Tradition*, Lexington, MA:Lexington Books, 1986.

Ogata, S., *The State of the World's Refugees: The Challenge of Protection*, New York: Penguin, 1993.

Parekh, B., 'Rethinking Humanitarian Intervention', unpublished paper, 1996.

Pease, K. and Forsythe, D., 'Human Rights, Humanitarian Intervention and World Politics', *Human Rights Quarterly*, 15(2), 290–314, 1993.

Pogany, I., 'Humanitarian Intervention in International Law: The French Intervention in Syria Re-examined',*International and Comparative Law Quarterly*, 35, 182–90, 1986.

Ramsbotham, O. and Woodhouse, T., *Humanitarian Intervention in Contemporary Conflict*, Cambridge: Polity Press, 1996.

Reed, L. and Kaysen, C. (eds.), *Emerging Norms of Justified Intervention*, Cambridge, MA: American Academy of Arts and Sciences, 1993.

Roberts, A., 'Law, lawyers and nuclear weapons', *Review of International Studies*, 16(1), 75–92, 1990.

Ronzitti, N., *Rescuing Nationals Abroad through Military Coercion and Intervention on Grounds of Humanity*, Dordrecht: Martinus Nijhoff, 1985.

Smith, M., 'Ethics and Intervention', paper given at the International Studies Annual Conference, London, March 1989.

Tesón, F., *Humanitarian Intervention: An Enquiry into Law and Morality*, Dobbs Ferry, NY: Transnational Publishers, 1988.

Thomas, C., *New States, Sovereignty and Intervention*, London: Gower, 1985.

Thomas, C., 'The Pragmatic Case against Intervention', in: Forbes, I. and Hoffman, M. (eds.), 1993, 91–103.

Trachtenberg, M., 'Intervention in Historical Perspective', in: Reed, L. and Kaysen, C. (eds.), 1993.

Vattel, E. de, *The Law of Nations or the Principles of Natural Law Applied to the Conduct and Affairs of Nations and of Sovereigns*, Dobbs Ferry, NY: Oceana Publications, 1758/ 1964.

Verwey, W., 'Humanitarian Intervention under International Law', *Netherlands International Law Review*, 32, 357–418, 1985.

Victoria, F. de, *De Indis et De Jure Belli Relectiones*, Washington DC: Carnegie Institute, 1532/1917.

Vincent, R., *Nonintervention and International Order*, Princeton: Princeton University Press, 1974.

Vincent, R., *Human Rights and International Relations*, Cambridge: Cambridge University Press, 1986.

Wheeler, N., 'Pluralist and Solidarist Conceptions of International Society: Bull and Vincent on Humanitarian Intervention', *Millennium*, 21(3), 463–88, 1992.

6 Second Thoughts on First Principles

Hugh Beach

What is to be done about war in its contemporary form of inter-communal conflict now becoming a security dilemma for the whole world? It goes without saying that the best remedy by far is prevention. There is an obvious need for governments to promote tolerance of minority populations within their own borders and sometimes to grant some measure of autonomy. Countries must refrain from stirring up trouble among their own nationals living in other lands. (NATO's criteria for new membership explicitly include this point.) The setting of standards for rights of minorities would help, as would commonly accepted rules on citizenship. Again, NATO's criteria for new membership explicitly include this point and it is reflected in the recent treaty between Hungary and Romania. This requires both countries to protect the civil liberties and cultural identity of national minorities, particularly the use of their historic languages in education, the courts and administration generally.

Measures to promote economic and social development are equally fundamental. When things start to go wrong much can be achieved by early warning, preventive deployment of monitors and observers, conciliation and mediation. These measures have received much attention of late and figure largely in Dr Boutros Boutros-Ghali's *An Agenda for Peace* (1992). They are always preferable to the use of military force. But try as the international community will, only too often matters get out of hand and violence breaks out. The questions then to be addressed and which form the principal focus of this chapter are the following. Under what circumstances should intervention be attempted (or indeed withheld) and according to what principles should it be conducted?

Another of the great Helsinki principles is non-intervention in the internal affairs of other countries. It is stated explicitly that participating states will refrain from any intervention, direct or indirect, individual or collective, in the internal or external affairs falling within the domestic jurisdiction of another participating state, regardless of their mutual relations. Countries will accordingly refrain from any form of armed intervention or threat of intervention against another participating state. This clause was inserted, largely at the insistence of the Western powers, hoping it might slightly reduce the chance that the Soviet Union would again intervene in Eastern Europe as it had done in Hungary in 1956 and Czechoslovakia in 1968. But the principle is of far wider application. In Africa, for example, during the Cold War outside powers provided some of the most repressive regimes with arms and aid for no better reason than that their rival superpower was supporting another faction. The Americans supported Savimbi in Angola, Mobutu in Zaire, and Doe in Liberia. The Soviet Union supported Neto in Angola and Mengistu in Ethiopia. These regimes helped to bring already poor countries very close to the bottom of the UN Human Development Index. During the whole of this period a policy of non-intervention would have been far preferable. But over the past five years this situation has been turned on its head. The time is now ripe for quite different principles to be adopted, pointing towards legitimate and cooperative international interventionism.

The question of armed intervention on behalf of the international community in the internal affairs of a state, even against the wishes of the government of that state, in order to prevent widespread death or suffering amongst the population is certainly not a new issue. Rome grappled with the same problems in Dalmatia and Judaea during the 60s BCE as the international community does in those same regions today. The UN Charter, in Article 2(7), says bluntly that nothing contained in it shall authorise the UN to intervene in matters which are essentially within the domestic jurisdiction of any state. But it half-contradicts itself by saying that this principle shall not prejudice the application of enforcement measures under Chapter VII of the Charter. That Chapter relates not only to acts of aggression but also to threats to the peace and breaches of the peace. Until very recently it seemed as though this implied an international threat. Thus UN Security Council Resolution (UNSCR) 688 of 5 April 1991 described Iraqi repression of the Kurds and Shias as a threat to international peace and security. It was on the strength of this resolution that France, followed by the US, Britain and a number of other countries, took action with ground and air forces to compel the Iraqis to desist. But the supposed threat to international security was largely a pretext. On 3 December 1992, the Security Council (UNSCR 794) broke new ground by deciding to intervene in Somalia for strictly humanitarian purposes. There was not even a pretence of consent by the government of Somalia because such a government did not exist. There was negligible spill-over to other countries in the form of refugees. The plight of the Somali people was the sole rationale for invoking Chapter VII of the Charter, authorising the use of 'all necessary means' to establish a 'secure environment for humanitarian relief'. This meant in practice taking sides and acting with far from minimal force. A de facto Right of Humanitarian Intervention was thus beginning to emerge. The task of the UN forces in Bosnia was not described in terms of peacekeeping at all. Its task was to secure the delivery of humanitarian goods and services and to protect civilians in declared 'safe havens'. The deployment of UNPROFOR was carried out, initially at least, with the consent of the host states (Croatia, Bosnia, Macedonia). But its mandate was subsequently extended to include, for example, deterrence of attacks on safe havens and the occupation of key points on the ground to that end – with a clear flavour of Chapter VII enforcement. So during the past five years the view has been strengthening that where a state is inflicting upon its own people gross, flagrant and continuing infringements of their common humanity the international community has a right – some would even argue an obligation – to try and restrain it.

'JUST WAR' PRINCIPLES

The basis for a Christian ethical critique of these questions is to be found in the just war tradition, and this will 'serve as a framework for what follows. The American Catholic bishops, in a 'reflection' adopted in the fall of 1993 entitled *The Harvest of Justice is Sown in Peace*, gave a useful summary of the main components of the tradition, and their version is followed here.

Just cause

Force may be used only to correct a grave, public evil, i.e. aggression or massive violation of the basic rights of whole populations. And if we go back to the roots of just war doctrine we find Aquinas saying (*Summa Theologiae* II IIae 40,1):

...a just cause is required, namely that those who are attacked deserve it for some wrong they have done. So Augustine: 'We usually describe a just war as one that avenges wrongs, that is, when a nation or state has to be punished either for refusing to make amends for outrages done by its subjects, or to restore what it has seized injuriously. Among true worshippers of God those wars are looked on as peacemaking which are waged neither from aggrandisement nor cruelty but with the object of securing peace, of repressing the evil and supporting the good'.

Augustine is here thinking primarily in terms of wars between states (one can hear the distant echo of the Vandals hammering on the gates of Hippo); but otherwise his definition fits modern circumstances. If wickedness is being committed – people killed, populations uprooted – the use of force can be justified to punish the wrongdoers and avenge the wrongs. But Augustine goes further. While some punitive element may well be necessary, his emphasis on peacemaking (*pacis studio*) and supporting the good (*boni subleventur*) opens up much wider perspectives. In practical terms these motives cash out into the form of specific political objectives, such as:

- stopping the fighting or enforcing a ceasefire,
- preventing the forcible movement of populations, as in 'ethnic cleansing',
- enforcing the delivery of humanitarian aid and safe extraction of the sick and wounded,
- preserving safe havens, zones, demilitarised areas or open cities,
- restoring pre-existing boundaries or enforcing those newly agreed,
- setting up democratic institutions,
- or most ambitiously, establishing an international protectorate under UN control.

All of these 'causes' and no doubt many others could properly qualify as 'just' under Augustine's rubric. But it is obvious that the justice of a cause by no means guarantees a successful outcome.

Comparative justice

While there may be rights and wrongs on all sides of a conflict, to override the presumption against the use of force, the injustice suffered by one party must significantly outweigh that suffered by the other. One can see the point where conflicts between states are concerned. But internal conflicts are very difficult to adjudicate, because the rights and wrongs are seldom black-and-white even when viewed with hindsight by historians. Where many parties are concerned, the task becomes much harder. Where shall one find the facts? Instant media coverage is seldom free from bias. In Somalia the merits and crimes of the various factions were very far from clear-cut and it was precisely the decision to demonise Aideed which led the whole operation astray. In Rwanda it may be clear that responsibility for the main round of killings rested with the Hutus, but it has always been hard to say who was most to blame in Bosnia. Action ought not to be paralysed simply because significant comparative injustice cannot be established.

Legitimate authority

Only duly constituted public authorities may use deadly force or wage war. By this Aquinas meant that it is only the sovereign who has the right to go to war, not the barons or private warlords. Augustine goes wider when (as quoted by Aquinas) he says: 'The natural order conducive to human peace demands that the power to counsel and declare war belongs to those who hold the supreme authority'. Arguably, if one is intervening for the sake of international peace and good order, then only an international authority has the right to 'counsel and declare'. This could be a regional grouping, such as the Organisation for Security and Cooperation in Europe (OSCE) or even an ad hoc alliance as in the Gulf War. But all of these come ultimately under the jurisdiction of the United Nations, both in principle and as a matter of practical politics. It is clear that the United Nations is the supreme source of legitimacy where action in support of international peace and security is concerned, and it is emerging in that capacity in the case of internal disputes. The Security Council has mandated as many operations since the end of the Cold War as it had in the previous 40 years.

Right intention

Force may be used only in a truly just cause and only for that purpose. At first sight this looks like tautology: a simple restatement of the just cause criterion. In fact it goes much further. Augustine says (again as quoted by Aquinas): 'The craving to hurt people, the cruel thirst for revenge, the unappeased and unrelenting spirit, the savageness of fighting on, the lust to dominate and suchlike – all these are rightly condemned in wars'. This should warn us against several misleading motives. It should lead us to be wary of the surge of righteous anger when a city like Dubrovnik is shelled just because it is old and beautiful – and within range of guns: when a family is burned alive for belonging to the wrong religion. These things are horrible indeed, but with Northern Ireland on our conscience the English should be among the last to demand precipitate action. This principle should lead us to be cautious in applying Augustine's earlier remarks about avenging wrongs and punishing. To give a recent example, the Allies in the Gulf War set as their aim to evict Iraqi forces from Kuwait. They did not aim to break the power of the Republican Guards, still less topple Saddam Hussein. When they had succeeded in their limited aim they stopped: quite correctly in the opinion of this writer. The 'turkey shoot' of Iraqi troops escaping towards Basra was more than enough for most military stomachs. The *savageness of fighting on* was rightly eschewed. This notion of right intent can also be useful in weeding out vaguely expressed or inadmissible political objectives, for example:

- *Pour encourager les autres*: It has been argued that lack of firmness in one instance will encourage rogue regimes elsewhere to behave badly. If this is true then there is certainly no shortage of bad examples. But it is a cardinal principle of military aid to the civil power that such force as is used must address the here-and-now and can never be justified by recourse to its possible deterrent effects elsewhere and at some other time. It was no defence for Brigadier General Dyer to claim – though it may well have been true – that by shooting civilian demonstrators in Amritsar he had prevented the whole Punjab from going up in flames.
- *Machismo*: The press is prone to speculate whether such and such a leader is 'strong enough to act': 'Speak for America, Mr President'.

Both these arguments were used, as it happens, in a single article in the *New York Times* by Anthony Lewis (*International Herald Tribune*, 27 April 1993) urging tougher action in Bosnia. It should be clear how, from the point of view of right intention, they are inadmissible, as well as being quite hopelessly vague as a guide to military operations. Action for those sorts of reason would be, quite simply, immoral.

Probability of success

Arms must not be used in a futile cause or in a case where disproportionate measures are required to achieve success. Leaving on one side the question of proportion, since this rates as a separate criterion in its own right, this clause introduces a crucial point: that the practicability of what is proposed is a key element in formulating the ethical judgement. It is not a moral act to set the military off on a given course if they are likely to fail, however just the cause. To put in opposition the moral and the pragmatic is simply a theological howler. St Luke attributes to Jesus a saying to just this effect:

> Or what king will march to battle against another king without sitting down first to consider whether with ten thousand men he can face an enemy coming to meet him with twenty thousand. If he cannot then, long before the enemy approaches, he sends envoys and asks for terms.

> (Luke 14.31)

It is easy enough to list tasks for the military to carry out, in themselves perhaps quite legitimate:

- monitoring or enforcing a naval blockade or no-fly zones,
- protecting or fighting through a humanitarian aid convoy,
- monitoring or enforcing an open city, safe haven, or protected area for beleaguered populations,
- opening or keeping open an airfield or supply route,
- monitoring or enforcing a weapons exclusion zone,
- carrying out limited or punitive air strikes against the heavy weapons of one side, their ammunition dumps or command and control facilities,
- interdiction against bridges, key supply routes or other communication bottlenecks,
- bombing the civilian infrastructure of one side, including possibly the seat of government,
- attempting to kill a leader or capture him or her by *coup de main*,
- enforcing a general ceasefire,
- forcibly preventing 'ethnic cleansing',
- enforcing a new cantonal map, or even conceivably
- restoring the status quo ante,
- monitoring or enforcing withdrawal of troops, their disarmament and demobilisation,
- demining.

It is easy enough to list these things; we have heard talk of them all in recent years and many have been tried, albeit with varying degrees of success. No-fly zones have worked up to a point in Iraq although they had little practical effect in Bosnia. Arms embargoes are always leaky. The British Army in Bosnia almost always got its aid convoys through in the end by a mixture of cajolery, patience and cunning. Safe havens worked well enough for a time and then failed, spectacularly and humiliatingly, in the case of Srebreniça. Sarajevo airfield could not in practice be kept open by the UN nor could many supply routes. Limited air strikes were finally carried out on Bosnian Serb communication centres, ammunition dumps, radar-guided missile sites and latterly bridges, though deliberate efforts were made not to strike civilian factories, power stations and so forth or even to strike Serb front-line units in contested areas. Undoubtedly this played an important part in forcing the Serbs to negotiate at Dayton, Ohio. Monitoring or enforcing the withdrawal of troops has been the principal task of IFOR and demining forms an important part of that act. So a lot of experience is now accumulating. The point is that it would be quite immoral for the political leadership to order any of these military actions without heeding the military assessment of the likelihood of success. In the case of air action what would be the required number of sorties, the likely effectiveness, the effects of weather, the expected casualty rate and collateral civilian casualties, likely effects upon humanitarian operations, likely responses, military and otherwise, of the party being attacked? In the case of ground action it is vital to consider how many troops and of what kind are needed (infantry with or without armoured protection, forward air controllers, artillery radars), likely casualties to both sides, for how long the commitment can be expected to last, where the second, fifth or even fiftieth *roulement* will come from, how much it will all cost. And as the price of success mounts we must go on to ask how likely it is that the political constituency, nurtured on television, will lose patience and enforce a humiliating withdrawal, leaving things worse than if force had never been used. It is with this consideration in mind that the recent American *Presidential Directive 25* has emphasised the need for a credible 'exit strategy', thus avoiding open-ended commitments. It is easy to see why. But it is equally important to recognise that in many cases a reasonable prospect of success is attainable only over a long period. The United Nations Force in Cyprus has been there 32 years, without much progress being made towards a political solution. To say this is not to set pragmatism over against morality but to recognise an essential ingredient in the moral judgement itself. If what is proposed will not work then, however lofty the motive, the proposal is simply immoral. One can not, of course, claim that military forecasts of the likely outcome are necessarily infallible, quite the reverse. The military are often wrong, even on strictly military matters; how else can one account for the fact that, in all the wars of history, roughly 50 per cent of the generals have been losers? One is saying only that they must be asked and their answers heeded.

Last resort

Force may be used only after all peaceful alternatives have been seriously tried and exhausted. In other words if measures short of armed force would suffice then armed force should not be used. Articles 33 to 42 of the UN Charter describe a wide spectrum of measures available to the international community, starting with enquiry, mediation, conciliation and so forth, via diplomatic and economic measures up to demonstrations, blockade and 'other operations' by land, sea and air forces. Thus before the Gulf War both Houses of Congress authorised the President to use US armed forces only after he had certified that 'all appropriate diplomatic and other peaceful means had failed'. The point has been made by Sir Brian Urquhart that no determination about the adequacy of sanctions was ever made by the Security Council. This is a crucial point, but it also poses a difficult dilemma. In many cases it may be appropriate to use these various measures in chronological sequence, only moving up the ladder as and when softer approaches have been tried and failed. But in other instances it may be that to go in early and hard, albeit on a limited scale, might avert much bloodshed and suffering. For example it is widely argued that had the UN, led by the United States, committed ground troops with air support in the former Yugoslavia at a much earlier stage (for example to prevent the destruction of Vukovar by the Serbs in 1992) this could have nipped civil war in the bud. It implies a judgement at the outset that gentler methods are bound to fail and that recourse to the methods of last resort (albeit under the general rubric of minimum force) were better taken earlier than later. The term 'last resort' need not, on this reading, be understood chronologically. But the necessary decision-making will be very difficult and military advice will often be on the side of caution (witness the restraining influence of General Colin Powell in the American system). Everything hinges upon clear-sighted leadership at the international level.

Proportionality

The overall destruction expected from the use of force must be outweighed by the good to be achieved. This is the crucial consideration which, in a sense, subsumes all others. It is also arguably the most difficult. It was relevant, for instance, to the American preference in Bosnia for allowing the Muslims to import arms and for air attacks on targets of strategic importance to Serbia. If foreseeable consequences had included bringing existing humanitarian operations to a halt, enforcing the withdrawal of UN forces and perhaps prolonging the bloodshed this might have been a bad bargain. Of course proportionality involves weighing in the balance things which, even in theory, are incommensurable. How many Dutch lives was it worth to protect Srebriniça? Can one put a price on a principle? Yes, one does it every day so there is no dodging, and certainly there are no easy answers. One of the most notable features of recent years has been the way in which the issue of proportion has dominated at least the vocabulary of debate. Only very rarely have disproportionate interventions been threatened: by the Americans, for example, against Bosnian Serbs in summer 1995 and against Saddam Hussein a year later. After the event it is always claimed that targets have been hit precisely, civilian casualties minimised and the actions proportionate.

Non-combatant immunity

Civilians may not be the object of direct attack, and military personnel must take due care to avoid and minimise indirect harm to civilians. It is again notable the way in which everyone pays at least lip-service to this consideration (even the Russians in Chechnya!). More to the point is the way in which it was taken with all seriousness by the Allies in the Gulf War and the NATO bombings in Bosnia. But in a partisan style of conflict this is another very difficult line to draw. It is, of course, obvious that in this kind of war the contestants totally and systematically ignore this and almost all other laws of war, but that does not absolve the international community, quite the reverse. It can be argued that on this score, bombing of Serbian artillery and its ammunition, anti-aircraft sites and communication links was admissible; the Drina Bridges would have been doubtful; Belgrade absolutely not.

BIBLIOGRAPHY

Boutros-Ghali, B., *An Agenda for Peace*, June 1992, UN DPI/1247. New York: United Nations, 1992.
US Bishops, 'The Harvest of Justice is Sown in Peace', in: *Origins*, 9 Dec. 1993, Vol. 23, No. 26.

Part III
War by Other Means?
Wider Dimensions of the
Debate

In the third part of the book, the issues of alternatives to war and the wider dimensions of intervention are addressed. *Oliver O'Donovan* indicates that sanctions are not an easy alternative to war, but should be understood, continuing the development of Clausewitzian doctrine, as **'War by Other Means'**.

Barrie Paskins examines **'Intervention and Crimes against Humanity'** and shows the difficulties arising for those who are reticent about support for war, but committed to the defence of human rights.

Brian Wicker argues that breaches of the peace abroad require the capacity for international law enforcement. He therefore argues for development **'From National to International Policing'**.

7 War by Other Means
Oliver O'Donovan

WHAT IS MEANT BY 'WAR BY OTHER MEANS'?

In the introduction to his major work, *On War*, Carl von Clausewitz wrote his most quoted dictum: 'War is nothing but the continuation of policy with other means' (Clausewitz, 1993:77). What he meant by this, as he explained in his eighth book, was that war was not an intelligible enterprise apart from political reason. It had to be an 'instrument' of policy, and instruments always derive their intelligibility from the ends they serve. Read in this sense the dictum is the purest practical wisdom, and certainly supports the disciplining of war by morality. However, it has consistently been read as a slightly cynical observation; and that, I take it, is because Clausewitz relates war not to international justice but to 'policy'. This tends to suggest that warfare between sovereign states is an uncomplicated and unambiguous exposition of what state policy is all about. The appearance of purely self-interested national communities exercising their strength upon their neighbours' defences is a true disclosure of the self-contained purposes of the civil community. This Lockean hint Clausewitz develops in a somewhat romantic nineteenth century direction, adding his voice to the view that vitality and will are the truest realities, and that if war is the authentic prophet of national will, total war is the most outspoken form of authentic prophecy.

I want to reverse the order of the dictum and speak, instead, of the various ways in which we may continue *war* 'by other means'. For if Clausewitz thought that war discloses the true nature of state policy, then, I suggest, we should say that he got it exactly the wrong way round. The normal activities of the state disclose the true nature of war, and teach us to see it as an act of judgement, serving the need of the international community for just order. This reconstruction of the idea of war happens in two stages. The first is the disciplining of the resort to war and the means of war, bringing them under the threefold constraint of authority, proportion and discrimination. The second is the devising of intermediate means, which stand between serious political conflict and the outbreak of war, and provide a range of responses which will perhaps avert the necessity of resort to armed conflict.

We begin, then, with the idea of war as a pure expression of state power in support of state policy, and of total war as its most complete expression, and we learn to conceive of just war, as force put under the discipline, and in the service, of justice. But then we move from just war to 'war by other means', which is to say a flexible range of intermediate measures, which depend on the marginal possibility of resort to war but serve to keep it at arm's length.

This second stage is rather similar to the task of scaling down the language of punishment, so that we are not forced constantly to resort to the execution of criminals. And in each case we must say that we cannot devise intermediate means if we fail to understand what the extreme means were intended to accomplish. The search for intermediate alternatives to war must come after the decision that our wars should be just. If we begin from a posture of simple opposition to war, we will lose sight of this logical order by thrusting the search for 'some other way' to the fore. But 'some other way' to do what? Not just to 'discuss our differences', but to resolve issues of right justly and effectively. Intermediate means that are not designed to do this are not intermediate means at all. They are simply an excuse for avoiding the tasks of justice.

What are the true 'intermediate alternatives' that stand between parties in conflict and outright war? First, there is the symbolic language of diplomacy, which expresses judgement by such means as expelling diplomats, severing relations, lodging protests and so on. This language makes no direct appeal to power; but its effect is entirely derived from the fact of power and the possibility, which lies on the horizon, of deploying force. Such gestures act as warning indicators, and are an excellent example of how the ultimate possibility of force supports a proximate language which can proceed at a distance from force.

Diplomacy continues war by other means; but those other means are not acts of war. There are other kinds of alternative means which are, formally considered, acts of war, in that they involve the actual exercise of power beyond the sphere of political authority, yet are alternative to what we conventionally understand as acts of war. In the first place, there are uses of force that are designed to overcome opposition without directly intending fatalities. The deployment of tear gas, or of other incapacitating gases, is an example of this. In the second place, there are uses of power which are not uses of force. It is on the most controversial of these that I wish to concentrate: economic sanctions.

First of all, we must distinguish economic sanctions, as used by one hostile state, or a group of states, against another, from other and similar-looking gestures, which are, however, in a different moral category and do not constitute acts of power beyond the reach of political authority.

SANCTIONS

1 Not a selective refusal to trade

Sanctions are distinct from a *selective refusal to trade* with, or invest in, immoral businesses or sectors of business. Imagine a nation that makes a considerable export market out of addictive drugs; and consider the status of laws in other nations forbidding the import of, and banning trade in, those drugs. It would be wrong to construe those laws as a hostile act towards the exporting nation. The decision not to permit trade in such goods is intelligible solely on its own terms, and is logically independent of any decision about how to deal with nations that encourage the trade. It is a question of refusal to trade with immoral businesses. And the business may be immoral either because the goods it deals in are immoral or because those who run the business have no moral standing to do so. The trade in slaves may be prohibited because slaves ought not to be bought or sold; the trade in artefacts made by slaves may be prohibited because the vendors have no proper title to the property in which they deal. For similar reasons we ban a trade in ivory which depends heavily on the work of poachers and is, as such, environmentally destructive – even though, as some African countries remind us, it is possible to run a responsible trade in ivory which is actually beneficial environmentally. None of these prohibitions are acts of war, even though whole nations may be damagingly affected by them. And, in principle, they are *not discretionary*. Once the character of the improper business has become clear, there is a moral obligation not to trade with it, because one is required not to cooperate in wrong. It is, of course, *politically* discretionary for a government to criminalise such trading, as there always is an element of political discretion about the implementation of moral principle in law. But individual business people who understand the nature of the enterprises, and continue to trade with them, are acting wrongly.

What applies to trading applies a fortiori to investment. Trading is minimally cooperative; and we usually say that the purchaser of goods bears only a small responsibility to establish the bona fides of goods offered for sale in the market place – yet even so, that small burden of responsibility may require the boycott of scandalous goods. A greater burden of responsibility rests on those who invest, since investment is positively cooperative. One of the great disadvantages of arm's length dealing in the stock market, is that neither the investor nor the financial corporation who sells the unit trusts assumes responsibility for inquiring into the morality of the businesses concerned. But here, too, what is in question is the nature of the business itself, not the nature of the society or the state which supports it. In the term 'business', of course, we may include a whole sector of business in a given country, where conditions are inhuman or pay inadequate – relative to what is reasonably possible within that society. To know that workers on coffee plantations only take home so much a year, tells you nothing. You need to know what could be done, given good will, within the constraints of the market and the social setting; and only then do you know whether you are looking at an immoral sector of business.

Any measures of this first kind, whether legislated or voluntary, are directed against types of business practice. Legislation implementing them must be framed generically, specifying the kinds of enterprise involved. If, instead of such legislation, government were to act executively, naming the countries or companies involved, it would cross the line that separates selective refusal to trade from sanctions, and would commit itself to an act of war.

2 Not a policy of dissociation

Different from this first policy, and still distinct from sanctions, is the policy of *dissociation* from societies which tolerate or encourage behaviour unacceptable to the international community. Under this heading is included the severing of wider cultural, as well as business contacts, and this is done on a *non-selective* basis, irrespective, that is, of whether the activities in question are conducted immorally. Thus we have, in the past, refused sports contacts even with racially integrated sports associations in South Africa. The point of these measures is penal, but they fall short of an exercise of power, and so do not constitute a penal act of war. These measures aim to communicate to the society in question the disapproval in which it is held; and they are chosen for their symbolic and expressive power, rather than for any special guilt incurred within the activities that are suspended, and – more importantly – rather than for any leverage they may have upon the policies of that state. The penalty is informal; it operates at the sub-political level; and for that reason may often be conceived as part of an ongoing remonstrance with that society in which dissociation at one level (say, culture) is offset by continued communication at another (say, between religious leaders). In invoking such measures the future of the conversation, and the possibility of its actually having a beneficial effect, have to be borne in mind. Now, in my view it is important that societies should be able to communicate informal judgements on each other in a manner that stops short of state intervention. The reason for this is to protect society's moral reflection on international affairs from the constraints of *realpolitik* which inevitably affect a state. A society which cannot form, and express, judgements on its neighbours except when its government tells it to, is not a free society. For that reason I confess I see much good sense in the rather unpopular policy of the British government for many years, of encouraging, but not requiring, cultural gestures of dissociation from South Africa. Once government starts requiring hostile acts against another state, then a threshold of some importance has been crossed; and once it is crossed, the basis for selecting the measures must change. Its aim must be to impose judgement upon the recalcitrant offender, and its measures will be chosen precisely for their effectiveness in doing that. At that point you cross into sanctions.

3   Not acts of retorsion

Different again, and still distinct from sanctions, are what international lawyers call *acts of retorsion*. These are acts performed by states, which, though they are intended to be hostile, lie perfectly within the state's sphere of political authority and would not constitute an offence, whatever the circumstances in which they were performed. Examples might be: cutting off aid, refusing preferential access to domestic markets, banning arms' sales. All these things lie within the jurisdiction of the state. It does not lie within the jurisdiction of the state to prevent another state's growing rich, developing its trading, or arming itself; but it does lie within its discretion in the conduct of its own foreign policy to discourage these developments; and if a state is to carry through its foreign policy effectively, it must be able to command support from its citizens, including those who give aid, trade, or sell armaments.

Not all trade falls directly within the scope of a state's foreign policy; but the making of special treaties offering trading privileges does; and so does trade in arms, or in any other goods which may be instruments of hostility or oppression. Computer programs, for example, suitable for a police force needing to keep extensive records of dissidents, might be included in a trade ban with respect to a particular country in which the government judged that there was a police state. This ban is not, as such, an act of war, but an act of policy. (This is still the case when a number of states agree a common policy on banning arms' sales.) If, however, the government undertook active measures to prevent the disfavoured state from importing arms from other countries which would otherwise be willing to export them, then it would be more than an act of retorsion, and would have to be classified as a 'reprisal', which belongs within the category of 'sanction' as I am using the term.

WHAT THEN ARE SANCTIONS?

Sanctions are an act of war which does not involve the direct use of force. It employs the power of the state, or more probably of a number of allied states, in a way that would constitute an offence against the opposing state were it not for that state's prior offence which has given just cause for war. Sanctions are thus 'reprisal' rather than 'retorsion'. But I include general trade embargoes in the category of sanctions, in defiance of the international lawyers, who maintain that these cannot be reprisals because they would not be illegal otherwise. The moralist is in a happy position with regard to legal categories. He can plunder them at will, and then revise them as he chooses in order to purge them from the taint of sin! In this case I argue that everyone has a basic right of access to commerce with everyone else, subject only to such regulatory control as is necessary to protect the common good, and that a general ban on trade with a given country, even if not illegal in law, is overtly hostile and ought to be considered as an offence unless justified as an act of war.

The decision to impose sanctions is already a decision to make war. If we fail to acknowledge this, we will fail to ask the relevant questions about the justice of the sanctions, and these two questions in particular:

1 whether in the particular circumstances sanctions can be imposed in a way conformable to the restraints of just war;
2 whether in the particular circumstances sanctions are more appropriate than other modes of hostility.

Let us take first the question of conformability to just war restraints. Can sanctions be discriminate? And can they be proportionate?

CAN SANCTIONS BE DISCRIMINATE?

It is clear that sanctions can be indiscriminate; and that general economic sanctions are always likely to be indiscriminate. They strike directly at the ordinary, life-sustaining functions of the community. When used with great effect, they result in famine, the first victims of which are the poor and other vulnerable sectors of society – the sick, the old and children. We may be tempted to think them categorically immoral, for the same reason that biological warfare directed at the water supply is immoral. They attack the life of society as such, not the threat posed by the activities of the state to other societies. It is important to understand the structural difference between economic sanctions and the traditional siege. A siege used to be undertaken in order to inhibit troops from free movement. Civilians in a besieged city might starve; but that was not the point of the operation, and you would always have been happy had you been able to pin your enemy's forces down in a city which had been deserted by its civilian inhabitants. General economic sanctions, however, aim to reach the political will of the hostile government through the economic straits into which the population at large is thrown. If the population is unaffected by them, then the whole strategy has failed, since there was no other way in which they were going to persuade the government to change its mind. This is bad enough; but when the sanctions are directed against a government to persuade it to stop mistreating a part of its own population, as in the cases of Rhodesia and South Africa, there is the additionally distressing consideration that the first to suffer will quite probably be the very population it was intended to defend. We ought to notice that the argument which used to be held in support of general sanctions against South Africa – that if the black leadership was in favour of sanctions, it was not for us to be over-scrupulous about them – is without any force. We were answerable for the methods by which we chose to make war; and the black community was not entitled to offer us their children and elderly to use as weapons against the white government.

Into this unpromising picture, however, we can introduce a factor which allows some flexibility. Sanctions can be varied in their severity and in focus. Directed against investment, they may attack the capital on which the industrial organisation of a complex economy rests, and so destroy the society's prosperity, but may not attack its capacity to sustain a subsistence. Given certain types of economy, with a developed industrial sector on top of a capacity for food production that is essentially self-sufficient, general economic sanctions will not produce famine, though they may produce grave social disruption. And where the food production is not self-sufficient, the sanctions may be tailored to allow subsistence imports while still maintaining a stranglehold on capital and industrial resources. This is what the UN tried to achieve in the sanctions on Iraq. If general economic sanctions are deployed in this way, directly attacking capital and industry, not subsistence, may our negative judgement be mitigated, even though they are still formally 'indiscriminate'?

The classic just war theorists drew a sharp distinction between the claims of the innocent to their lives, and their claim to their property. Suarez, in a judgement that may strike us as cold-blooded, says: 'it is permissible to deprive the innocent of their goods, even of their liberty. The reason is that the innocent form a portion of one whole and unjust civil community'. However, 'innocent persons as such may in no wise be slain.' This, he argues, follows from:

> the difference existing between life and other possessions. For the latter fall under human dominion; and the state as a whole has a higher right to them than single individuals; hence individuals may be deprived of such property because of the guilt of the whole realm. But life does not fall under human dominion, and therefore no one may be deprived of his life save by reason of his own guilt.
>
> (Suarez, 1944:817)[1]

When we have recovered from shock of his permission for taking slaves as reparations (though only of non-Christians, and even heretics are not to be included!), we may perhaps see some good moral sense in Suarez' refusal to extend to the property of non-combatants that immunity from direct attack that he extends to their lives. The argument that wealth 'falls under human dominion' may be paraphrased like this: the power to accumulate wealth depends on the state's protection of an advanced social organisation; property-owners are such by virtue of the conditions the state has maintained, and to that degree their property is not inalienably their own, in the sense that their lives are. This argument may be compared with one that is sometimes heard, that the wealthy are *ipso facto* complicit in the oppression of the poor. This stronger argument seems to me to be badly overstated but to have a grain of truth in it. Wealth as such is not a form of aggression; and if it were, then the wealthy would, as such, be combatants, their lives and not merely their property forfeit. But wealth may sometimes depend on aggression, even on an aggression that is not that of its owners; or it may depend on political conditions which have permitted aggression to take place unchecked; and for these reasons it cannot be viewed, as it is in the Lockean tradition, as a kind of extension of the person, enjoying the same immunities that the person enjoys.

We may note in passing that this argument in favour of general economic sanctions, when limited to direct attack on capital and industry rather than subsistence, implies a view of the so-called 'principle of double effect', to which the distinction between direct and indirect attack appeals. If we may attack the property of non-combatants directly, then this is a case to which the principle of double effect does not apply. It does not matter that this kind of attack is 'indiscriminate'. But if there are cases to which the principle of double effect does not apply, then it is not, as has usually been claimed, a general formal rule governing all cases of ambiguity in moral choice. It is a rule that applies only, or primarily, to the taking of innocent life, and cannot confidently be extrapolated beyond this sphere (cf. O'Donovan, 1994:192–3).

CAN SANCTIONS BE PROPORTIONATE?

Moving on to the second question, it is clear that general economic sanctions can be disproportionate. They take longer than military action to have effect, and they expose societies to various consequential ills with long-term implications, including the breakdown of civil order. The experience of Britain in imposing sanctions, in cooperation with the UN, on the rebel regime in Rhodesia in 1965 is illuminating. When the rebellion occurred, the government of the day resorted to sanctions because it was not confident of popular support for a cumbersome military operation in Central Africa against colonial settlers with whom there was a strong feeling of kinship. Extravagant hopes were entertained of the speed with which sanctions would 'bring the rebel regime to its knees' – 'weeks rather than months' was one unfortunate prediction. In fact it took ten years, and part of the cost was the slow collapse of Rhodesia-Zimbabwe into a civil war conducted by guerrilla methods which inflicted extensive suffering on innocent victims both white and black. The 'success' of sanctions in this case was somewhat Pyrrhic, and suggests strongly that an initial military endeavour, however difficult to mount, would have been more prudent. Certainly it would have given the new state of Zimbabwe a better start in life. I assume in this argument that not a single death was directly attributable to sanctions (which would class them as indiscriminate). The deaths caused indirectly over the space of ten years should be weighed against the likely cost of an immediate military operation. It is hard to think that they do not appear disproportionate as a result.

It is clear from this that the decision to impose sanctions presupposes a conviction that they are the appropriate means of war for the circumstances. Much of the problem surrounding Western sanctions against South Africa sprang from the idea that sanctions were an alternative to war, rather than an alternative mode of war. Western powers, though they might have offered military aid to the front-line states if they had become involved in a South African civil war, were not ready to contemplate direct military involvement themselves. This meant that the question was not put in the form that it should have been: whether sanctions were the appropriate means for performing an act of judgement against the South African regime.

It is arguable that, in fact, they were the appropriate means. Sanctions commend themselves as a means of fighting a war of intervention, in which the *causa belli* is internal to the nation-state, so that the international community have a comparatively weak *locus standi* in international law for pursuing a quarrel. Wars of intervention are not ruled out legally, if conducted under UN authorisation, by the UN Charter. The Security Council is entitled to concern itself with any 'dispute the continuation of which is likely to endanger the maintenance of international peace and security' (Article 33), which includes internal disputes within states when they are of such an order as to draw other states into conflict with them. Morally, too, we may say that there should be no outright bar on a war of intervention, given sufficient cause. Nevertheless, there is a strong presumption against wars of intervention, based on respect for the authority of each state to govern its people; and this presumption is appropriately acknowledged by a preference for hostilities which do not involve armed intrusion onto the hostile state's territory.

CONCLUSION

Intervention into a state's internal conflicts, then, is one type of cause for which sanctions appear especially appropriate. Another is when military operations would face severe logistical impediments – though perhaps this is the most treacherous type, as we shall argue. A third is to provide a first, and mild stage in the hostilities, to bring moderate pressure to bear to achieve a settlement, if possible, before the resort to arms becomes necessary. This was the use to which sanctions were appropriately put before the Gulf conflict. But that case illuminates two general principles very clearly. In the first place, economic sanctions raise least problems when directed against a developed industrial economy which is adequately self-sufficient in food production to maintain its subsistence. By the time that military operations began in January 1991 it was claimed by Iraq that 4000 people from vulnerable sectors of the population had, in the course of six months, died of conditions related to undernourishment; and although this information came from a tainted source, independent observers of the flow of rural refugees leaving Iraq for Jordan thought it not improbable. Sanctions were, as was claimed at the time, 'working' – but working in precisely the way one does not want them to work, undermining subsistence rather than capital. In the second place, then, the Gulf experience demonstrated the necessity of having it clearly in mind what was to be done if sanctions failed to achieve the purpose within tolerable limits of damage to the community. A decision has to be made at the point of imposing sanctions what the next step will be – whether to abandon the attempt altogether or to go forward to military activity.

And here we see why it is 'treacherous' to impose sanctions in situations where military action faces insuperable obstacles. If there is no further stage in the hostilities that can be envisaged, the temptation will be to maintain the sanctions indefinitely, even after the point at which they can be seen to be inflicting indiscriminate destruction on the population. The temptation will be even worse if it has never been admitted in the first place that sanctions are an act of war, and they are interpreted, in bad faith, merely as a kind of 'statement' of disapproval. A belligerent has a duty to bring the warfare to a decisive conclusion. A besieging army may have to attempt to storm the garrison in order to end the privation and misery within it, even if it would suit its own purposes much better just to sit there until there was no one left alive. Similarly, those who impose sanctions ought to reckon with the possibility that they may have to take other action to bring their economic siege to an end. The attraction of sanctions to a population which loves strong moral statements but hates war is a possibly fatal one, liable to tempt us into grave immorality.

NOTE

1.   Author's own translation from *de caritate* 13.7.15 (*Opus de triplici virtute theologica*).

BIBLIOGRAPHY

Clausewitz, C. von, *On War*, (ed. & trans. M. Howard, P. Paret), London: Everyman's Library, 1993:77.
O'Donovan, O., *Resurrection and Moral Order* (2nd edn), Leicester: Apollos, 1994:192–3.
Suarez, F., *Opus de triplici virtute theologica*, 1621, reproduced in: *Selections from Three Works by Francisco Suarez*, Vol. 1, Classics of International Law, Oxford: Clarendon Press, 1944.

8 Intervention and Crimes against Humanity
Barrie Paskins

Crimes against humanity were crisply defined in the Charter under which the Nuremberg Trial was conducted. In addition to traditional war crimes and the alleged crime of aggression, the defendants at Nuremberg were accused and convicted of:

> Crimes against humanity: namely, murder, extermination, enslavement, deportation, and other inhumane acts committed against any civilian population, before or during the war; or persecutions on political, racial or religious grounds in execution of or in connection with any crime within the jurisdiction of the Tribunal, whether or not in violation of the domestic law of the country where perpetrated.
>
> (Charter of the International Military Tribunal, Article 6)

All states agree that such actions are criminal and they are identified as such in contemporary international law. Let us refer to them somewhat oversimply but not too misleadingly as 'genocide'. Genocide is universally condemned and the UN system includes a Commission whose special responsibility it is to combat genocide.

Unfortunately, genocide is politics by other means. For example, 'ethnic cleansing' has proved to be an atrociously efficacious method of effecting partition in the former Yugoslavia. Despite its illegality, genocide is widely felt to be an effective political instrument so we can talk sense about it only by considering its place in political life.

Genocide is all too often perpetrated by states. To deal with the crimes of any state is very difficult. It is all the harder because every state is a member of a very exclusive club, the interstate system, and as such has a vested interest in preventing outsiders from interfering in interstate relations. Moreover, we individual human beings have a deep stake in the interstate system. On reflection, we find it very difficult to be sure that we want to intrude upon interstate relations. Appalling though it is in many ways, the interstate system has a certain logic to it, and enough historical weight and achievement to make one unsure that one wants to undermine its ground rules for any reason whatever, even to curb genocide.

To see the difficulty, let us recall in outline the nature and achievement of the interstate system. In the years before 1648 Europe was convulsed by catastrophic warfare that was in part religious. In the Treaty of Westphalia the European powers agreed to implement the principle that in future *cujus regio ejus religio* – the ruler would determine the religion of his or her subjects *and the other powers would accept this decision as final.* No state would *intervene* in such matters. Although no one at that time could say that religious matters were unimportant, states nevertheless agreed to regard them as the internal affairs of each particular state.

The full implications of this agreement were not and could not have been foreseen at the time. In the centuries since 1648 the non-intervention principle which was adopted then has grown to be the basic ground rule of international relations. It has become a *constitutive* principle, in that the answer to the question of what a state is makes vital reference to the mutual recognition of states, their acceptance that each has a legitimate sphere of internal affairs with which all the others are required not to interfere.

Non-intervention has grown since 1648 in two ways. First, the original agreement to avoid interfering in religious questions has come to include many other spheres of state activity, such as economic and social policies from nationalisation and privatisation to abortion and euthanasia. Second, the originally European limits of the system have been overcome. It is now universal. Every part of the human world is subject to the jurisdiction of states which stick together as members of the interstate system. Even Antarctica and the Moon fall within this universal jurisdiction, in that what may be done there is determined by international law which states have created and have the power (given the political will) to enforce.

Non-intervention thus makes itself felt everywhere that human beings can live and everywhere that we can be the victims or perpetrators of crimes against humanity. Knowing as we do that states are all too willing sometimes to perpetrate genocide and sometimes to acquiesce in it or to appease its perpetrators, do we want to repudiate the basic principle of non-intervention? I think we do not. I suspect that on reflection we all tend to believe that Westphalia was a positive achievement, that it is desirable for each state to have a recognised sphere of internal affairs in which other states are required not to interfere. This, I take it, is one of the commitments which defines the practical problem of crimes against humanity.

An intellectually elegant solution to the problem would be self-regulation by states: that there should be within the system of states an institution whose special responsibility it is to ensure that crimes against humanity are prevented or punished. Experience suggests, however, that this solution does not work. The scandalous history of the UN's Genocide Commission indicates strongly that states cannot be trusted to police themselves (see, for example, Kuper, 1981). Nor should we be quick to wax indignant about this. Each state has a great many kinds of problem with which to grapple and its political agenda is tightly constrained by the private priorities of its subjects. There are not many votes in policing genocide, so it is not surprising that other priorities override the need to curb crimes against humanity.

An extremely inelegant solution to the problem is direct action by individuals or non-state actors. One possible model for this is the International Brigade of the Spanish Civil War. The British and French governments had every right to lend military assistance to the Republican government of Spain in its hour of need against Franco's fascist rebellion. To have lent the necessary assistance to a fellow state would not have infringed the principle of non-intervention: states are at liberty to give help to fellow states as they see fit in dealing with internal security problems. Rather than exercise their sovereign right to assist Spanish democracy, the British and French governments did nothing. Faced with this calamitous failure of responsibility, individuals took it upon themselves to go and fight in the International Brigade. It is imaginable that individuals should likewise take it upon themselves to go and fight against genocide. Would this be desirable?

There are at least three drawbacks. First, however well meaning these individuals might be, their chances of making serious inroads against the perpetrators of genocide are likely to be very slim. If their opponents are a professional army they stand a good chance of being wiped out with no one the wiser. Second, there is a deep problem about whom they represent. The status of the International Brigade was, in theory at least, relatively clear-cut in that they were fighting in the service of Spain's established and legitimate government. If a group of individuals were to take it upon themselves to fight for (say) the Kurds then the *point* and *meaning* of their action as well as its practical efficacy could not but be in doubt. Third, because genocide is politics by other means, private individuals taking up arms in defence of the victims of crimes against humanity would be very likely to be drawn perhaps unwittingly into political causes of which they might thoroughly disapprove. For example, in all too many cases of crimes against humanity the victims are divided against one another by vicious factional in-fighting. Outsiders would find it very difficult if not impossible to escape involvement in such complications and this too might easily affect not only the effectiveness but also the meaning of their actions.

It seems to me just about conceivable that there could be a legitimate non-state intervention against genocide by an organisation analogous to that of the International Brigade. But I think it is very unlikely. Its chances of effective action – of stopping or punishing the criminals – would be so slight that it would be most plausible as a symbolic intervention and the difficulties of making clear what it was symbolising would be formidable. The likelihood is that it would achieve no more constructive engagement in the target country than Che Guevara managed in his fruitless attempt to make revolution in Bolivia without Bolivian political roots.

Private, individual action need not, of course, follow the model of the International Brigade. We as consumers can operate formidable boycotts if we choose to do so – I wonder how many readers of this page are at this moment sitting on chairs made of wood harvested by the Khmer Rouge. As citizens we can write to our Members of Parliament or other political office-holders in order to push particular cases of crimes against humanity up the political agenda of our particular country. Some situations are so relatively straightforward that actions of these kinds can be straightforwardly constructive. In other situations, acute political dilemmas may be worsened. It can happen, for example, that our government under pressure from us forces an important ally to relent in its (genocidal) struggle with internal opponents and the result is that the allied government collapses and is replaced by a far more destructive regime. These days so much political information is available and non-state human rights organisations are so sophisticated that it seems to me that we as individual citizens stand a good chance of making relatively well-informed decisions about which causes to press upon the attention of our political leaders.

Supposing we have identified some reasonably clear-cut example of crimes against humanity. What should we press our government *to do?* One important kind of case, I suggest, is that in which the victims of the crime are fighting back and we (or our government) can identify a reasonably cohesive fighting force to support. Under these circumstances, it seems to me, there is a possibility of legitimate intervention. We could, for example, give training to the resistance fighters; we could arm them; we might give them refuge from which to plan and conduct operations. These would, of course, be extremely provocative actions. They could be regarded as tantamount to war. If it suited all sides to regard them as something other than war then such measures could nevertheless commit or draw us on to further actions which would unmistakably amount to war. Indeed, to be effective symbolically or coercively, such actions would very often need to leave open the possibility of degenerating into war, for in many cases the perpetrators of crimes against humanity will be persuaded to desist only by the prospect of having to fight *us*.

It is necessary to be brutally emphatic about this. There is a long established tendency to define 'intervention' as being a set of military measures short of war. Vincent (1974) provides a thorough discussion. There are two good reasons for entertaining such a definition but numerous bad ones. One of the good reasons is that it is sometimes realistic to intervene in the internal affairs of a state in ways that do not involve military measures at all – for example, by freezing the bank accounts of corrupt political leaders. Such actions should not be called war and 'intervention' is a good word for them. Second, it can occasionally be effective to take military measures which really are short of war, such as sending an aircraft carrier into sensitive areas of international waters to demonstrate concern or resolve. This too might sometimes amount to intervention short of war. But the hard cases for which we need a clear-cut vocabulary in which to question and lobby our political leaders are those in which the possibility of war is in practice unavoidable even if all the parties to the conflict are eager to avoid the word 'war'.

The obvious terminology to use is that of the just war tradition. To be just, a war must be for a just cause. Resistance to, punishment and perhaps prevention of crimes against humanity all constitute eminently arguable just causes for war. To be just, a war must be the last resort. This requirement is likely to be met when the cause is genocide for states are unlikely to be eager to fight to protect foreigners from genocide – all other options are very likely to have been tried first. There must be legitimate authority. These days many people would like to say that war can be legitimate only if it is approved by the UN. There are two reasons for thinking that this is an over-stringent requirement as regards crimes against humanity. First, the very same interests which have made the Genocide Commission such a scandalous failure can be counted on to obstruct even the most manifestly just of wars against genocide. Second, the UN ideology which holds that only wars of individual and collective self-defence can be legitimate has to be challenged if we are to think seriously about using force against genocide, for many crimes against humanity do not seriously threaten anyone outside the state concerned. If force is to be used (as a last resort) against the perpetrators of crimes against humanity then the possibility of action by individual states or coalitions of states needs to be recognised as not being subject to veto by any member of the Security Council or General Assembly who happens to find the action impolitic.

The other just war principles, such as non-combatant immunity, reasonable prospect of success and right intention would all need careful discussion in a fuller account of intervention against the perpetrators of crimes against humanity. In this brief essay, however, another issue seems to me more pressing. I said just now that many crimes against humanity do not seriously threaten anyone outside the state concerned. This is obviously the case so far as modern thinking about international relations is concerned. In the years since the Treaty of Westphalia we have become so accustomed to the thought that the world consists of separate sovereign states that it is mere common sense that genocide is often an internal matter which affects the neighbours only if the victims are strong enough to flee to the border and to cross it, making the problem an international one.

Although this is common sense nowadays, it derives from an understanding of international relations which cannot but seem questionable to anyone who has an informed commitment to the ideas that underlie the just war tradition. According to these ideas, the state exists for the common good, that is, for the good of all human beings. It is for the good of all that there should be a plurality of states rather than just one, not least because a single world government is not only unattainable but also extremely undesirable because of the very real possibility of its becoming a universal tyranny or collapsing into universal civil war. It is for the good of all that each state should concentrate primarily on the well-being of its own subjects (all of them). It is for the good of all that states should recognise one another as having legitimate spheres of internal affairs that are to be immune from interference by other states. On the other hand, it by no means follows from the desirable limited sovereignty of states that any state should have the right to subject its subjects or anyone else to crimes against humanity. The division of the world into separate states is not an end in itself but a means to a deeper good and it can easily happen that a state fails so badly relative to the proper purposes of states as to become liable to legitimate coercion and/or replacement.

According to this cosmopolitan sort of understanding of international relations, every crime against humanity is automatically of concern to every state because every state exists to protect and further the common good – the good of every human being including the victims of the crime. If these people are being killed or otherwise tormented by their proper protector, then the universal political order is being violated and every state needs to consider how to respond. Each state needs to consider, for example, whether it ought to offer refuge to the victims if it is unable or unwilling to fight on their behalf. Of course, offering them refuge might be politically foolish in that it might deliver the very objectives that the criminals are seeking (for example to expel an unwelcome racial minority). But this confirms the point that according to a cosmopolitan understanding of international relations all crimes against humanity are an inescapable problem for every state – if we do not want to offer refuge, what do we propose? The most politic action might be war!

The picture of our problem that I am suggesting makes some very debatable assumptions. I assume that information is good enough these days for us, the citizens of democratic states, to identify crimes against humanity. I assume furthermore that there is a workable intellectual framework for thinking about the proper use of armed force in such cases. The just war principles are, I assume, definite enough to enable us to ask all the right questions with the possible result that we find ourselves, probably as members of an organised pressure group, a non-state actor, urging one or more states to use military force which may or may not fall short of war. The UN orthodoxy that the only legitimate cause of war is defence against aggression is, I take it, unacceptable, for every crime against humanity is in principle such a grave offence against the universal political order as to be a possible cause of just war. If possible we will of course avoid all military measures. It is possible that military measures can fall short of war, if it is agreed that training and equipping just rebels is intervention short of war. Alas, it is also possible that the one thing needful to halt, punish or perhaps prevent crimes against humanity might be a just war.

I sympathise with some of those who doubt that these assumptions are sound. Perhaps politics is too murky and manipulative for us to see clearly enough to be able to commit ourselves to a just war for any purpose, even such an apparently just purpose as resisting the evil of crimes against humanity. In that case, I suppose, our only option is the deeply uncomfortable one of solidarity with the victims. Perhaps we should go to be with them not as an armed International Brigade but as a religious witness, to die with them, submitting to the will of God, offering no resistance to evil. Though this is a real, reputable possibility I believe that more straightforwardly constructive options are also available.

BIBLIOGRAPHY

Kuper, L., *Genocide: Its Political Use in the Twentieth Century*, Harmondsworth: Penguin, 1981.

Vincent, R. J., *Nonintervention and International Order*, Princeton: Princeton University Press, 1974.

9 From National to International Policing

Brian Wicker

THE NEED FOR AN INTERNATIONAL POLICE FORCE

The moral and legal conundrum of intervention arises today because of potential conflict between the principle enshrined in Article 2(7) of the UN Charter, which we may call the 'libertarian' principle, and the principle enshrined in Chapter VII, namely the principle of 'law and order'. I call the first principle 'libertarian' because it embodies the belief that, as far as is consonant with the common good, people should be allowed to do what they like within their own territory – whether it be in the private home, the local community or the nation state – without interference from any higher or external authority. Now the principle of 'law and order' comes into conflict with the 'libertarian' principle when tension between people within a single territory – whether in the home, the town or the nation – dictates that action must be taken to prevent the conflict from threatening the legitimate interests of the neighbours, or even for the good of those fighting among themselves. It may sometimes dictate that for the sake of the common good, force from a higher authority be used to prevent or quell the disturbance, even against the will of those fighting each other.

So much for platitudes. My argument is that humanity has now arrived at a stage where vast segments of our planet and its inhabitants have to be regarded as constituting one community for certain 'law and order' purposes. We need a new kind of police force to deal with new kinds of threat to law and order in whole regions, continents, even perhaps the globe itself. Boutros Boutros-Ghali's *Agenda for Peace* calls for just such a force to be set up. He says it should consist of armed contingents from the member states to be made available on a permanent basis, both as a deterrent to potential troublemakers and as a force able to meet threats posed by them. Unfortunately he assumes these forces have to be military in character, culture and composition. I think this is a mistake. What he is really asking for is an international police force.

Now a modern police force is much more than a posse of men well armed enough to put down public disorders where they occur. It must also be a detective organisation able to spot the beginnings of trouble; a community-based organisation able to prevent potential violence from spilling over into actual violence; and a body equipped to deploy resources in a diplomatic and preventive rather than in a combat mode. And of course, behind the police there must stand an independent judiciary, appointed and equipped to give a fair trial to, and punish, people duly convicted of offences.

All of these elements are implied by Boutros Boutros-Ghali's *Agenda for Peace*. The question is: how do we get there? Perhaps a study of how domestic police forces within modern states have arrived at their present state of effectiveness might throw some light on this question. In putting forward this argument I shall concentrate on the emergence of the police in England to illustrate my thesis.[1]

DEVELOPMENT OF A NATIONAL POLICE FORCE IN ENGLAND

Most people tend to think that the police exist to catch criminals. So the first point to make is that in the Western world police forces emerged in order to deal with public disorders: food riots, demonstrations, workingmen's crowds. Secondly, in England at any rate they were created precisely as *substitutes* for military forces. Thirdly, before they could come into existence strongly held 'libertarian' principles had to be overcome. Fourthly, it was a long time before communities saw any need to pay for the police they needed. Yet fifthly, despite their libertarian principles, the ruling classes slowly came to accept the institution of a modern police force (including a detective branch) because the alternatives seemed to them clearly worse. Sixthly (London excepted) the police were accepted only because they were controlled by, and accountable to, a locally-elected body representing the community to be policed. All of these points are directly relevant to any attempt to create a police force on the international plane.

During the public disturbances of the late eighteenth century in England, it was usual for the military to be called out. But there were always difficulties. The local militia under the command of a local landowner could not be expected to act with impartiality, even if the law itself was fair (which it often was not). The only alternative seemed to be a standing army. But as Blackstone wrote, 'our laws know no such state as that of a perpetual standing soldier, bred up to no profession than that of war'. A standing army was but a temporary excrescence 'bred out of the distemper of the state' (quoted in Palmer, 1988:61).[2]

Calling out the army always had its problems. Soldiers sometimes found themselves condemned by military law if they refused orders to shoot into a crowd, and condemned by civil law as murderers if they obeyed (cf. Palmer, 1988:65). In the face of such dilemmas, there was always the temptation for the authorities not to act quickly enough, or not to act at all. Indeed in many eighteenth and nineteenth century riots the public authorities must stand accused of negligence rather than of acting too quickly or too brutally. Palmer sums up the situation after the Gordon riots thus:

> Where there was no strong civil power, there had to be, in times of crisis, military force...Creation of a strong regular police force would break this pattern by preventing the deterioration, which had traditionally required military aid. But so long as an efficient police remained a concept abhorrent to free-born Englishmen, the daily disorderliness of freedom and the emergency interposition of troops would continue. 'Your true Englishman', remarked Dr. Charles Burney after the riots, 'is never so happy as under a bad government'.
>
> (cf. Palmer, 1988:87)

Even when employed as substitute policemen, military forces had no training in non-lethal crowd control. Cavalry were not useful in city streets, while foot soldiers tended to have to use the flats of their sabres against crowds, thus showing that their equipment was not well fitted to the task of policing. Worse still, the kinds of rewards that soldiers normally expected for their work – glory, honour, loot – were not to be got out of riot control. On the contrary soldiers could expect insults in the press, attacks in parliament and possibly conviction in the courts for their pains.

In the period between Waterloo and the passing of the Reform Act of 1832 movements for suffrage reform, for trade unions and other popular causes led the authorities to think harder about the best way to contain trouble. The model of policing already established in colonial Ireland was at hand to suggest some alternatives to the established pattern of the local 'posse' backed by the use of military power. But the key to the acceptance of a police force introduced by Peel's Metropolitan Police Act of 1829 was a change in attitudes by the ruling classes. Until then, they had been in the forefront of opposition. 'Freeborn Englishmen' did not need a professional police force. But now they began to see things differently. As the *Tory Review* put it, 'police, in our view of the subject, when rightly understood...is the base on which men's liberties, properties and social existence repose' (cf. Palmer 1988:293). The *Review* berated what it called a 'despicable apparatus [that is, the current system of law enforcement] which, in cases of the slightest importance, can do nothing without the backing of red-coats and bayonets', and demanded that 'the public good...is entitled to some weight in the scale'. In short, the ruling elite had come to see that the introduction of a professional police force was in their own interests. But in the end it was in the interests of the public too.

Outside London, police came into existence under the control of local bodies in the main towns and cities. But one of the continuing difficulties was the refusal of many local authorities and taxpayers to pay for law and order in their own localities. In a crisis the military could always be called in, and then the government would pay. Furthermore local people often had good historical reasons to be suspicious of police with their foreign connotations of spying and surveillance. And in many places innovation was not an urgent necessity. 'If it ain't broke why fix it?' was sometimes a legitimate attitude to adopt (cf. Palmer, 1988:402). So progress was slow and patchy.

Yet irresistible pressures were bringing communities closer together, creating a greater sense of 'one nation'. The combined effects of the canal, the railway, the telegraph, the post office, the national newspaper, the improved road network, the interdependence of local economies and new industries were transforming England into a national 'village'. The railway, in particular, was having a major impact on the logistics of law enforcement. Thus during the 'Plug Plot' disturbances of 1842 (part of the Chartist challenge) Manchester was flooded with 2000 soldiers (there being no proper police there as yet) within 48 hours, by means of trainloads of troops despatched from London and Liverpool. This marked an unprecedented advance in what we would now call the capacity for 'lift' (cf. Palmer, 1988:457).

In the end parliament was able to force the most recalcitrant counties and towns into organising professional forces of law and order and paying for them. Even then however, there was resistance to the concept of a 'detective' branch designed to anticipate and prevent, and not just put down, disturbances. Such a branch smelt of 'spying' and was resisted in many places in England long after the main battle had been won.

APPLICATION OF LESSONS TO THE INTERNATIONAL LEVEL

In tracing the emergence of a police force within one country I have suggested a number of key points. First of all, the police emerged largely in response to large-scale public disorders: 'breaches of the peace' to use the words of Chapter VII of the UN Charter and of *Agenda For Peace*.[3] Secondly, in many places, community leaders and city fathers were suspicious of the concept of a police force, and refused to raise the money for it locally, defending their opposition on the principle of 'non-interference'. Thirdly when there was little threat of public disorder in their own neck of the woods, they could see no good reason for having a police force paid for out of local funds to deal with disorders in some other neck, especially since they would have no say in its control. However, the limitations and unsuitability of using the military to deal with public disorder were becoming ever more obvious as food riots, workers' demonstrations, demands for political rights and so on, especially in the cities, grew in intensity. Non-lethal techniques for putting down riots and affrays were being practised in London, and their merits as alternatives to using the military were understood more widely. So gradually the idea of a professional police force, using minimum force within an established code of procedure, became acceptable as the least bad option, even to the most independently-minded city fathers as they contemplated the ineffectiveness of current arrangements.

Just as the rapid unification of England during the industrial revolution – turning it from a patchwork of largely independent towns and counties into something like a single political and economic community – both required and made possible the emergence of a police force, today irresistible forces are at work on the global and regional scales which simultaneously make possible and require the creation of a global police force. Some of these forces are at least potentially benign: for example, the environmental and commercial pressures which are increasingly making national frontiers porous if not irrelevant. Others are clearly malignant: for example the arms and drugs trades, and the internationalisation of organised crime. Yet others could be either, or both: such as the world's increasing vulnerability to penetration by the electronic media and the spread of a homogenised and sanitised world culture. Benign, malignant or neutral, these forces are enormously powerful in the modern world.

I have dwelt at some length on the historic difficulties encountered in setting up a democratically controlled police force in one country. Yet in the end, the overwhelming need to set up a new kind of police force, based on a new legal framework, and with a new code of conduct quite distinct from the military model, overcame these difficulties. A mixture of cajolery, bribery and coercion eventually led to the creation of a police system for the whole community which, at least in theory – doubtless only ideally in practice – had the following features:

(1) day-to-day management and control at local and regional level, under partly elected bodies (except in London) who themselves appoint the 'chief constable';

(2) a network of professional codes, organisation and contacts between localities, which together with a good deal of central control help to ensure a tolerable degree of uniform practice and cooperation over the whole country;

(3) training in the use of non-military, and especially non-lethal, methods for dealing with public disorder ('affrays' and so on);

(4) a high proportion of costs paid out of local taxation, but with grants from the centre;

(5) cultivation of good relations with the community to be policed;

(6) strong influence by central government on matters affecting national policing issues and policies, through grants of money and a system of national inspectors to guarantee efficiency.

All of these features can and must be translated into the necessary elements of an international police force able to deal with large-scale 'affrays': that is, conflicts commonly regarded by the participants as 'wars'. What we are talking about here is the construction of a 'flying squad' of police under central control especially designed to deal with emergencies that are beyond the resources of the local community: that is, the individual state(s). In Europe, the concept of a flying squad has already taken hold, in two forms: the 'rapid reaction force' consisting of military units drawn from different states under the NATO umbrella, and the 'Franco-German Corps' consisting of an integrated international force drawn from several states but fully amalgamated into a single unit. Unfortunately both share the grave fault of being essentially military in culture and character, and designed in the first place to deal with defence against aggression rather than breaches of the peace. (The military's object is 'winning' fights, while that of the police is stopping them.) Furthermore, the concept of a NATO-based 'rapid reaction force' is essentially that states offer units to the force which they are not sure what to do with. Since these units exist anyway, states are prepared to 'lend' them to the NATO force at no great extra expense to themselves.

As I have pointed out, police have usually emerged out of the failure of the military to cope with public disorder, because of an inevitable cultural mismatch between criminal problems and military solutions. The Bosnian crisis is a case in point. Europe has obviously failed to live up to its need for a policing operation capable of dealing with an 'affray' which has taken on the appearance, simultaneously but self-contradictorily, of a civil war *and* of an international aggression. Of course a police action capable of dealing with a Bosnian-scale crisis would have to be able to deploy force on a scale undreamt of by any democratic police department.[4] But this difficulty should not permit us to delude ourselves as to its essential character, as a force designed to restore law and order, not to 'win' in a duel of sovereign opponents.[5]

A commonly stated objection to the notion of an international 'flying squad' is that it would imply the creation of a world government. Not surprisingly at this point the familiar reservations about non-interference in the internal affairs of self-sufficient communities, the old reluctance to understand what is happening, rear their ugly heads. But world government is not the point. The objection arises only if it is assumed that nothing but highly centralised police forces, on the French model, can work properly. Certainly the question of management and control is crucial, and would involve considerable loss of sovereignty: but not necessarily much more than is envisaged in the UN Charter when it speaks in Article 47 of a 'military staff committee'. This committee, consisting of the chiefs of staff of the 'Permanent Five' Security Council members (P5), with the addition of invited representatives from other states, was supposed to be answerable for a complex multinational force put at the disposal of the UN for international security purposes. It was to work out 'the strategic direction' of the forces, although 'questions relating to the command of such forces' were to be 'worked out subsequently' (presumably because of objections by some states to their own forces being commanded by foreigners). What is needed now, however, is a UN 'police staff committee', consisting of experienced senior police officers from various states. But one thing is clear: this committee could not work if it were dominated by the P5. For the essential point of a democratic police force is that it is impartial in enforcing adherence to the law, and is not working for any particular interest or set of interests. An international flying squad could not be set up until the UN Security Council itself had been made more representative of the international community, making its members more equal and more representative in power and influence. At the very least, the P5 veto would have to go.

Such a committee would not only have to set a 'strategic direction' for the flying squad: it would have to ensure a common police culture, drawing on the best practices of policing irrespective of origin: a massive task. And clearly there could be no question of some units refusing to work except under their 'own' superintendents.[6] The committee would be encouraged to set up 'regional subcommittees' to supervise regional flying squads which might be better able to deal with the sorts of 'affray' which their own region is subject to than would a squad mainly coming from another cultural world.

Whether such a 'flying squad' needs to be a permanent standing force is open to question.[7] There are grave objections to standing forces which have nothing particular to do much of the time. In England, police are frequently called in from various local forces to deal with large-scale emergencies. But this only works because of a high level of common culture, interoperable equipment and relatively straightforward liaison between senior officers. The same would be necessary in the international flying squad (as indeed it would be for any multinational military force). But certainly a permanent planning and liaison staff based at the UN, together with a permanent staff college for the training of international policemen, would be necessary.

In addition to an international 'flying squad' of (presumably armed) police able to sort out global 'affrays' there needs also to be a new kind of 'interpol': that is, a detective and intelligence branch. This too would have to come under the UN 'police staff committee'. But since its work would be highly political – to detect the beginnings of civil disturbances such as we have seen from Bosnia to Rwanda and to report its findings to the committee, and thence to the Security Council where appropriate – it would have to be extremely carefully managed, to avoid the sort of suspicions that the English harboured concerning spies and informers. The problems of the British in getting intelligence in the course of policing Northern Ireland are doubtless instructive here. I am not qualified to discuss them in detail: merely to note that they exist and would have to be coped with in some way on the international plane.[8] There is a range of proposals for a UN 'police force' ranging from the type of force to stop international affrays as discussed here (cf. Brian Urquhart 'If the United Nations is for real, give it a Police Force') to the more limited goal of a force designed to protect humanitarian workers operating in the field.[9]

I am not qualified to discuss the sorts of equipment an international flying squad would need to have available to it or be able to use. It seems obvious that the scale of the 'affrays' it would have to deal with, sometimes involving thousands of troops and a lot of weaponry, would inevitably mean that it would have to be able to mount quite elaborate operations with a good deal of heavy equipment – armoured personnel carriers for example. But heavy offensive weaponry would presumably be unnecessary, since their use would normally mean that the threshold between policing and open warfare had been crossed. Disarming the Serbs in Bosnia of their heavy guns was 'police' work, but air strikes were surely not.

CONCLUSION

The problem with the concept of just intervention at the present time is its political, legal and moral ambiguity. What are we to say about it as long as the necessary legal machinery does not exist? Where should we stand on intervention during the period when the conditions for its proper application are only slowly evolving? I think it would be a mistake to dismiss intervention altogether as being wholly inadmissible until all the legal conditions have been fully met. For it seems likely that continuing to intervene, or preparing to intervene, will be required for the successful evolution of the necessary machinery. It is a chicken and egg problem. That is, unless the international community continues to be exercised, in a practical way, with humanitarian intervention by doing what it can to intervene successfully even under the unsatisfactory conditions currently prevailing, the whole process of creating adequate international machinery for the apprehension and punishment of international criminals may grind to a halt. Then the balkanisation of the Balkans may well turn into the balkanisation of all Europe, not to mention of Africa, South Asia and the former Soviet Union. So we have to live, for the time being, in an ambiguous and uncomfortable moral limbo, supporting the practice of intervention wherever it seems to be practicable and necessary, provided that it is working in the right direction: namely, helping to promote rather than hinder the creation of a system of international policing that works. Being able to discern that direction, amid the confusions of contemporary politics, is what political leaders are paid to do. Let us make sure that we pay only those who can do it.

NOTES

1.   I rely heavily here on the monumental work by Stanley Palmer, *Police and Protest in England 1780–1850* (Palmer, 1988).

2.   Blackstone was reacting to the abuses of military power by the later Stuarts (under James II the army rose from 2000 to 30 000) as well as to the huge standing armies of France (150 000 men), Austria (100 000), and Prussia (80 000).

3.   The 'Peelers' in Ireland were originally called the 'Peace Preservation Police', cf. Palmer, 1988: 328–30.

4.   David Chuter has written in the 1994 *Brassey's Defence Yearbook* on the size of force needed to meet Boutros Boutros-Ghali's requirements as set out in *An Agenda For Peace*. His conclusion, summarised in another article, is that 'it is difficult to see how the force could be any smaller than 50 000 men' (Chuter, 1994:11).

5.   cf. Dobbie, 1994:141: 'The peacekeeper to peace-enforcer is as referee to football player... One (sc. peace-enforcer) is there to win, the other to ensure fair play'. However, the analogy of peacekeeper to 'referee' is misleading in so far as the peacekeeper is also supposed to be a kind of police officer, who is authorised to restore law and order, not merely to see fair play. This insight is partly expressed by Mackinlay (1994), where he says that given the doctrinal void that has existed at the UN in this field, the international community now needs to 'define the new domain of collective activity *between* peace keeping and enforcement' (my italics). While Mackinlay rarely speaks of this new activity as 'policing' there are hints at it in his account of the tasks of the

'multifunctional force': e.g. 'a UN soldier has the same approach as a policeman enforcing the law...He will uphold it regardless of which party is challenging him' (Mackinley, 1994:159).
6. cf. Mackinlay, 1994:157: 'To succeed, they must provide a structure for coordination in which the key players will agree to submit to a common procedure in which their jealously guarded autonomy will be diminished'.
7. cf. Roberts, 1994:115–16.
8. cf. Smith, 1994:174–92.
9. Urquhart, 1994. cf. Roberts, 1996:67 ff. on the latter proposal.

BIBLIOGRAPHY

Berdal, M., 'Fateful Encounter: The United States and Peacekeeping', *Survival*, Vol. 36, No. 1, Spring 1994, 30–50.

Chuter, D., 'Boutros-Ghali's Army? Proposals for a United Nations Military Force', Council for Arms Control, *Bulletin* No. 15, August 1994, 11–15.

Dobbie, C., 'A Concept for Post-Cold War Peacekeeping', *Survival*, Vol. 36, No. 3, London: IISS, Autumn 1994.

Mackinley, J., 'Improving Multifunctional Forces', *Survival*, Vol. 36, No. 3, London: IISS, Autumn 1994.

Palmer, S., *Police and Protest in England 1780–1850*, Cambridge: Cambridge University Press, 1988.

Roberts, A., 'The Crisis in UN Peacekeeping', *Survival*, Vol. 36, No. 3, London: IISS, Autumn 1994.

Roberts, A., *Humanitarian Action in War: Aid, Protection and Impartiality in a Policy Vacuum* (Adelphi Paper 305), London: IISS & Oxford University Press, 1996.

Roman Catholic Bishops of England and Wales, *The Common Good*, London: Bishops' Conference, 1996.

Smith, H., 'Intelligence and UN Peacekeeping', *Survival*, Vol. 36, No. 3, London: IISS, Autumn 1994, 174–92.

Thompson, E.P., *The Making of the English Working Class*, Harmondsworth: Pelican, 1968.

Urquhart, B., 'If the United Nations is for Real, give it a Police Force', *International Herald Tribune*, 23 May 1994.

Part IV
Geopolitics, International Law and Intervention

In the first of three chapters, *Comfort Ero* and *Suzanne Long* address the issue ***'Humanitarian Intervention: a New Role for the United Nations?'***

Correlli Barnett warns, in his energetic chapter, ***'Use of Armed Forces as an Instrument of Policy'***, against military intervention except for defence of vital national assets.

In a presentation on ***'Post-Cold War Illusions and Daunting Realities'*** *Richard Falk* argues that hopes for a new world order have not been fulfilled. He seeks to outline how international law and humanitarian motivation can be used to address perceived shortcomings of a realist paradigm.

10 Humanitarian Intervention: a New Role for the United Nations?

Comfort Ero and Suzanne Long[1]

Since the end of the Cold War the United Nations has found itself increasingly engaged in wrestling with domestic conflicts. But such cases as intervention in northern Iraq, Bosnia and Somalia have raised complex and difficult questions for the UN of a legal, normative and political kind, in dealing with issues that were once considered 'essentially within the domestic jurisdiction of states'. Perhaps the most complex and difficult question facing the United Nations today is this: under what circumstances is humanitarian intervention by the international community justified? Can the international community intervene by force in order to put an end to serious human rights violations? Or should the international community abide by the prohibition of the use of force embodied in Article 2(4) of the United Nations Charter? This chapter argues that there is no commonly accepted new approach or thinking on humanitarian intervention aimed at stopping the gross and widespread violations of human rights. The debate on the 'right to intervene' remains in a state of flux, partly because members of the UN have remained attached to the doctrine of non-intervention, and partly because the defining cases of northern Iraq, Bosnia and Somalia can be disregarded as precedents and do not necessarily herald an emerging customary law.

In most of the cases of humanitarian intervention that have arisen since the end of the Cold War, for example Iraq/Kurdistan (April 1991); the former Yugoslavia (August 1992); Somalia (December 1992); Rwanda (June 1994) and Haiti (July 1994), the United Nations has been pressed to redefine the limits of what will be perceived as legitimate involvement in the internal affairs of member states. Not only are there concurrent crises, but the pattern of recent experiences is that even the most 'internal' of issues tends to have international repercussions, because of the pressures on neighbouring states caused by floods of refugees across the borders. There is no consensus as to whether there exists a right to intervene in a sovereign state in order to alleviate human sufferings or to stop major human rights abuses. Clearly, something important is going on. Faced with the dilemmas posed by intra-state conflict and the increasing, though selective, attention given to it by the world's media, states are being forced to revise the UN's rationale, methods and procedures. For this reason, it makes sense to take a look at the whole phenomenon of humanitarian intervention, to assess the traditional legality of this old concept, and 'how the end of the Cold War has brought about a transformation in the political situation of the United Nations, so that the possibility of humanitarian intervention may no longer be discounted' (Greenwood, 1993:35).

This chapter addresses the legal and normative issues surrounding the debate on humanitarian intervention, but also notes the extent to which these are affected by the political factors that face the UN within this area. In discussing the role of the UN in such interventions, we shall first consider the status of humanitarian intervention within international law prior to the United Nations Charter. Specifically, we shall comment on the nineteenth century theories and practices which are more relevant to the contemporary debate. Room, however, needs to be made for the human rights implications of the natural law theories, especially as these still generate debate amongst promoters of human rights and state-centred theorists in their interpretations of the United Nations Charter. In a later chapter (Chapter 13), we focus on the three United Nations operations which have often been used to serve as examples of humanitarian intervention. These are northern Iraq, the former Yugoslavia and Somalia. More specifically, we concentrate on the Security Council resolutions – 688, 770 and 794 – which are said to have formed the basis for humanitarian intervention. Conditions or criteria for humanitarian intervention will be briefly considered. All three humanitarian operations raise practical issues as well as important legal issues.

HUMANITARIAN INTERVENTION

The term 'humanitarian intervention' is occasionally used in a very broad sense to cover non-forcible action for humanitarian reasons. However, for the purpose of this chapter, the discussion is being limited to military humanitarian intervention, or the use of armed force for humanitarian reasons.[2] Anthony Clark Arend and Robert Beck state that humanitarian intervention may be considered as 'the use of armed force by a state (or states) to protect citizens of the target state from large-scale human rights violation there' (Arend and Beck, 1993:113). Ian Brownlie defines humanitarian intervention as 'the threat or use of armed force by a state, a belligerent community, or an international organisation, with the object of protecting human rights' (Brownlie, 1974:217). According to Nick Lewer and Oliver Ramsbotham, to count as humanitarian, 'the intervention must be (a) a response to actual or threatened denial or violation of basic or fundamental human rights', along with innocent civilians that have been deliberately starved by actions or inactions of belligerents, (b) 'undertaken with a view to remedying the situation, and (c) carried out in the name of the international community' (Lewer and Ramsbotham, 1993:25). In other words humanitarian intervention can be defined to mean a military operation whose primary purpose is the relief of human suffering. Although the difficulty remains of determining what kind of human rights abuses are at issue and on what scale they must occur to trigger intervention, all three definitions point to the use of force in cases of (extreme) human rights violation.

THEORY AND PRACTICE BEFORE THE CHARTER

Debates on 'a right to intervene' have had a long and distinguished history stretching back to antiquity. Much discussion has taken place within the legalist paradigm. Traditional international law, one could argue, constitutes a serious obstacle to humanitarian intervention, for the doctrine of state sovereignty and non-intervention in the internal affairs of other states has deep roots in customary international practice. The principle of non-intervention finds its first explicit manifestation in the writings of Christian Wolff (1794) and Emmerich de Vattel (1758) and had acquired general recognition by the nineteenth century. However, the international legal order of this period was characterised by certain exceptions to the rule and some theorists of international law argued that customary international law recognised two grounds on which states could intervene in another state. First, a state could intervene 'to protect the lives and property and material interests of its nationals abroad' and second, a state could 'intervene in situations where another state mistreated its own citizens in a way falling so far below the general standards recognised by civilised peoples as to shock the conscience of mankind' (Fonteyne, 1973:198). In the course of the nineteenth century, the Great Powers threatened or carried out intervention in a number of cases on the stated grounds of protecting foreign nationals or Christians facing massacre or brutal repression. Many of these cases concerned the conduct of the Ottoman Turks, in Greece (1827–30), Crete (1866), and Bosnia-Herzegovina and Bulgaria (1876). In 1860, after the massacre of thousands of Christians in Syria, France was expressly authorised by a protocol between the Great Powers to intervene to halt the bloodshed and 6000 French troops landed in Syria for this purpose.[3] However, all these cases were mainly rescue missions of foreign nationals, or based on self-interest, or mere diplomatic protest. They failed to satisfy the basic principles of humanitarian intervention which involve severe human rights violations, exhaustion of all other remedies, disinterestedness, proportionality and cooperation with relevant international organisations (Donnelly, 1984:314). A study of so-called humanitarian intervention in this period reveals that most occurred in situations where the humanitarian motive was outweighed by a desire to protect property or to enforce socio-political and economic instruments of the status quo. Despite the state practice of the nineteenth century, it is debatable whether humanitarian intervention was clearly established under customary international law. Many scholars opposed this doctrine, more it seems, from fear of political abuse than on consideration of the principle (Fonteyne, 1973:199).

By the twentieth century there was still a strong support for the principle of non-intervention. The League of Nations did not provide for a right to intervene. Among the conventions during the inter-war period (1918–1939), the 1928 Convention on the Duties and Rights in the Event of Civil Strife prohibited intervention even by nationals of one state in the affairs of another state. Similarly, the 1933 Montevideo Convention on the Rights and Duties of States maintained that no state had the right to intervene in the internal or external affairs of any state.

THE CHARTER PRINCIPLES

After the Second World War, the principle of non-intervention continued to play a prominent role within contemporary international law. This concept holds that states are obligated to respect one another's sovereignty. Non-intervention, as it has developed over the last several centuries, positively protects the powers of a state and its sphere of jurisdiction without foreign intervention. The prohibition of state-sponsored interference directed against an established government is based on various grounds. To some, it is inherent in the general principles which define the international system, such as the doctrines of sovereignty, the sovereign equality of states and of self-determination of peoples. The UN Charter is silent on humanitarian intervention.[4] Article 2(4) of the Charter forbids the use of force by states and can only be overridden in cases of individual or collective self-defence (Article 51). Article 2(7) of the Charter prohibits intervention by the UN in 'matters which are essentially within the domestic jurisdiction of any state', but the second half of that article does allow for the possibility of 'enforcement measures under Chapter VII', thereby declaring the situation one of threat to international peace and security.

Legal scholars have debated the legitimacy of using force against tyrants engaged in gross violations of domestic human rights, one fear being that a dangerous precedent would be set. Opponents of humanitarian intervention have argued that human rights can be seen as being permanently subordinated to the UN's primary responsibility of maintaining international peace and security (see Akehurst, 1984; Brownlie, 1974 and Ronzitti, 1985). These opponents maintain that Article 2(4) cannot be interpreted as allowing for a right of humanitarian intervention, either because that norm bans virtually all uses of force, or because allowing the exception would open the door to unacceptable abuse. Furthermore, Article 2(7) of the Charter has been referred to by these opponents to refute the possibility of humanitarian intervention. Ian Brownlie represents the views of many opponents of humanitarian intervention when he states:

> In the lengthy discussions over the years in United Nations bodies of the definition of aggression and the principles of international law concerning international relations and cooperation among states, the variety of opinions canvassed has not revealed even a substantial minority in favour of the legality of humanitarian intervention.
>
> (Brownlie, 1974:218–19)

Some support for this is provided by declarations passed in the resolutions of the United Nations General Assembly.[5] However, it should be noted that while the declarations appear to support those who oppose humanitarian intervention, they do not have any legally binding effect. Supporters of humanitarian intervention argue that this kind of intervention does not contravene Article 2(4), since 'such an act would not constitute an assault on the territorial integrity or political independence of the affected state' (Rodley, 1992:21). (See also Reisman and McDougal, 1973:167–95 and Lillich, 1974:229.) Their position is further enhanced by the fact that, if the Security Council so determines, it is authorised to use force against a recalcitrant state. Some interventions may fall under Chapter VII provisions since it is quite possible that a grave violation of human rights could constitute a threat to peace. In this regard, Article 39 is of special importance, since it gives the Security Council the right to determine 'any threat to peace, breach of peace or act of aggression'. We are of course reminded by legal theorists, including Greenwood, that, prior to 1991 and the end of the Cold War, political considerations prevented any realistic possibility of humanitarian intervention:

> When the United Nations did commit forces to a State in order to prevent massacres or other humanitarian disasters (for example, in Cyprus and the Congo during the 1960s), it did so with the consent of the government of that State. The forces concerned were peace-keeping forces, which in most cases operated only with the consent of all the parties concerned.
>
> (Greenwood 1993:35)

To some extent the new political environment has also permitted a new emphasis on human rights and the principles of intervention to safeguard them.

THE EVOLVING EMPHASIS ON HUMAN RIGHTS

The UN Charter has of course mirrored the uneasy balance between the cardinal principles of non-intervention and respect for human rights, and in this regard the Charter is not without contradictions. Primarily an organisation whose main function was to maintain peace between states, the UN included among the purposes stated in its Charter the promotion of values within them such as respect for human rights. The second article guarantees territorial integrity and the inviolability of national boundaries. It was based on the notion that the internal political, economic and social structure and practices of a state were no other state's formal business. More importantly, human rights have often been viewed as a matter 'solely' within states' domestic jurisdiction. However, there are a number of articles (as well as documents such as the Universal Declaration of Human Rights) and the flow of human rights conventions[6] that oblige governments to protect the human rights of their populations.[7] Their principles reflect the competing theories of international law since the period of Grotius.

Human rights were viewed by some writers as being derived from a natural law which is based on those freedoms that humanity was believed to have enjoyed. The leading natural law theorist Hugo Grotius (1583–1645) is often cited as providing the first 'authoritative statement of the principle of humanitarian intervention – the principle that exclusiveness of domestic jurisdiction stops when outrage upon humanity begins' (Lauterpacht, 1946:46). Although reluctant to sanction the recourse to war, Grotius considered as just resort to war to prevent the maltreatment by a state of its own subjects (Lauterpacht, 1946:46). Grotius saw law as being derived from principles of justice which had a universal and eternal validity and which could be discovered by pure reason. Thus the law of nature:

> ...is a dictate of right reason, which points out that an act, according as it is or is not in conformity with rational nature, has in it a quality of moral baseness or moral necessity; and, that, in consequence, such an act is either forbidden or enjoined by the authority of nature, God.
>
> (Grotius quoted in Duke, 1994:29)

Grotius is often cited as arguing that the readings of the Laws of Nations should begin with the individual (P. Remec quoted in Vincent, 1990:243).[8] Within the writings of Grotius rights had a central place and no society could be preserved without the recognition of rights (Vincent, 1990:244). Grotius' view lasted until the eighteenth century when his work was superseded by the writings of Wolff and Vattel and the later positive orthodoxy of the nineteenth century. Within this period, it was argued that law was man-made, thus law and justice were not the same thing. Applied to international law, with which we are concerned, this approach considered the actual behaviour of states and their interaction with one another. Human rights were seen as derived from and regulated by internal laws which were decided upon by internal tribunals (Duke, 1994:30). Publicists within the positivist school saw states as being exclusively the subjects of international law and individuals merely as objects.

The differences between the naturalist and positivist schools of thought were brought into play when the Charter was drawn up in 1945. Attempts to accommodate both schools within the Charter still raise debates in present day discussions on human rights and the legal foundations for the use of force in cases of their gross violations. Reisman and McDougal, in making the case for humanitarian intervention, underscore the moral philosophical dimension and draw out the natural law position in present day discussions by arguing that:

> the validity of humanitarian intervention is not based upon the nation-state oriented theories of international law; these theories are little more than two centuries old. It is based upon an antinomic but equally vigorous principle, deriving from a long tradition of natural law and secular values: the kinship and minimum reciprocal responsibilities of all humanity, the inability of geographic boundaries to stem categorical moral imperatives and, ultimately, the confirmation of the sanctity of human life, without reference to place or transient circumstances.
>
> (Reisman and McDougal, 1973:168)

In other words, there are higher values affirmed in customary international law that take precedence over principles of non-intervention. This, however, again raises the old classic question facing those falling outside the natural law tradition of 'whence come' these higher values?

Human rights lawyers and activists have long contended that violations of human rights are a matter of universal concern. Indeed the evolution of human rights law and thinking over the last 40 years has been marked by the development and acceptance of universal standards of human rights, even if procedures to hold governments accountable for such violations have not yet been accepted. As early as 1948, the Genocide Convention showed that the international community recognised that there were limits to national sovereignty and that the international community had a responsibility to act to prevent genocide. The United Nations

Charter also includes various articles which further highlight international responsibility for the protection of human rights. For example Article 55 of the Charter commits all members to 'universal respect for, and observance of human rights', while Article 56 provides that 'all members pledge themselves to take joint and separate action in cooperation with the Organization for the achievement of the purposes set forth in Article 55'. Beyond the provisions laid down in Articles 55 and 56, the Charter's conception of human rights was articulated in detail in the General Assembly Resolution 2174 (III) of 10 December 1948, entitled, 'The Universal Declaration of Human Rights'. The preamble emphasised the Charter's conception of the inseparability of human rights and peace. Article 28 states that, 'Everyone is entitled to a social and international order in which the rights and freedoms set forth in [the Declaration]' can be fully realised. Article 30 goes on to state that, 'Nothing in this Declaration may be interpreted as implying for any State, group or person any right to engage in any activity or to perform any act aimed at the destruction of any of the rights and freedoms set forth herein'. It can be argued that of all the Articles the most exigent in regard to humanitarian intervention are Articles 3 and 5. Article 3 provides that '[e]veryone has the right to life, liberty and security of persons'. Article 5 states that '[n]o one shall be subjected to torture or to cruel, inhuman or degrading treatment or punishment'.

Despite the numerous articles and declarations, debates between human rights (or suffering) and non-intervention have generally been decided in favour of the latter. However, the scope of the human rights regime has been growing to the extent that human rights violations can no longer be said to belong to the *domain reservé* of states irrespective of Article 2(7). The former United Nations Secretary-General, Javier Pérez de Cuéllar, raised the importance of human rights when he stated that, '[i]t is now increasingly felt that the principle of non-interference with the essential domestic jurisdiction of States cannot be regarded as a protective barrier behind which human rights could be massively or systematically violated with impunity' (Pérez de Cuéllar 1991:12). His successor as Secretary-General, Boutros Boutros-Ghali observed in his oft-quoted June 1992 report *An Agenda for Peace* that: 'The time of absolute and exclusive sovereignty... has passed; its theory was never matched by reality' (Boutros-Ghali, 1992:12). Finally, as an international legal expert, Ved Nanda, noted in a testimony before the US Congress; 'consequently, international human rights issues transcend a nation's claim that they are exclusively within the domain of its domestic concern. A nation no longer can maintain that the treatment of its own citizens is exclusively within its own jurisdiction' (Nanda, 1991:23). Put together, these three views raise the difficult question of how such values are determined. Member states may attach priorities to human rights issues and there has been considerable disagreement over what constitutes grave or major human rights violations. Much of the public debate on these questions has been dominated by European or North American positions which may not reflect the views of Asian, African or Latin American states. The UN's consideration of human rights issues nevertheless takes account of all views, as the 1993 Vienna Conference demonstrated,[9] and rejects the notion that there is a hierarchy of human rights. Until recently Western states have emphasised civil and political rights over and above economic, social and cultural rights but all states accepted the Vienna Declaration that:

> All human rights are universal, indivisible and inter-dependent and inter-related. The international community must treat human rights globally in a fair and equal manner, on the same footing, and with the same emphasis.
> (World Conference on Human Rights, 1993, para. 5)

This evolution in the human rights regime has added to the climate which has encouraged states to consider new kinds of humanitarian operations by the UN, notably the deployment of forces to protect humanitarian activity where there is widespread suffering. It is not yet possible, however, to argue that the examples comprise a new customary legal framework of interventionist behaviour. Indeed the new development has been controversial.

NOTES

1.   An earlier version of the study subsequently expanded into chapters for this book was written by Comfort Ero for the UN and Conflict Programme, UNA, March 1994 and revised for presentation at a joint meeting of the Council on Christian Approaches to Defence and Disarmament and Council for Arms Control Working Group on Ethics and Intervention, January 1995.

We are indebted to participants at that meeting and the anonymous referees for their comments and to Josh Arnold-Forster for his help and support. While not expressing any policy of the United Nations Association this article reflects the continuing and necessary debate in the NGO community on these issues. The paper was first published in *International Peacekeeping*, Vol.2, No.2, Summer 1995, pp.140–56. Permission to publish has been granted.

2. There are other types of intervention which do not require the use of force and may be carried out by other bodies, such as NGOs, the UN High Commission for Human Rights or UN specialised agencies e.g. humanitarian work conducted by the Quakers during the Nigerian civil war and Amnesty International Reports on torture in various countries. These are often categorised as non-official coercive, official coercive, official coercive non-military and official coercive military forms of humanitarian intervention (see Lewer and Ramsbotham, 1993).

3. The various incidents are described in Franck and Rodley (1973:275–305, esp. 277–83). See also Reisman and McDougal (1973:179–83).

4. During the Cold War period, no action was taken by the UN Security Council in civil conflicts, such as Angola, Mozambique, Nigeria and Sudan, to name but a few.

5. For example, the Declaration on Principles of International Law Concerning Friendly Relations and Co-operation Among States in Accordance with the Charter of the United Nations stated in the eighth preambular paragraph: 'the practice of any form of intervention not only violates the spirit and letter of the Charter, but also leads to the creation of situations which threaten international peace and security.' *United Nations General Assembly Resolution. 2625 (XXV)*, 24 Oct. 1970. Similarly, in 1974 there was a condemnation of intervention in a UN document which classified the following as 'aggression': 'The invasion or attack by the armed forces of a State of the territory of another State, or any military occupation, however temporary, resulting from such invasion or attack...', Article 3(a) of the Declaration of the Definition of Aggression, approved by the *UN General Assembly by Resolution 3314 (XXIX)*, 14 Dec. 1974.

6. See, for example, the Declaration on the Granting of Independence to Colonial Countries and Peoples, *General Assembly Resolution 1514 (XV)*, 14 Dec. 1960; Convention on the Elimination of All Forms of Racial Discrimination, *General Assembly 1965*, 21 Dec. 1965; International Convention on Civil and Political Rights, *General Assembly Resolution 2200 (XXI)*, 16 Dec. 1966.

7. It should, however, be noted that there is debate among lawyers as to whether or not the Declaration has any legally binding effect.

8. While Grotius did promote the right of the individual, he may also be counted as a non-interventionist because of the deference he showed to sovereign authority and the maintenance of international order.

9. On 25 June 1993, representatives of 171 countries adopted the Vienna Declaration and Programme of Action of the World Conference on Human Rights, which was a common plan for the strengthening of human rights around the world. The Vienna Declaration marks the culmination of a long process of review and debate over the current status of the human rights machinery in the world.

BIBLIOGRAPHY

Akehurst, M., 'Humanitarian Intervention', in: Bull, H. (ed.) 1984, 95–118.

Arend, A. and Beck, R., *International Law and the Use of Force*, New York: Routledge, 1993.

Boutros-Ghali, B., *An Agenda for Peace*, June 1992, UN DPI/1247. New York: United Nations, 1992.

Brownlie, I., 'Humanitarian Intervention', in: Moore, J. (ed.), 1974, 217–52.

Bull, H. (ed.), *Intervention in World Politics*, Oxford: Clarendon Press, 1984.

Bull, H., Kingsbury, B. and Roberts, A. (eds.), *Hugo Grotius and International Relations*, Oxford: Clarendon Press, 1990.

Donnelly, J., 'Human Rights, Humanitarian Intervention and American Foreign Policy: Law, Morality and Politics', *Journal of International Affairs*, Vol. 37, No. 2, 1984, 311–28.

Duke, S., 'The State and Human Rights: Sovereignty versus Humanitarian Intervention', *International Relations*, Vol. XII, No. 2, 1994, 25–48.

Fonteyne, J., 'Forcible Self-help by States to Protect Human Rights: Recent Views from the United Nations', in Lillich, R., (ed.), 1973, 197–222.

Franck, T. and Rodley, N., 'After Bangladesh: The Law of Humanitarian Intervention by Military Force', *American Journal of International Law*, Vol. 67, No. 2, 1973, 275–305.

Greenwood, C., 'Is There a Right to Humanitarian Intervention?' *The World Today*, Vol. 49, No. 2, 1993, 34–40.

Lauterpacht, L., 'The Grotian Tradition in International Law', *British Yearbook of International Law*, Vol. 23, 1946, 1–53.

Lewer, N. and Ramsbotham, O. *'Something Must be Done': Towards an Ethical Framework for Humanitarian Intervention*, University of Bradford: Department of Peace Studies, 1993.

Lillich, R. (ed.), *Humanitarian Intervention and the United Nations*, Charlottesville: University Press of Virginia, 1973.

Lillich, R., 'Humanitarian Intervention: A Reply to Ian Brownlie and a Plea for Constructive Alternatives', in: Moore, J. (ed.), 1974, 229–51.

Moore, J. (ed.), *Law and Civil War in the Modern World*, Baltimore: Johns Hopkins University Press, 1974.

Nanda, V., 'A United Nations Convention on the Right to Food, Humanitarian Intervention, and the UN Response to International Disasters – An International Law Perspective' (Testimony before the House Select Committee on Hunger), US Congress, 30 July 1991.

Pérez de Cuéllar, J. *Report on the Work of the Organisation from the Forty-fifth to the Forty-sixth Session of the General Assembly*, Sept. 1991, DPI/1168–40923, New York: UN Department of Public Information, 1991.

Reisman, M. and McDougal, M., 'Humanitarian Intervention to Protect the Ibos', in: Lillich, R. (ed.), 1973, 167–96.

Rodley, N., 'Collective Intervention to Protect Human Rights and Civilian Populations: The Legal Framework', in: Rodley, N. (ed.), 14–42.

Rodley, N. (ed.), *To Loose the Bonds of Wickedness: International Intervention in Defence of Human Rights*, London: Brassey's, 1992.

Ronzitti, N., *Rescuing Nationals Abroad through Military Coercion and Intervention on the Grounds of Humanity*, Boston: M. Nijhoff Publishers, 1985.

Vattel, E. de, *The Laws of Nations on the Principles of Natural Law*, 1758 (ed. and trans. Fenwick), C. G. Carnegie Classics of International Law, Washington DC: Carnegie Institute, 1916.

Vincent, R.J., 'Grotius, Human Rights, and Interventions', in: Bull, H., Kingsbury, B. and Roberts, A. (eds.), 1990, 241–56.

Wolff, C., *Jus Gentium Methodo Scientifica Pertractatum*, 1794, (ed. and trans. Drake, J.H.) Carnegie Classics of International Law, New York: Oceania, 1964.

World Conference on Human Rights, 'The Vienna Declaration and Programme of Action', UN Pamphlet. DPI/1394–39399, New York: UN Department of Public Information, 1993.

11 Use of Armed Forces as an Instrument of Policy[1]

Correlli Barnett

'The Use of Armed Forces as an Instrument of Policy' – when I gave the original lecture to the Royal College of Defence Studies (RCDS) in January 1996 on which this chapter is based, I was tempted simply to utter the word 'Chechnya' and then go off to the pub with the Commandant! What perhaps gives that rather feeble joke an extra point is that I had used it to begin my lecture this time the previous year. There we were, 12 months on and Chechnya was still just as apposite as a dreadful warning about the unpredictable and uncontrollable nature of the military option. In contrast to my co-panellist, who was a distinguished international do-gooder, I am no more than a strategic historian; and it is as such that I approached the topic. All I would claim for strategic history is that it can help us to understand the dynamics of power and leverage, and in this way serve as a guide to the likely future course of particular current problems.

For instance, just over four years ago, on the same platform at the RCDS, I was contending that conflicts fuelled by religious or communal hatred or by territorial rivalry could not be solved in midstream by the liberal cure-alls of compromise and reconciliation, or outside mediation by the UN or whoever else. They could only be brought to an end by means of one party to a conflict first imposing its will militarily on the other or, in some cases, by mutual acceptance of a stalemate. In other words, I saw the then Vance-Owen mission to the former Yugoslavia and the Baker mission to Israel and the PLO as equally doomed to failure. And so it proved. Moreover, from the beginning of the civil war in the former Yugoslavia I argued against Britain or any other outside party committing a single soldier to the ground, on the score that committing that single soldier would lead us eventually and inevitably up to our necks in the mire. So it has also proved.

Study of strategic history also convinced me that outside intervention in Yugoslavia would actually prolong the civil war, by thwarting a quick Serb victory, and encouraging the Bosnians and

Croats not to accept defeat. In 1995, General Mackenzie, the UNPROFOR commander in Yugoslavia back in 1992, said exactly the same thing on television. Let me quote him: 'The conflict would have been over a year ago, if the UN had stayed out. One side would have won, the other would have lost.'

In the event, it has taken four years of conflict and the covert arming of the Bosnians before a military stalemate at last made outside mediation practically possible. Clausewitz would not have been surprised.

In the case of Israel and the PLO, the Baker mission did indeed fail, as I predicted. There did of course subsequently take place the deal between Arafat and Rabin. But, even so far as it goes and so long as it lasts, this deal only marks in reality a belated Arab acceptance of their cumulative defeat in four wars with Israel. It also marks, if you like, the acceptance by the current Israeli government that the de facto armistice that has endured since the Yom Kippur War did *not* provide a firm base for Israel's long-term security. Clausewitz (and Mao Tse-tung) were right – peace has once again grown out of the barrel of a gun.

You could say the same about the present armistice in Northern Ireland – clearly the product of a military stalemate between the IRA and the British security forces. All this by way of recommending to you so unfashionable an approach to international relations as thinking strategically; or, to put it another way, realistically appreciating the dynamics of power and conflict.

The title of this chapter is 'The Use of Armed For*ces* as an Instrument of Policy' – *not* 'Armed *Force*'. It is a key distinction. You can use armed forces as an instrument of policy without necessarily employing armed *force*. To give a simple historical illustration, Hitler used armed forces as an instrument of policy very successfully in the Czechoslovakian crisis in 1938. He used armed force as an instrument of policy in the Polish crisis in 1939 with ultimately catastrophic results. Let us next consider the phrase, 'As an instrument of policy'. Whose policy? What policy? In pursuit of what interests, or objectives? And in what world strategic environment?

To take the strategic environment first, the facts before our faces tell us that we do not live in a political 'world community', nor is there a 'new world order', as liberals in the West seem to believe. What instead does exist is a world arena for rivalry between myriad human groups – nation states certainly, but also ethnic groups, religious groups, social·groups, transnational industrial combines in market competition with each other, special interest groups such as big business on the one hand and Greenpeace on the other.

What is more, there exists a fundamental global divide between technologically advanced and therefore rich people, and the backward and therefore poor. This is not only a divide between 'first-world' and 'third-world', but also within 'first-world' societies in the form of the 'underclass'. So we actually see armed forces deployed in inner city streets as an instrument of domestic policy. Some world community!

I suppose that the only real 'world community' or 'world order' that exists today lies, firstly, in the globalisation of markets, including stock markets, and, secondly, in information technology (IT) – the Internet, e-mail, satellite television. Needless to say, traditional political institutions like the nation state or even NATO and the UN are quite irrelevant to these revolutionary developments, which simply bypass them. In fact, far from political institutions and armed forces exercising any influence over the IT revolution, that revolution powerfully influences them.

For instance, I hardly need to emphasise to you that real-time television coverage now constitutes a major constraint on the use of armed force by 'first-world' countries. Viewers are entirely turned off the idea of military intervention by the spectacle of the dead and wounded, whether their own soldiers or the civilian victims of air attack, as in the case of pictures of Iraqi women and children transmitted by CNN during the Gulf War, or the scenes of carnage and confusion in Chechnya. We all know that American public opinion will not sanction any use of America's vast military might that would entail more than a handful of casualties.

Yet paradoxically the spectacle of civilian suffering also makes the TV viewer feel that 'something must be done' – such as putting in 'peacekeeping' soldiers. In the case of Yugoslavia, this popular emotion exercised a decisive pressure on Western governments. Here then is a crucial puzzle of today's strategic environment for the reader to evaluate.

Now I would like to turn to the questions of whose policy and what policy, with what objectives, we are considering armed forces as the instrument of. For a start, it is perfectly evident that armed forces, and indeed armed force, in the hands of ruthless terrorists have proved a tremendously effective instrument of a policy of overturning an existing regime. I think here of the Irgun Zvai

Leumi in Palestine in the 1940s, or the PLO or the IRA in the 1970s and 1980s. After all, the IRA's political front, Sinn Fein, enjoys only a tiny minority vote in the North of Ireland and an even smaller one in the Irish Republic. Yet thanks to the bomb and the Armalite, Sinn Fein's profile in the current peace negotiations is far more prominent than those of Irish political parties which actually enjoy mass support.

The point is that militant subversives are in no way shackled by law, or squeamishness about innocent victims. Whatever their own tally of dead, they are sustained by a fanatical belief in a righteous cause. The very opposite of all this is the case with the state apparatuses which seek to defeat terrorists. I can recall only two cases since the Second World War where armed forces as the instrument of state policy have defeated armed forces as the instrument of revolutionary politics – the Mau Mau in Kenya and the Communist guerrillas in Malaya. By contrast we saw the total and ignominious failure of the French and American attempts to use military means as an instrument of policy in Vietnam; and of the Soviet attempt in Afghanistan.

But what of armed forces or even armed force as an instrument of the general policy of a major nation state today? When I say 'policy', I mean what I term 'total strategy'. Total strategy encompasses and relates together such different factors as defence policy, foreign policy in the traditional sense, the promotion of trade and industrial development, even education – in other words, all the things that make for a country's security and prosperity.

Governments can and do misjudge the make-up of their total strategy and get things terribly wrong. One can adduce as examples Imperial Germany and the Third Reich's overemphasis on the military card and the accompanying fatal bungling of foreign policy, or the Cold War-era Soviet Union's ultimately self-destructive attempt to maintain the role of military superpower from the resources of an essentially Third World economy. We may even note in passing the contradictions within present US total strategy, between the panoply of advanced military technology displayed in the Gulf War on the one hand, and, on the other, the huge American balance of payments deficit, the Japanese conquests in the American home market, the industrial rust-belts, the highly criticised American education standards and the Third World squalor of American inner cities.

But in any event the scope for the use of armed forces, let alone armed force, as an instrument of a nation state's total strategy has become more and more restricted during the twentieth century. Up to 1918 it was universally accepted as legitimate for states to use the menace of their armed forces as peacetime leverage behind their foreign policies. It was no less accepted as legitimate that a state could go to war in pursuit of its interests as it saw them. But since the end of the First World War and the setting up of the League of Nations, the free employment of armed forces and armed force by one state against another as a positive instrument of policy has been criminalised – finally and definitively by the judgements in the Nuremberg Trials in 1946.

The constraining restrictive effect of this on the usefulness of armed forces as an instrument of state policy has been pretty devastating. For instance, it is perfectly within the capabilities of Western airpower to destroy the opium crops of Pakistan and the golden triangle in Burma, or the coca crops of Colombia, so solving the desperately serious drug problem at source in short order. A hundred years ago Western nations would not have hesitated to resort to military force in such a case, and to hell with the sovereignty of the countries where the drugs were grown. But today this is politically quite out of the question. I make no judgement about it; I simply state the fact.

So just about the only remaining legitimate purely *national* use of armed forces lies in the direct defence of the national territory, or the territory of an alliance of which the state is a member – whether by means of deterrence, as with NATO during the Cold War, or, if necessary, by a fighting response to actual attack, as in the case of Britain and the Falklands War. However, this basic defensive necessity does not constitute a pursuit of national policy, in the sense of furthering the total strategic interests of a state.

What therefore strikes me is the impotence of armed force today as a component of a nation's total strategy; or, if you like, the cost-*in*effectiveness of armed for*ces* relative to other components. Let me give you one notable example: Great Britain since the Second World War. To telegraph a complicated story, Britain has spent about twice the proportion of GNP on defence as would have been needed for her own direct security. Why? Answer: In order to support her pretensions to be a world power, or at least to exercise global 'influence'. Remember her huge military presences in the Middle East and Far East. But this swollen defence expenditure has disastrously squeezed back investment in modernising Britain's industries and infrastructure, as well as sharpening her balance of payments difficulties.

What has been the total-strategic return on this British defence expenditure in support of her pretensions to a world role? There was none: it was all loss – and not merely of industrial investment and foreign exchange. For those expensive overseas military and political 'presences' once deemed indispensable have vanished one by one.

Yet in this same postwar period, Britain's main industrial rivals, Germany and Japan, spent exactly zero per cent of GNP on defence until the 1950s, and then only half or less of the British proportion of GNP. They were free to put their resources into the re-equipment of their industries and infrastructure. Their chosen leading card of total strategy was thus economic success and power, not an outdated hankering over a world political role buttressed by armed forces. Whereas the Deutschmark became the hardest currency in the world, the pound sterling dwindled into funny money, devalued again and again. What use, compared with the Deutschmark, have been Britain's 'out-of-area' armed forces and commitments as leverage in the international economic and financial fora which have now become so much more important than traditional diplomacy? What use were they when it came to negotiating to join the Common Market in 1963 and then again in 1970?

It would be interesting, I think, to examine the present cost-effectiveness of the American armed forces and American global deployments as a tool of American total strategy in the post-Cold War era. Can it really be said, for example, that Somalia was sufficiently important to the American people's wealth and security as to be worth putting ashore 20 000 marines to try to sort out a few local warlords? Can it really be thought that the Haitian regime, however unpleasant, constituted a threat to the United States? Is the survival of Bosnia-Herzegovina really so important to the US as to warrant locking up 20 000 soldiers in its preservation? And which of America's global spread of garrisons, air bases and fleets actually protect either valuable American markets or sources of raw materials, or are essential to the security of the American continent?

Rich though America still is, I do wonder if there are not lessons she could draw from the Soviet delusion, or perhaps even more the British delusion, that the imperial red across the map of the world signifies assets, when in fact it can all too easily signify unprofitable commitments. I leave this to the reader to ponder.

In any case, the employment of armed forces as a continuation of policy by other means has always entailed heavy risks and disadvantages, and this is equally true today of military interventions in the guise of some altruistic purpose under the UN. Use of armed forces can all too easily look like a short-cut route to a political solution, a quick in-and-out job. Yet, once started, the process of using armed forces, even more so armed *force*, is subject to dangerous unpredictability and uncontrollability. To cite a notorious example, all the belligerent nations of 1914 believed that victory would be won in six weeks, and that the soldiers would be home for Christmas. In 1941 Hitler believed he could crush the Soviet Union in a couple of months. The campaign in fact ended in the ruins of his own capital four years later. In 1967 – as I think it was – Washington believed that American military technology in massive strength could combine harvest Vietnam from South to North in time for the next presidential election. We all know how that one turned out.

Bosnia-Herzegovina is another obvious example. When the first small contingent of British peacekeeping troops were sent in, did anyone in Whitehall imagine that four years later Britain would be deploying there no fewer than 13 000 soldiers – and that in support the Royal Navy would be deploying its largest single task group? You can think of other direct lessons – like the Soviet campaign in Afghanistan, or Menachem Begin's foray into Lebanon in 1982, or the Indian Army's peacekeeping mission to Sri Lanka a few years ago; or of course, the Russian invasion of Chechnya.

In short, military history tells us that short and sharp walkovers like the Gulf War – which was a kind of updated Battle of Omdurman, where we had the Gatling gun and they did not – are rare indeed.

So much then for armed forces as the instrument of national policy. But what about the international organisations – the UN and NATO; the European Union? Here the questions of what policy and whose policy, and with what objectives become even more apposite. The North Atlantic Treaty was signed when an offensive by the Red Army in Europe seemed all too possible. The Treaty therefore committed the signatories to take appropriate action in such a contingency, 'including the use of armed force'. In other words, the purpose of the Treaty and later the Organisation was specifically limited and defensive, designed to confront a single common threat.

With that threat apparently vanished, the members of NATO have been trying to invent a new purpose for the Organisation – such as so-called 'peacekeeping' outside their own territories, and acting as a military agent of the UN. Seen in this light, enforcing the present peace deal in the former Yugoslavia appeared to be a marvellous opportunity for NATO. Yet the deployment there of a field army of 60 000 goes far beyond the terms of the North Atlantic Treaty, which limit collective action to the single contingency of armed attack on one or more of the signatories. Have any of the parties in the Yugoslav civil war launched an armed attack on any NATO member state?

'The Use of Armed Forces as an Instrument of Policy' – but what or whose is NATO's policy in the former Yugoslavia? Surely it cannot be that NATO powers have deployed a field army in an area of peripheral strategic importance just for the sake of preserving the rump state of Bosnia-Herzegovina? Where for example is the profit to a hard-up country like Britain in gutting the British Army's frontline strength in order to help garrison a region where we have virtually no investments, markets or sources of energy and raw materials? So I would urge that when, and if, NATO escapes from its entanglement in the former Yugoslavia, its members should revert to the strict terms of the Treaty. For who can tell what other costly Yugoslavias may be over the horizon?

This leaves me with the UN, the white hope of liberal internationalists, but in my judgement a diplomatic and military quicksand. Again, let us go back to the original nature of the UN. It was set up first and foremost to prevent interstate aggression, which its predecessor, the League of Nations, had failed to do. What is more, it was then overwhelmingly dominated by the West. So it was clearly in the interests of the Western great powers to be permanent members of the Security Council. But today the UN – no longer dominated by the West – shoves its fingers into civil-war messes like Bosnia, Rwanda, Cambodia, wherever. As a result, permanent membership of the Security Council has come to mean burdensome political and military obligations rather than diplomatic advantage. I simply cannot understand why Germany, for example, wishes to become a permanent member – apart from that weasel word 'prestige'. In short, for first-world countries at least, the UN as a security insurance policy is now all premiums and few, if any, benefits.

This becomes the more evident if you look at the regional distribution of the conflicts with which the UN currently concerns itself. For that pattern does not at all coincide with the pattern of the three great world industrial blocs – North America, Europe and the Pacific Rim – and where no blue berets are to be found.

It would therefore seem to me that the one remaining useful purpose of belonging to the Security Council today is to prevent the UN being turned any further into a global nanny trying to sort out local troubles wherever they occur; and instead to bring it back to its original limited purpose – that is, the prevention of major interstate aggression. Otherwise we may all find ourselves again and again pressured into using our armed forces as an instrument of policies which in no sense serve our own total-strategic interests.

But how should we define such interests? We should always remember, as Britain sometimes fails to do, that an 'interest' is not necessarily an asset, especially when the so-called interest is actually a commitment or obligation without hope of a return in terms of either wealth or national security. In other words, 'interests' should be identified in the same hard-nosed 'bottom-line' way as would an industrial combine. A nation state is not a branch of OXFAM. High-minded waffle about world peace being our interest will not do.

My final word of advice to nation states and alliances alike would therefore be: do not commit a single soldier, aircraft or warship anywhere, except to protect your own truly vital interests, including your own territory. Do not deploy them in action except in defence of your own territory, your citizens or your material assets against actual attack. Otherwise you will be sorry.

NOTE

1. This chapter is based on the author's Royal College of Defence Studies Lecture, 17 January 1996.

12 Post-Cold War Illusions and Daunting Realities

Richard Falk[1]

THE JURISPRUDENTIAL PREDICAMENT

Most of the international literature on intervention ignores geopolitical pressures and constraints. Such a failure has several serious consequences for our capacity to understand and act in specific situations. Part of the neglect of geopolitics is a matter of apologetics, and part a matter of wishful thinking.[2] The apologetic part overlooks the extent to which interventionary claims are exclusively mounted by powerful states that have often in the past put forward self-serving rationalisations for their questionable uses of force to coerce weaker countries with what appears to be an anti-humanitarian net effect. A recent controversial instance would be the economic coercion maintained by the United States against Cuba for several decades in the form of sanctions. It is rather strange but those international law specialists who think of themselves as realists when describing the predominance of power in international society tend still to talk as if the most powerful states in the world can be taken at face value when they purport to act as altruistic agents of change with respect to the assertion and implementation of humanitarian claims.[3] Neither international relations nor practice lends much support to such a benevolent role for Great Powers, nor, it should be added, does the evidence support the opposite view that geopolitically motivated action will never confer humanitarian benefits. Conclusions either way are persuasive to the extent that their assessment is particularised by reference to the characteristics and effects of particular interventionary claims. But there should be no illusions about the independent weight that is to be accorded humanitarian factors.

When Vietnam invaded Cambodia in 1975, presumably mainly for security reasons, but effectively removed a genocidal regime from power, it was widely condemned. Vietnam was called upon to withdraw by the United Nations despite the danger that, by so doing, it would revive the influence of the Khmer Rouge. The successor Cambodian government installed as a result of the Vietnamese intervention was precluded from representing Cambodia in the United Nations. The anti-Vietnam posture was based purely on geopolitical calculations despite the extremity of opposing humanitarian considerations, namely, that it was more important to avoid the extension of Vietnamese influence and to placate China (then hostile to Vietnam) than to relieve the people of Cambodia from the grotesque burdens being imposed on their lives. Such priorities may seem extreme, but they are not anomalous when it comes to disclosing the relative impact of geopolitical and humanitarian claims on the behaviour of leading states and hence, through their influence, of international institutions under their control.

There is another kind of geopolitical pressure operative in the years since the end of the Cold War; the *avoidance* of intervention even in the face of extreme humanitarian emergencies. The United States has been in the critical role of decisive leader with respect to the clarification of geopolitical concerns. Since its experience of encountering violent resistance in Somalia, followed by a domestic firestorm of criticism in the United States, there has operated 'a Mogadishu syndrome' which has suggested that humanitarian interventions that take the form of involvement on the ground risk serious military confrontations. In reaction the United States has scaled back drastically its willingness to act directly or indirectly to restore peace and normalcy to afflicted societies except by way of applying diplomatic muscle to hasten negotiations among adversaries as in Bosnia, the Middle East, and even Northern Ireland.[4] This US reluctance has also expressed itself in terms of rigid limits both on the duration of its commitment even to the implementation of the Dayton Agreement that it brokered, and of an unwillingness to make open-ended financial commitments in such settings, and by a particularly notable resistance to desperate requests for even low-level UN operations to prevent the renewal of genocidal violence in Rwanda and its outbreak in Burundi. Thus, in some important sense the geopolitics of humanitarian intervention has recently worked mainly to *discourage* action at the regional or global levels premised on responses that are reflective of attitudes of collective responsibility and compassion. It is the anti-interventionary geopolitical mood that has been as much the occasion for critical commentary as earlier it was the interventionism associated with American foreign policy, in particular, but geopolitics in general.[5]

There is also the utopian side of the ledger in these settings, with moralists and legalists naively urging governments to do what is right without any feeling for the political constraints which surround such demands. One result is frustration and bitterness which come with the discovery that governments will not generally act in a substantive manner against their material interests to any great extent, as shown by the unhappy fate of East Timor and Tibet – forcibly and brutally annexed against the clearly expressed will of their peoples. At the same time, agitation by transnational civil groups on such issues prevents the legitimation of oppressive arrangements that cannot be reconciled with minimal conceptions of self-determination and human rights. The basic compromise in these settings is to avoid substantive opposition, but to engage in some sort of symbolic action that to varying degrees withholds full approval. Another utopian tendency is terrible disappointment with the role of international law, finding it impotent to overcome the torments of peoples, and entire nations, trapped in such humanitarian emergencies. Both of these effects tend to divert attention from the constructive, if modest, roles of international law, as well as from the contributions that can be made through other avenues seeking to exert political influence. In essence, the only way to induce action in support of such humanitarian claims is to generate enough countervailing power to overcome geopolitical inhibitions; domestic protest in the key countries of the United Kingdom and the United States succeeded in doing this with respect to instituting a sanctions campaign to weaken apartheid during the early 1980s, thereby providing the political context for an effective transnational campaign that drew upon humanitarian arguments but did not rely upon them to achieve change. In this regard, mobilised domestic and transnational pressures responsive to humanitarian emergencies can alter the geopolitical calculus to a considerable extent, especially as most political leaders are preoccupied with holding on to domestic power. A famous instance, the interpretation of which is itself a matter for continuing controversy, involved the levels of United States support for the early period of Israeli statehood, that is, prior to 1967 when Israel became more of a strategic partner, despite the risks that were taken that might have weakened crucial ties with oil-rich Arab countries in the Middle East. Obviously, the impact on geopolitical calculations is greatest in a democratic country such as the United States where a well-financed, deeply committed constituency that imaginatively mobilises its resources for a sharply focused campaign and has enough of a perceived connection to domestic political balances in the United States to be a serious factor can exert pressure that will confine foreign policy within rigid parameters that make little geopolitical sense if considered purely by reference to international goals. The Cuban exile community has been remarkably effective in its efforts to maintain US pressures on Castro's Cuba despite the undermining since 1989 of geopolitical pretexts for a hostile relationship.

If international law, following the broad outlines of the New Haven approach associated with the work of Myres McDougal, Harold Lasswell, and more recently, Michael Reisman, is to be associated with some kind of conjointness between the authority to act and the capacity to implement, then the application of international law to the theory and practice of humanitarian intervention is highly problematic *in the current global setting*.[6] Recent experience in Somalia, Rwanda, Liberia, Burundi, Chechnya, and most of all, Bosnia and Croatia, are suggestive of both the growth of authoritative claims to act on behalf of the international community and of the absence of the capabilities to translate those claims with any consistency into outcomes that vindicate the undertaking. There is, thus, a serious gap between claim and performance with a tendency to deform the implementing policy and its agents of enactment. Does this suggest the wisdom of a higher threshold of non-intervention despite the presence of humanitarian wrongs that need to be corrected? Does it also underscore the importance of differentiating actions by states and interstate actors such as the United Nations and NATO from transnational civic initiatives that are carried out by independent associations of citizens?

At issue, also, is the fundamental Westphalian question of representation. It has been useful and generally reliable to treat the constituted government as the authoritative representative of the people, the subject of international law. Furthermore, with reason, the manipulation of counter-elites to obtain invitations and mandates to intervene, which was standard Soviet practice (as in Czechoslovakia in 1968 and Afghanistan in 1979), reinforced the view that only the legitimate, internationally recognised government has the authority to grant consent for the entry of an outside force with an interventionary mission.

But this neat Westphalian view has been eroded in a variety of respects as a result of recent practice. For one thing, if the oppressed people of a country can validate interventionary force by welcoming their own liberation, then the voice of formal governmental authority can be cast aside rather abruptly; such is the implication of an alleged emergent right of democracy or the state-shattering practice of self-determination accompanying the breakup of the Soviet Union and Yugoslavia.[7] Also, if there has been a collapse of government, there is no authority to grant or withhold consent, and forcible entry can be claimed, as it has been, by reference to the objective conditions of complex humanitarian emergency. But what if those empowered to represent are also the perpetrators of crimes against humanity? These leaders are simultaneously treated as negotiating partners and potential war criminals. This is the puzzle created by the 1995 Dayton Peace Agreement. It suggests that diplomacy should be less confined to its traditional governmental parameters. Instead of treating only figures such as Karadzic and Milosevic as negotiating partners there should have been discussions with 'representatives' of these peoples who did not endorse or participate in crimes of state or seek to establish states along ethnically pure lines. The feasibility of such an alternative course of action is uncertain at best. Governmental leaders, even if associated with criminal practices, may alone possess representational capacity by having sufficient control over the sentiments and capabilities of the peoples, and it would be meaningless to deny their representational authority. Such an acknowledgement of realities has led to the acceptance of both the PLO and the IRA as necessary participants in their respective peace processes, but without the Bosnian overlay of potential indictment for previous terroristic activity.

Once that overlay exists, as is the case in relation to Bosnia, it poses a fearful dilemma: the intention to prosecute those responsible for war crimes seemingly can neither be dispensed with, nor implemented, and this indeterminacy imperils the move from war to peace, and makes the process appear vindictive to some, hypocritical to others. It is notable that even with the resumption of IRA terrorism in February 1996 there are as yet no suggestions from responsible negotiating actors that perpetrators be treated as 'war criminals' because in this instance the British government has sought to protect the population by a substantive commitment rather than to abandon protection and offer those exposed to violence the symbolic solace of a future war crimes tribunal.[8]

This issue of reconciling Westphalian notions of representation and legitimacy with post-Westphalian ideas of personal criminal accountability of agents of state power are at the very centre of the difficulties surrounding the contemporary compromise between geopolitics and morality in the setting of 'humanitarian intervention'. The move to institute war crimes proceedings in this instance of Bosnia (and more casually, Rwanda) reflected the relative unwillingness of the Great Powers to use their capabilities directly, by way of the United Nations or through NATO, to prevent ethnic cleansing in the former Yugoslavia or genocide in Rwanda, but especially Bosnia, during the 1991 to 1994 period. Being unwilling to act substantively when it counted most, the political pressures to act in some manner acknowledging the humanitarian challenge produced a variety of symbolic gestures, including the establishment of a war crimes tribunal in The Hague, an arms embargo, sanctions against Serbia and safe havens in Bosnia. These measures had a range of effects, but overall an ambiguous, if not a perverse, impact on the underlying wrongdoing. They shared the common feature of responding for the sake of humanitarian goals but not being committed to devoting major resources to increase prospects that the response would be effective.

The standoff between the authority to intervene and the lack of capabilities to do so effectively raises serious questions about support for the purported legality (and even morality) of given instances of humanitarian intervention. Indirectly, as well, it suggests that at this stage of international society the doctrine of non-intervention provides a generally more constructive foundation for exerting the influence of international law than does an emphasis of the sort contained in Boutros Boutros-Ghali's oft-quoted passage in *An Agenda for Peace* to the effect that sovereignty in the sense of territorial supremacy is being eroded as a principle of world order. This is not a mere jurisprudential quibble. The policy concerns here are at least four-fold, and are not altogether internally consistent:

- upholding the sovereign rights of weak states, by stripping further the pretensions of legality away from interventionary diplomacy of an essentially geopolitical character, as was the case with the Panama intervention of 1989, that is, protecting states against dubious interventionary claims even if backed by some humanitarian considerations;[9]
- avoiding punishing the victims and weakening tendencies toward reconciliation, by acknowledging the inability and unwillingness of leading states and international institutions (as now constituted) of an inter-governmental character to intervene effectively for

predominantly humanitarian purposes in most circumstances of acute distress;[10]

- challenging the artificial line of sovereign deference that is now drawn to give Russian intervention in Chechnya, or Iraqi intervention against the Kurdish regions of northern Iraq, a different, more internal legal and geopolitical status than Russian intervention in Georgia or, formerly, in the countries of Eastern Europe;
- accepting the view that, despite the unevenness of international practice, it remains beneficial to maintain maximum and flexible support for the alleviation of suffering and the establishment of peace, and thus avoiding a highly selective, and inconsistent, doctrine of humanitarian intervention.

This line of analysis suggests a reconvergence of authority and effectiveness in relation to humanitarian claims as evaluated in context, thereby both reinforcing sovereign rights and norms of non-intervention, but also endorsing a limited option of humanitarian intervention. Such an approach opens the way for humanitarian assistance in many, but not all, circumstances, and recognises that the actors in the current phase of the Westphalian structure must often make tragic choices between diplomacies of interventionism and reconciliation. It further admits that the latter is possible only in the absence of strong strategic interests on the part of major states, or with the existence of a mobilised domestic constituency that is pushing humanitarian concerns onto the foreign policy agenda in a manner that overcomes a purely geopolitical assessment of interests.[11]

In advocating such a position it is obvious that major, and likely unfortunate, uncertainties exist in relation to the adoption of a more permissive approach to interventionary options. No one can answer the 'what if' questions about various recommended interventionary initiatives alleged to support humanitarian goals. Would an early minor NATO action of bombing the gun emplacements around Sarajevo have lifted the siege sooner and led to a much quicker, less devastating 'peace'? Or would such action have led to a bloody Serbian retaliation against vulnerable UN forces prompting their removal or to a spread of the violence to new arenas in the Balkans?[12] Did the creation of the safe havens negligently contribute to ethnic cleansing and the containment of refugees or was it a genuine good faith effort to provide sanctuary and protection for a portion of the entrapped Muslim population of Bosnia? Clearly the

inability to defend adequately several of the six safe havens contributed to the impression of UN impotence and culpability, and
probably suggested that, had the level of Serb aggressiveness
been anticipated, support for the safe haven concept would not
have been forthcoming. These fundamental issues are what post-
modernists (in the deconstructionist mode) are fond of calling
'undecidables'. The vigorous debates generated reveal little about
the probabilities and much about the sensibilities of participants in
the debate.[13]

MAKING HUMANITARIAN INTERVENTION HUMANITARIAN

My argument has been that with the end of the Cold War there has
been a notable shift in interventionary diplomacy away from purely
geopolitical interventionism in the direction of support for humanitarian claims to alleviate human suffering. This shift has been
expressed especially strongly in US foreign policy, both as directly
enacted, and as channelled through the United Nations and, to
some extent, NATO.

From a purely normative perspective of law and morality this shift
in interventionary practice is a welcome development, but it has
foundered in key instances because it was based on a very shallow
commitment of resources and will, underestimating the burdens
associated with successfully carrying out humanitarian diplomacy.
Earlier geopolitical interventions had also frequently failed because
they engendered a combination of indigenous, nationalist resistance
and counter-intervention organised by opposed geopolitical actors.
Thus, interventionary success should never be equated mechanically
with money, weapons, or even ground forces.

Interventionary experience suggests a number of conclusions
with respect to humanitarian emergencies. First of all, the best
opportunity, given available levels of capability to avoid acute
suffering is normally to become seriously engaged in a preventive
mode, providing a symbolic presence, substantial economic relief,
and making constructive diplomatic intermediary services available.
Secondly, external encouragement of nationalist tendencies toward
self-determination needs to be balanced effectively by adequate
protection of human rights.[14] Thirdly, once battlefield results have
produced a stalemate or antagonists have reached a point of

disillusionment with armed struggle, outside diplomatic moves and military forces can play a valuable catalytic role in encouraging and implementing a peace process. Fourthly, during the phases of most intense humanitarian emergency in the absence of a suitable interventionary response by states and international institutions, a maximum effort should be made to support transnational and grassroots initiatives without compromising their independence, especially those with a non-violent, reconciling orientation. Fifthly, a critical geopolitics is needed to convince those who dominate decisions about the allocation of resources that investments in conflict-prevention, human rights (including economic, social, and cultural, as well as civil and political) and conflict-resolution are conducive to global stability and prosperity; whether such a critical geopolitics is presented as 'a new realism' or as an abandonment of realism is not of great importance compared with altering the make-up of decisions and understanding about what counts for individual and collective well-being at this stage of international political life.

It is the contention of this chapter that these five directions of policy have been insufficiently emphasised in the years since 1989 with the consequence that there has been an unhealthy move from an initial unfounded enthusiasm for 'humanitarian intervention' to a more recent unwarranted disillusionment. As a result, by and large, even allowing for some specific successes and mixed outcomes (as in Somalia) the net impact of humanitarian diplomacy has been perceived to be, and in several instances has been, anti-humanitarian. The challenge now is to rededicate our energies to increase the prospect of humanitarian interventions serving humanitarian goals.

NOTES

1. An earlier version of this chapter was published as part of: Falk, R., 'The Complexities of humanitarian intervention: A new world order challenge', *Michigan Journal of International Law*, Vol. 17, No. 2, Winter 1996, pp.491–513. Used with permission.
2. Such a distinction owes a great deal to Koskenniemi (1989).
3. Compare for instance the realist tone of Thomas M. Franck's *Nation against Nation* with his support for an emergent norm entitling peoples to democratic forms of governance, Franck (1992).

4. It also lends support to preventive efforts as in Macedonia where a symbolic military presence under UN auspices has so far successfully sought to avoid any spillover of the warfare that could spread further the conflicts in Bosnia and Croatia.

5. See Barnet (1972) and Kolko (1994).

6. See Hedley Bull's important argument that international society lacks sufficient solidarity at this time to support collective ventures for the public good on a global level such as humanitarian intervention or criminal accountability of governmental officials, cf. Bull (1966).

7. This recent self-determination practice means that in situations other than decolonisation peoples previously entrapped within a state have been acknowledged by the international community as entitled to engage in struggle to establish by an act of secession their own independent state; these developments are difficult to assess as they have also been the occasion for establishing 'ethnic states' that are violently and cruelly 'cleansed'.

8. Such an observation is not to be confused with an overall endorsement of the British role; indeed, Major's tilt toward Unionist sentiments in Ulster for domestic political gain in British elections may well have upset the balance within the IRA that had earlier opted for a ceasefire combined with the prospect of all-party negotiations. On the misuse by Britain of the political space during the ceasefire to pursue 'the war' by other means, see the meaningful article by Woollacott (1996).

9. See Rumage (1993).

10. Humanitarian interventions might become more feasible in a wider class of instances if the UN or a regional actor were given the financial and peacekeeping resources to act with far greater independence of geopolitical priorities, or if geopolitics was reconceived to incorporate acute humanitarian emergencies for the sake of overall global stability and investor confidence; the essence of this point is grasped by comparing the mobilisation of resources to address the Iraqi challenge in the Gulf crisis with that occurring in response to the Serb challenge in Bosnia.

11. As argued, such pressures can work for or against intervention, and in normative terms, are a wild card as played in specific circumstances.

12. The retrospective claims made in light of NATO bombs bringing the Serbs to Dayton need to be tempered by the realisation that their impact occurred after Milosevic had abandoned maximalist Serb goals in the war and after the military build-up of Croatia and Bosnia changed the realities on the ground; without a far more detailed analysis of causal responses at various stages of the conflict it is exceedingly difficult to draw any firm conclusions about what would have happened had bombing occurred sooner. What is clear is that the United States and other actors undertaking such earlier bombing would have had to have been bureaucratically prepared in advance to cope effectively with the political fallout arising from possible failure of bombing to achieve its intended results and with possible Serb retaliatory actions.

13. To some extent the deontologically minded are drawn to positions that seem intrinsically right, acting to oppose ethnic cleansing, while the consequentially minded are drawn to positions that seem contextually sound, given likely effects of proposed actions; some combination of perspectives is

probably most likely to produce results that are both responsible and responsive, but in what apt combination it is impossible to codify in any useful way.

14. The German recognition of Croatia and Slovenia in 1991 was in this sense anti-humanitarian even if it did support strong majoritarian claims of self-determination; ethnically or religiously mobilised majorities pose severe human rights challenges to dissident minorities, especially as in Croatia and Bosnia, where varying interpretations of recent historical experience engendered plausible fears and established political space for opportunistic politicians to play their own minority nationalist card, as Milosevic did to such devastating effect in both Croatia and Bosnia.

BIBLIOGRAPHY

Barnet, R.J., *Intervention and Revolution: The United States in the Third World,* London: Granada, 1972 (1970), 1st US edn. 1968.

Bull, H., 'The Grotian Conception of International Society,' in: Butterfield, H. and Wight, M. (eds.), *Diplomatic Investigations,* Cambridge MA: Harvard, 1966, 51–73.

Franck, T.M., 'The Emerging Right to Democratic Governance,' *American Journal of International Law,* Vol. 86, 1992, 63ff.

Kolko, G., *Century of War,* New York: The New Press, 1994.

Koskenniemi, M., *From Apology to Utopia: The Structure of International Legal Argument,* Helsinki: Lakimiesliiton Kustannus, 1989.

Rumage, S.A., 'Panama and the Myth of Humanitarian Intervention in U.S. Foreign Policy: Neither Legal nor Moral, neither Just nor Right,' *Arizona Journal of International & Comparative Law,* Vol. 10, 1993, 1ff.

Woollacott, M., 'Finding the Bone of Contention,' *The Guardian,* 17 Feb. 1996, 14.

Part V
Tried and Found Wanting? The United Nations under Scrutiny

In the fifth part of the volume, actual case studies of the performance of the United Nations and the 'international community' are addressed. *Comfort Ero* and *Suzanne Long* develop three studies and seek to draw lessons from them in **'Cases and Criteria: the UN in Iraq, Bosnia and Somalia'**.

David Fisher applies the just war criteria to the Bosnian case in **'The Ethics of Intervention and the Former Yugoslavia'** and concludes that there was indeed a moral case for robust use of military force.

In **'Rwanda: the Media and the Message'** *Comfort Ero* and *Suzanne Long* examine the role of the UN and media presentations of recent events in Rwanda.

13 Cases and Criteria: the UN in Iraq, Bosnia and Somalia

Comfort Ero and Suzanne Long

One of the most significant developments in the practice of humanitarian intervention today is the use of United Nations forces to protect humanitarian operations where there is widespread human suffering. This has led to a new kind of operation, especially in Bosnia-Herzegovina and in Somalia (Boutros-Ghali (d), 1995:10). The increasing number of UN operations mandated to meet emergency humanitarian needs, trying to ensure safe delivery of aid and seeking to deter attacks on civilians, with action culminating in collective use of force, has been the most controversial development.

NORTHERN IRAQ

This trend began with the UN Security Council resolution on 5 April 1991 (SC/RES/688) and the international community's military intervention in northern Iraq in the immediate aftermath of the Gulf War to establish 'safe havens' to protect the Kurdish minority from the Iraqi army. It was in response to the massive influx of Kurdish refugees into southern Turkey and northern Iran as a direct consequence of Saddam Hussein's repression. The resolution made reference to the Security Council's responsibility for maintenance of international peace and security, and subsequently linked widespread human rights violations within a country to Chapter VII of the UN Charter. Although the idea of linking human rights to international peace and security is not new, it represented a significant development and departure from previous UN attitudes on the right to intervene.[1] Jarat Chopra and Thomas Weiss have argued that the case of the Kurdish 'safe havens' signalled a new willingness in the international community to legitimise humanitarian intervention (Chopra and Weiss, 1992).

But the action taken over Iraq is not only an exception, it is also an inappropriate example for establishing a general guideline for humanitarian intervention. First, as Adam Roberts stated, 'no right of purely national intervention on humanitarian grounds, without Security Council authority, was recognized' (Roberts, 1993:437). The resolution made no specific reference to Chapter VII, and its wording does not mention any collective measures or expressly authorise or endorse the allied intervention. Secondly, Resolution 688 should not be seen as the Security Council preparing to treat every violation of human rights as coming under Chapter VII. Many within the Council feared that this resolution could set a precedent for future UN interventions and that it was incompatible with Article 2(7) of the Charter. This has made the value of the resolution unclear as a precedent for a link between human rights and an Article 39 determination (Sarooshi, 1994:8). Only ten members voted in favour of the resolution. Cuba, Yemen and Zimbabwe opposed it, while China and India abstained, not wanting the resolution to go beyond declaratory condemnation (Rodley, 1992:29). China went on to explain its reason for abstaining after expressing its concern for the refugee flows into Turkey and Iran:

> However this is a question of great complexity, because the internal affairs of a country are also involved. According to paragraph 7 to Article 2 of the Charter, the Security Council should not consider or take action on questions concerning the internal affairs of any State. As for the international aspects involved in the question, we are of the view that they should be settled through the appropriate channels. We support the Secretary-General in rendering humanitarian assistance to the refugees through the relevant organisations.
>
> (*UN Doc. S/PV.2982*, 5 April 1991, Provisional 55–6)

The third reason why this operation does not serve as a useful framework is due to the particular circumstances in which the allied operation occurred. It has to be recalled that Iraq was still under Security Council sanctions and a series of mandatory resolutions under Chapter VII. To a certain extent, the legal basis for Resolution 688 can be found in Resolution 678 of the previous November which was made in the light of Iraq's invasion of Kuwait. It was this act of aggression which allowed for subsequent military operations and the creation of enclaves for the Kurdish peoples.[2] This resolution therefore does not provide a general basis for humanitarian intervention. Finally, James Mayall argues that action was only taken to protect the Kurds because 'the attention devoted by the Western media to the plight of the Kurds . . . threatened the political dividends that Western governments had secured from their conduct of the [Iraq–Kuwait] war itself' (Mayall, 1991:426, 428).

BOSNIA

In many ways the situation in the former Yugoslavia also fails to provide a precedent for humanitarian intervention, if only because the political choices which confronted the United Nations were difficult to make and because of the reluctant attitude shown by member states in trying to find a solution to the conflict. It was not until 13 August 1992, in Resolution 770, that the UN finally recognised that 'the situation in Bosnia Herzegovina constitutes a threat to international peace and security and that the provision of humanitarian assistance in Bosnia Herzegovina is an integral element in the Council's efforts to restore international peace and security in the area'. It expressed its deep concern of 'reports of abuses against civilians imprisoned in camps, prisons and detention centres'. The mandate for the peacekeeping operation in the former Yugoslavia, United Nations Protection Force (UNPROFOR), gave some specific Chapter VII enforcement authority to assist in the delivery of humanitarian relief and to deter attacks on safe areas, even though the presence of UNPROFOR was, initially at least, with the consent of the host states (Bosnia, Croatia, Macedonia and Serbia). The initial UN peacekeeping forces were deployed under Chapter VII. The Security Council reaffirmed its demand that all parties stop fighting and called upon states 'to take nationally or through regional agencies or arrangements all necessary measures to facilitate in coordination with the United Nations' the delivery of humanitarian assistance in Bosnia. The 'safe areas' concept in Bosnia-Herzegovina gave the United Nations a humanitarian mandate under which the use of force is authorised, but for limited and local purposes. It was not, however, designed to bring the war to an end. As Boutros-Ghali argued, 'even though the use of force is authorised under Chapter VII, the United Nations remains neutral and impartial' (Boutros-Ghali (d), 1995:10).

In spite of the Security Council authorisation, members of the UN were more reluctant to use force in the former Yugoslavia than in the Gulf for a variety of reasons. First of all, there was the argument that member states were reluctant to use force, because of a perceived lack of national interests in doing so. The second reason was the view that, unlike the Gulf, the use of force by the UN might not necessarily achieve the objectives of the operation. That is, they were not going to be able to use force to impose a peaceful settlement, a point later to be recognised by the Secretary-General in Somalia. To this must be added the point that many countries feared being entangled in a complex and open-ended conflict which might involve long-term military commitments within the region. Thirdly, there was the argument that no clear or common Western policy existed on what the future of the Balkans should be. This was clearly illustrated in the question of lifting the arms embargo on all parties to the conflict, an issue on which the Western European countries and the United States disagreed deeply.

SOMALIA

Finally, in Somalia, where the Government had collapsed in a civil war continued by armed factions, Security Council Resolution 794 (1992), acting under Chapter VII of the Charter, authorised 'all necessary means to establish as soon as possible a secure environment for humanitarian relief operations in Somalia'. Once again, the same familiar diplomatic language of *all necessary means* was a euphemism for authorising military force. It should, however, be noted that fear of a pattern being set led the UN to stress the 'unique character of the present situation in Somalia' and the 'complex and extraordinary nature' which 'requir[ed] an immediate and exceptional response' (*Preamble, Security Council Resolution 794, 3 Dec. 1992*). The Security Council also authorised the deployment of United States forces to deputise on its behalf to secure a safe environment for the work of humanitarian NGOs and relief operations. The United Nations and subsequent Security Council resolutions on Somalia directly linked human rights issues to a threat to international peace and security. In an earlier report to the Security Council (March 1992), the Secretary-General had declared that the crisis in Somalia posed a threat to international peace and security under Article 1 of the UN Charter since '[t]he countries of the region – Djibouti, Ethiopia, Kenya and the Sudan – some more than others, are beset by problems that are largely common to all. As a result, the exacerbation of conflict in one of the countries of the region could have serious consequences in one or more of the others' (Boutros-Ghali (b), 1992). Later on in that same year, the Secretary-General explicitly stated the possibility of the situation in Somalia falling under Chapter VII of the Charter:

> At present no government exists in Somalia that could request and allow such use of force. It would therefore be necessary for the Security Council to make a determination under Article 39 of the Charter that a threat to the peace exists, as a result of the repercussions of Somali conflict on the entire region, and to decide what measures should be taken to maintain international peace and security.
>
> (Boutros-Ghali (c), 1992:3)

This letter led to the authorisation contained in Resolution 794 and prior resolutions, and the creation of the Unified Task Force (UNITAF) involving around 38 000 troops from over 20 countries and the launching of Operation *Restore Hope*. UNITAF ceased to operate in May 1993. As a result of Security Council Resolution 814, the UN took control of the operation. However, just like the coalition operation in northern Iraq, Somalia should not be regarded as a satisfactory precedent or model for future interventions. This was a country with no government at all – the UNITAF deployment was not carried out against the wishes of the authorities but in their absence.

CRITERIA FOR INTERVENTION

In the last few years, and particularly since the Gulf War (1991), there has been increasing demand that the international community *should* intervene in order to safeguard human life when governments are unable or unwilling to do so. If the principle of humanitarian intervention is to be accepted, however, then the question arises about the criteria to be used in deciding when and in what form such intervention should be applied. There are no criteria developed by the UN for guiding decision-making in cases of humanitarian intervention. Without any established, objective criteria for humanitarian intervention, the question about the credibility and legitimacy of the UN, particularly of the Security Council, will be raised. More importantly, criteria are necessary to reduce the selective nature of UN humanitarian intervention action and to avoid the perception that decisions are largely dictated by the political interests of the Permanent Five (P5). Possible criteria could be stated as follows:

(1) Military humanitarian intervention should be undertaken by a competent authority, in this case the United Nations, or by other recognised international bodies, authorised by, and acting on behalf of, the United Nations.

(2) Humanitarian intervention should take place only when violations of human rights are extremely serious, involving the systematic violations of the most basic rights. This criterion, however, needs much more detailed consideration as it remains the fundamental area of disagreement.

(3) Military humanitarian intervention should proceed only when all other appropriate measures outlined in Article 41 of the UN Charter have been implemented and have failed to bring about the cessation of human rights violations.

(4) The intervention should be proportionate to direct and urgent needs, and should not be enlarged further and extended longer than these needs warrant.

(5) The intervening forces should begin their withdrawal as soon as reasonably possible. The intervention should be seen as a short-term measure which responds to the *immediate* requirements of those in need or danger until such time as a political accommodation can be organised through international arrangements.

(6) There should be minimal impact on the authority structure within the target state except where the cessation of human rights violation is dependent upon the removal of those holding power. Humanitarian intervention is based on the preservation of life. It is not the purpose of the interventionary forces to do anything more than enforce the stipulations of international treaties pertaining to human rights. Of course, in practice, interventionary forces have other objectives which may or may not coincide with the protection of human rights principles.

These are important factors which must be taken into consideration when discussing the principles and forms of humanitarian intervention. However, Claire Palley states that legal principles should be added to any criteria to assist the UN in decision-making:

'Such principles are implicit in humanitarian law and in general international law'. Palley recognises 'that legal principles do not dictate decisional outcomes: all they do is encourage consistency and predictability by drawing the attention of those responsible to relevant considerations' (Palley, 1994:7).

CONCLUSION

The UN's humanitarian role has changed dramatically since the end of the Cold War. UN actions in Iraq, Somalia and Bosnia have been hailed by some as defining a new 'right to intervene' and as setting a precedent which challenges the idea of the sovereignty of individual states. The watershed is said to have come in April 1991 with Security Council Resolution 688 when the Iraq case generated a new type of humanitarian activism within the UN (Kono, 1994). The UN had determined that the human suffering facing the Kurds in Iraq threatened international peace and security. This was followed by Resolution 770 which provided UN military protection for humanitarian convoys in Bosnia. The situation in Bosnia was such that all states and other actors were entitled to use 'all measures necessary' to provide humanitarian assistance. Then came Resolution 794 which, following the breakdown of order in Somalia, authorised UN troops to use 'all necessary means' to secure the unimpeded distribution of aid. Such interventions in the domestic affairs of a state would have been unimaginable five years earlier. The UN has shown itself willing to take enforcement action in the last resort to assist the victims of a humanitarian emergency where there is no existing government (as in Somalia) or where the existing government refuses to consent to UN action despite the scale of emergency (as in Iraq).

Whilst humanitarian intervention has become an issue that can no longer be ignored by the UN and its member states, there is an increasing reluctance amongst some of its members to become involved in interventions of this nature beyond the confines of their national interests. The increasing involvement of the UN in situations of human suffering is to a considerable extent dependent upon how its member states perceive their own national interest. Although UN interventions in Iraq, Bosnia and Somalia have produced various methods for humanitarian intervention, the international community is increasingly reluctant to use them, as the recent case of Rwanda eloquently testifies. The P5, as well as other large and small regional states of the UN, are attached to the principle of state sovereignty and the doctrine of non-intervention. As yet, the concept of humanitarian intervention remains embryonic. It has only been invoked in the aftermath of a war (as in northern Iraq), or in a situation where a government collapsed and sovereignty could be said to no longer exist (as in Somalia). The basic legal justification for all the three cases mentioned above was determined by whether it could be a 'threat to the peace'. At best, this can be seen as a matter of perception. As stated above, Article 39 of the Charter authorises the Council members to make their own judgement. The phrase, 'threat to the peace' is the 'magic formula' that allows the Council to overcome the restriction of Article 2(7).

But this position is becoming much more complex especially with the recent developments in modern broadcasting. To a large extent outside government control, the media have delivered real-time broadcasts from particular parts of the world directly to the living rooms of the general public. This has had, and will continue to have, an effect upon how governments react to events. Anthony Parsons argues:

> Had it not been for the heart-rending television pictures, there would have been no coalition intervention in Iraqi Kurdistan in 1991...no American led incursion into Somalia in 1992... [and] probably no humanitarian deployment in 1992 of UN troops in Bosnia. In each case public reaction to the horrors brought into our living rooms overcame governmental caution.
>
> (Parsons, 1995:186)

It is still unclear what impact these three operations will have on the theory and practice of humanitarian intervention. Certainly they have generated a debate and led to a re-examination of an old issue that concerns law, politics and morality. However, at present the thinking on humanitarian intervention is in a state of flux and the emergence of customary law is subject to the political interests of member states of the UN, which appear reluctant to establish precedents. And although model criteria for intervention have been discussed here, it is impossible to predict what new criteria, if any, will actually emerge within the United Nations over the next few years.

NOTES

1. In the past, the UN has adopted sanctions against those guilty of grave violations of human rights, such as Southern Rhodesia (Zimbabwe), *S/Res./253, 1428th Mtg*, 1961 and South Africa, *S/Res./418, 2046th Mtg*, 1977.
2. Resolution 678 had stated that the Security Council was, 'Mindful of its duties and responsibilities under the United Nations for the maintenance and preservation of international peace and security', *Security Council Resolution 678*, 29 Nov. 1990.

BIBLIOGRAPHY

Boutros-Ghali, B., (a) *An Agenda for Peace*, June 1992, UN DPI/1247, New York: United Nations, 1992.

Boutros-Ghali, B., (b) 'The Situation in Somalia: Report of the Secretary-General', UN Security Council Documents: S/23693, 11 March 1992.

Boutros-Ghali, B., (c) 'Letter to the President of the Security Council', UN Security Council Document: S/24868. 30 November 1992.

Boutros-Ghali, B., (d) *An Agenda for Peace*, second edition with the new supplement and related UN documents, New York: United Nations, 1995.

Chopra, J. and Weiss, T., 'Sovereignty Is no Longer Sacrosanct: Codifying Humanitarian Intervention', *Ethics and International Affairs*, Vol. 6, 1992, 95–117.

Kono, T., 'The UN Intervention in Iraq: Implications for Human Rights and Sovereignty'. Paper presented at the Academic Council of the United Nations System Annual Conference, The Hague, Netherlands, 1994, 1–32.

Mayall, J., 'Non-intervention, Self-determination and the New World Order', *International Affairs*, Vol. 67, No. 3, 1991, 421–9.

Palley, C., 'On the Question of the Role of the United Nations in International Humanitarian Activities and Assistance and Human Rights Enforcement, Bearing in Mind the Principles of Non-intervention', *Commission on Human Rights: Sub-Commission on Prevention of Discrimination and Protection of Minorities*, UN Document: E/CN.4/Sub.2/1994/39, 15 June 1994.

Parsons, A., *From Cold War to Hot Peace: UN Interventions 1947–1994*, London: Michael Joseph, 1995.

Roberts, A., 'Humanitarian War: Military Intervention and Human Rights', *International Affairs*, Vol. 69, No. 3, 1993, 429–49.

Rodley, N., 'Collective Intervention to Protect Human Rights and Civilian Populations: The Legal Framework', in: Rodley, N. (ed.), 1992, 14–42.

Rodley, N. (ed.), *To Loose the Bands of Wickedness: International Intervention in Defence of Human Rights*, London: Brassey's, 1992.

Sarooshi, D., *Humanitarian Intervention and International Humanitarian Assistance: Law and Practice*, The Wilton Park Papers, No. 86. London: HMSO, 1994.

14 The Ethics of Intervention and the Former Yugoslavia

David Fisher

The dilemma facing the West in the former Yugoslavia in recent years was well encapsulated in a cartoon that appeared in *The Guardian* newspaper entitled 'The Bosnian Drill'. In the cartoon a squad of soldiers is being drilled by a sergeant who is bellowing out the command: 'On the order "Something", "Do Something!"' In recent years there were many calls for something to be done but few, if any, were clear as to what it was that needed to be done.

Part of the difficulty has been the lack of an agreed ethical framework against which the many and diverse calls for intervention can be judged. Nor is this lack surprising since, during the long years of the Cold War, the demands of prudence, morality and law appeared conveniently to conspire to rule out – other than very exceptionally – military interventions in the affairs of other states. Given the risk of nuclear escalation, it was deemed too dangerous to intervene; and intervention would breach the sanctity of the state protected both by moral custom and international law. Indeed, the international order established after the end of the Second World War was founded on the principle of non-intervention, as enshrined in Article 2(4) of the UN Charter: 'All members shall refrain in their international relations from the threat or use of force against the territorial integrity or political independence of any State'.

With the ending of the Cold War and the rediscovery of the diverse utility of military force, intervention has once more become a practical political option. There are, however, as yet no clearly agreed ethical guidelines to help determine when it might be appropriate. For Christians, such an ethical framework is furnished by the complex body of thought known as the just war tradition. That tradition – developed over the years from Augustine to Aquinas and continued into this century – seeks to provide guidance on when the use of military force might be permissible and, in particular, when and how wars should be conducted. The relevance of this tradition to intervention may not at first be apparent because of the sheer variety of interventions, many not involving warfare at all: there are diplomatic and economic interventions as well as military. Its relevance is certainly most clearly discernible in relation to military interventions, while it is perhaps of little relevance to diplomatic. Most interventions, including economic sanctions, can, however, involve the threat or application of physical harm against civilians, which can even result in loss of life: they are hence activities that require careful ethical appraisal.

The just war tradition prescribes the circumstances in which a state may legitimately resort to war – the *jus ad bellum*; and the way in which the war should be conducted – the *jus in bello*. The *jus ad bellum* prescribes that war is permissible if and only if: war is declared by a competent authority; as a last resort, all available peaceful means of settling the dispute having been tried and failed; a just cause exists; the harm judged likely to result from the war is not disproportionate to the likely good to be achieved, taking into account the probability of success. The *jus in bello* adds two further conditions governing the conduct of war: the harm judged likely to result from a particular military action should not be disproportionate to the good to be aimed at; and non-combatant casualties should be minimised (Fisher, 1985: chapters 2–3).

The first requirement that war should be declared by a competent authority is usually interpreted within the tradition to mean a government of a state, reflecting the fact that we regard the wielding of military force as the monopoly of governments, not individuals. More recently, it has been argued that the use of military force for interventions needs to be authorised by the United Nations. UN sanction would certainly constitute competent authority – it is thus a sufficient condition. Whether it is always necessary is perhaps open to debate. There have been some interventions, for example Tanzania's intervention in Uganda in the 1970s, that appeared justified but were not sanctioned by the UN. In any case, this does not represent an issue for the West's intervention in Bosnia since this is clearly a UN authorised operation.

The second requirement – that military interventions should be undertaken only as a last resort – reflects the fact that the application of military force, even in a limited mode, can have harmful, even lethal, consequences. It is, therefore, clearly appropriate that other ways of achieving the objective should also have been considered. It does not, however, follow that the use of military force in a limited mode (for example to assist a humanitarian, food-distribution operation) should never be undertaken in preference to other measures, since the latter can sometimes, as illustrated by economic sanctions, pose a greater threat to human life than limited military force.

Indeed, it is arguable that economic sanctions have tended to be imposed by the international community too readily on the grounds that they are an easy low-cost option. This may be true of selective, carefully-targeted sanctions such as an arms embargo, although even the latter can, as its application to the former Yugoslavia has shown, have unintended consequences favouring one belligerent against another. The imposition of more general economic sanctions is, however, far from low cost to the populace upon whom they are imposed, who may thereby be faced with widespread hardship and even starvation and death. The imposition of such indiscriminate harm would at least require a very compelling justification in terms of some overriding good that could only be achieved thereby. Given the poor success rate of general economic sanctions in achieving their objectives, the readiness with which they have been applied is difficult to justify. It may be morally preferable to use limited military force carefully targeted against military objectives before applying such an indiscriminate weapon as general economic sanctions. Indeed, it is arguable that one of the lessons of Bosnia is that military force has typically been applied too little, too late and that a more deliberate use of force early on could have prevented many of the deaths that have taken place. I shall have more to say on this later.

The third and crucial condition of the just war theory is that there should be a just cause for the use of force. As the sixteenth century writer Victoria put it: 'there is one and only one just cause for waging war viz. an injury received' (Victoria:13). Until recently, most interpreters of the just war tradition have applied this in a very restrictive way to legitimise only individual or collective self-defence against aggression, as provided for by Article 51 of the UN Charter.

On this basis, the coalition operations to eject the Iraqi aggressor from Kuwait were clearly justified. Subsequent allied operations to protect the Kurds in northern Iraq or the Shiite Muslims in southern Iraq were not. Nor were allied operations in the former Yugoslavia. Insofar as international opinion now considers such actions to be justified, there has clearly been a shift in our thinking, with a readiness to interpret what constitutes a just cause less restrictively than in the immediate past. The question is whether such a relaxation is justified.

It is salutary to recall that the restrictive interpretation of what constituted a just cause that has characterised the latter half of the twentieth century reflected not just the caution induced by the nuclear stalemate of the Cold War era. It was also grounded in the European experience in the first half of the century of the devastating effects resulting from the interventions of great powers in the affairs of smaller states, including that of the Habsburgs in the affairs of Bosnia-Herzegovina. The importance of respecting state boundaries has been well argued by Michael Walzer:

> Now, the boundaries that exist at any moment in time are likely to be arbitrary, poorly drawn, the products of ancient wars. The mapmakers are likely to have been ignorant, drunken, or corrupt. Nevertheless, these lines establish a habitable world. Within that world, men and women (let us assume) are safe from attack; once the lines are crossed, safety is gone... It is only common sense, then, to attach great importance to boundaries. Rights in the world have value only if they also have dimension.
>
> (Walzer, 1977:57–8)

All of this does, I think, establish a strong moral presumption against intervention. Any intervention stands, therefore, in need of a very compelling justification if it is to be sanctioned. Assisting a country defending itself against aggression constitutes the paradigm just cause for intervention. The closer an intervention approximates to this paradigm the more readily may it be justified.

A frequent past pretext for interventions has been to support one or other side in a civil war. Does this constitute a just cause? On its own, I think not. The case against such interventions was well put by the nineteenth century writer Montague Bernard:

> Of two things, one: the interference in the case supposed either turns the balance, or it does not. In the latter event, it misses its aim; in the former it gives superiority to the side which would not have been uppermost without it and establishes a sovereign or a form of government, which the nation, if left to itself, would not have chosen.
>
> (Bernard, 1860:21)

Suppose, however, that one of the parties to the dispute has successfully established its bona fides in representing a distinctive political community and has gained control of a sizeable area of territory. It is only being prevented from achieving full nationhood by a repressive colonial or imperial power. It could perhaps be argued that this case moves closer towards the self-defence paradigm, with the repressive colonial power approximating to the role of the external aggressor, and to that extent, intervention on behalf of the oppressed community could be considered legitimate. Suppose further that an outside power has moved to prop up the crumbling imperial regime and so crush the movement for national liberation. In that event, support for the struggling nation could be regarded as a special case of the self-defence paradigm and so justified.

This was certainly the view of John Stuart Mill who argued in favour of intervention in the case of Hungary's revolt against the decaying Habsburg Empire in 1848–9:

> ...when, the Hungarians having shown themselves likely to prevail in this struggle, the Russian despot interposed and, joining his force to that of Austria, delivered back the Hungarians, bound hand and foot, to their exasperated oppressors, it would have been an honourable and virtuous act on the part of England to have declared that this was not to be, and that if Russia gave assistance to the wrong side, England would aid the right.
>
> (Mill, 1873:261–2)

Suppose next that intervention is contemplated in a civil war not to assure victory to one side or the other but rather to try to prevent further bloodshed by keeping the warring factions apart and so impose a kind of peace; or to prevent one or other or all parties to the dispute from perpetrating large-scale abuses of human rights. Such operations constitute what is currently called 'peacemaking'. The aim of bringing peace to a war-torn region by using superior force, perhaps under the authority of the United Nations, to hold apart belligerent parties could certainly constitute a just cause for intervention, as could interventions to prevent the large-scale abuse of human rights. Whether, in practice, such intervention would be justified would, however, depend on whether the next requirement of the just war theory could also be satisfied, that is, whether there was a reasonable prospect of achieving such a laudable objective at proportionate cost. It is on these grounds that peacemaking operations, including those in the former Yugoslavia, have often been resisted: the fear is that the intervening party may simply get sucked into the civil war without achieving the objective of bringing peace or preventing suffering.

Both of these conditions are far more readily satisfied where what is at issue is peacekeeping, that is, the use of military force to enforce a peace settlement or truce already entered into. The objective of peacekeeping would certainly constitute a just cause, as would humanitarian interventions of the kind undertaken by allied troops in Bosnia designed to provide military protection for humanitarian aid convoys.

Humanitarian interventions can thus range from such limited operations via more formal peacekeeping operations up to peace-making operations designed forcibly to persuade a belligerent to desist from abusing human rights. Such humanitarian motives may furnish prima facie just causes for intervention. The burden of proof for any intervention must, however, rest with its advocate: for any intervention is a regrettable breach of the integrity of a sovereign state, with potentially harmful consequences.

Where what is at stake is an abuse of human rights on a limited scale and/or where redress is available within the legal system of the state concerned, external interference would not be warranted. On the other hand, where a people is threatened with large-scale torture and/or massacre, even, at the extreme, amounting to geno-cide, the prevention of such suffering would constitute a just cause for intervention. In such circumstances humanitarian intervention would be ethically permissible. Indeed, it is at least arguable that where it is readily within our power to prevent appalling suffering, intervention is not merely ethically permissible, it may even be ethically required. The two conditions which, as I have argued in an earlier chapter (Chapter 2), are key to an attribution of moral responsibility – that what is happening is within our control and consented to by us – would both appear to be present. For if it is readily within our power to prevent genocide it is *ex hypothesi* within our control; and yet, if we fail to do anything to prevent its occurrence, are we not in a sense consenting to what is happening? And if so, is it not perhaps our duty to intervene and prevent the appalling suffering?

Even if there is a just cause to intervene, the next condition of the just war theory must also be met: the harm judged likely to result from a resort to military force is not disproportionate to the likely good to be achieved, taking into account the probability of success. This a crucial condition. It is always important before military force is applied to have made a careful assessment of the likely consequences to ensure that the good to be achieved will, indeed, outweigh the harm (often unintended) that may result. Hastily prepared and ill-conceived interventions – undertaken for however worthy a motive – would not therefore be sanctioned by the just war tradition.

Such then are the requirements of the just war theory that have to be met before force is resorted to and hence before any military intervention is undertaken: the *jus ad bellum* requirements. There are two further conditions that have to be satisfied in the conduct of any military operation – the so-called *jus in bello* conditions: the harm judged likely to result from a particular military action should not be disproportionate to the good aimed at; and non-combatant casualties should be minimised.

These then are the conditions of the just war tradition, all of which would have to be satisfied if an intervention is to be justified. How did the allies' actions in the former Yugoslavia measure up against these criteria?

The use of military force to protect humanitarian aid convoys – the original basis for allied intervention in Bosnia – would appear justified. On the other hand, the declaration of safe areas without making available the means to protect them would not: for however just the cause, this would not legitimise an intervention that had inadequate prospect of success. This lacuna was, however, remedied by the London Conference in July 1995, following which the remaining safe areas were successfully protected by the use of air power in Operation Deliberate Force.

Air power was, moreover, applied in a way consistent with the principle of non-combatant immunity, with only military assets targeted. (And insofar as these military assets, such as ammunition dumps, were important to the Serbian ability successfully to conduct ground operations during a crucial phase of the war, this was an important factor in the success of the air operations.) Operation Deliberate Force also complied with the requirement of proportionality, despite the claim of the air commander that the force to be applied would be disproportionate. For by this was meant merely that the quantum of force applied might exceed that used in the incident (the shelling of the marketplace in Sarajevo) that occasioned the onset of the operation. The proportionality of the principle of proportion is, however, forward-looking, designed to ensure that the harm resulting from any military action is outweighed by the good achieved. And insofar as one of the key objectives of Operation Deliberate Force was the lifting of the siege of Sarajevo it succeeded and the good achieved did surely outweigh the harm caused.

These operations also helped contribute towards the Dayton Peace Agreement and subsequent insertion of the NATO Implementation Force to keep the peace so painfully achieved. This peacekeeping operation is justifiable on just war principles.

The allies' actions in the former Yugoslavia appear thus on the whole justifiable against the just war criteria. What does, perhaps, give more pause for concern is whether we may not have been guilty less of sins of commission than of omission. For, as argued earlier, if it is readily within our power to prevent genocide, it may be not merely ethically permissible, it may be our duty to take action so to do. The doubt must inevitably persist as to whether, by taking more decisive action earlier on, the West could perhaps have prevented more of the suffering that ensued. The injured stranger we were called upon to help in the Gospel story lay on the road to Jericho. He or she could equally have been lying on the road from Split.

BIBLIOGRAPHY

Bernard, Rt. Hon. M., *On the Principle of Non-Intervention: A Lecture*, Oxford & London: J.H. & J. Parker, 1860.

Fisher, D., *Morality and the Bomb*, London: Croom Helm; New York: St. Martin's Press, 1985.

Mill, J.S., 'A Few Words on Non-intervention' in *Dissertations and Discussions*, New York: 1873, III.

Victoria, F. de, *De Indis Recenter Inventis et de Jure Belli Hispanorum in Barbaros* (W. Schätzel, ed.), Tübingen: J.C.B. Mohr (Paul Siebeck), 1952.

Walzer, M., *Just and Unjust Wars*, London: Allen Lane, 1977.

15 Rwanda: the Media and the Message
Comfort Ero and Suzanne Long

Since writing our previous chapters (Chapters 10 and 13) early in 1995, we have witnessed a growth in the literature on humanitarian intervention. Much of this literature has been both critical and prescriptive, largely as a direct consequence of the tragedy in Rwanda (see for example: the Steering Committee of the Joint Evaluation of Emergency Assistance to Rwanda, 1996; Jones, 1995; Prunier, 1995; Destexhe, 1994a,b; and Vassall-Adams, 1994). The debate, Jones suggests, has focused on the 'possibilities and limits of international humanitarian action in the post-Cold War era' and methods 'to shift the resources of the UN, diplomatic, and NGO communities towards a regime of early warning and preventive diplomacy' (Jones, 1995:232). As a contribution to what is essentially a period of reflection, both by academics and practitioners, we address again three interrelated issues that were discussed in our previous chapters: (1) the realities of the political context and the influence of the media; (2) the capacity of the United Nations in managing and resolving internal conflicts and (3) the relationship between non-governmental organisations (NGOs) and the military in humanitarian operations.[1]

THE POLITICS AND MEDIA COVERAGE OF INTERNAL CONFLICTS

The perceived failures and the political complexities surrounding the international community's response to Rwanda has led to a renewed focus on the gap between what we ought to do and what is politically feasible, or what is 'ethically desirable and what is politically likely and possible' (Hoffmann, 1995:45). As a consequence of the crisis in Rwanda, there is a need to find possible alternatives to narrow this gap in the face of increasing human tragedy. However, any understanding of the initial political inaction over Rwanda must be seen in the context of the events in Bosnia, but more significantly in the US, and later UN, Somalia operation during 1992 and 1994. The failure of this operation effectively ended the euphoria of the collective action that was said to have surfaced during 1991 and 1993 in the aftermath of the Gulf War. What is now defined as the 'Somalia Syndrome' – 'a fear of committing international forces to ill-defined missions of humanitarian intervention' – now largely frames the minds, not just of US policy-makers, but Europeans also (Shiras, 1996:108). Consequently, as Rwanda emerged within the international arena, 'any notions about intervening militarily to guarantee access to civilians caught in the throes of war, ethnonationalism, or human rights abuse were replaced by more realistic assessments about the limits of such actions' (Weiss (b), 1995:171). It seemed that the high expectations of a 'better' world had been replaced by the cynicism of politics or the limitation politicians placed on what they could do. As Hoffmann states:

> the imperative of doing good had yielded to a far more pessimistic appraisal: 'there is little good we can do, and some good we try to do produces more harm than good – so let us above all not do harm, even if it means caring less about doing good.'
>
> (Hoffmann, 1995:33)

An explicit example of how the Somalia operation dictated all subsequent actions within the area of humanitarian intervention or the broader subject of collective intervention can be found within the pages of the *Presidential Decision Directive (PDD) 25* (1994). Issued by the Clinton administration, this document effectively 'represented [a] 180-degree policy reversal...away from..."assertive multilateralism"' and a limited US military participation in future UN operations (Weiss (b), 1995:179). Largely as a result of the growing lack of political support both within the administration and the Republican Party towards UN operations, PDD 25 signalled the end of what President Bush had previously defined as 'a new world order'. Essentially, the directive set out several imperatives, the most explicit being direct US national interests, which effectively undermined future participation of US troops in new operations. Alain Destexhe, Secretary-General of Médécins Sans Frontières, suggests that the main reason for any lack of commitment from the international community towards Rwanda can be found in the Somalia operation: 'the international fiasco in Somalia and the deaths of more than 30 professional soldiers so shocked the American public that the Clinton administration had to rethink its foreign policy' (Destexhe (b), 1994:10; see also Weiss (b), 1995:179).[2] The political sensitivity stemming from Somalia, especially when Western military casualties were involved, inevitably led to a reconsideration of the merit of collective intervention in internal conflicts. Witness the following criteria as laid down by Malcolm Rifkind, the then British Secretary of State for Defence, to determine the United Kingdom's future participation in what is defined as 'Defence Role Three' (that is, 'wider security interest through the maintenance of international peace and security') in the annual *Statement on the Defence Estimates* (1995:27):[3]

> The degree to which our national interests are directly engaged. In particular, the deliberate commitment of our forces to conflict will require our national interests to be seriously under threat. The interest and involvement of those organisations of which we are a member, and of our major partners. Whether the use of forces represents the most suitable response to the crisis. Whether there are clear and achievable objectives. For crisis management operations, whether there is a political process to which the parties are committed which offers a reasonable hope of resolution of the crisis. Whether the mandate of the operation is precise and finite. The extent to which our forces are already committed elsewhere. Whether we have confidence in the safety and security of our personnel.
>
> (*Statement*, 1995:29)

This list of conditions strongly reflects that found within the US Presidential Decision Directive.

What tends also to motivate politicians, but is not a factor to which they readily admit, is intense media coverage, or what has been dubbed the 'CNN Factor', in deciding when to intervene in a conflict. The influence of the media is more apparent when politicians are seen to be indecisive or have no clear policy objective in resolving conflicts. According to Kofi Annan, the then Under-Secretary-General for Peacekeeping:

> ...when governments have a clear policy, they have anticipated a situation and they know what they want to do and where they want to go, then television has little impact. When there is a problem, and the policy has not been thought through, there is a

knee-jerk reaction. They have to do something or face a public relations disaster.

(quoted in Gowing, 1994:19)

How far the media influence or determine the decision-making process of states is widely disputed, but Rwanda and ongoing conflicts in Bosnia and Somalia, have illustrated the significant effects of visual images on the minds of politicians.[4]

In an extensive analysis on the impact of the media, Nik Gowing questions how far it pressures or distorts foreign policy decision, concluding that '(f)uture . . . television coverage of the proliferation of regional conflicts will create emotions but ultimately make no difference to the fundamental calculations in foreign policy making' (Gowing, 1994:87). But Gowing does recognise that to a certain extent, the visual images and the public support they generate, can wield political action: 'there is no doubt that *some* policy makers' real-time TV coverage does have a defining role in policy' (Gowing, 1994:84, 38–77).[5] But can human tragedies wait for what is essentially the lens of the Western media to determine its seriousness, before states are compelled to take decisive actions? The media themselves are selective about which conflict to cover; witness the limited coverage over the civil wars in Liberia and Sierra Leone. But also consider how it arouses domestic opinion when the international community is seen to fail in resolving a conflict:

> The 'CNN factor' is a double edged sword: it can pressurise governments into hastily conceived and open-ended military interventions, yet with equal rapidity, pictures of 'body-bags' arriving home can lead to public disillusionment and calls for withdrawal.

(Wheeler and Morris, 1996:140)

Despite the position of the media, this does not remove the perennial problem of state action in alleviating widespread human tragedies. Among the objective difficulties in dealing with what the title of this edited book suggests are conflicts in 'some corner of a foreign field', is the lack of anything approaching a consensus among member states of the United Nations. The incoherent mixture of statements, or the failure to develop anything like a political solution to ending internal conflicts, has hampered the performance of the UN in areas like Rwanda. As Hoffmann states, 'disagreements among states about the purposes that international intervention ought to seek tend to result either in the avoidance of hard cases or hard choices, or in minimalist or fuzzy UN resolutions' (Hoffmann, 1995:46). The lessons of the last few years are important for the future of collective intervention, whether US or UN led. They force us again to resurrect the old question of political will, and to ask how states determine what is in their national interest. Unfortunately, while we wait for the political leaders to decide what actions to pursue, the United Nations, charged with the task of global peacekeeping and humanitarian assistance, is criticised for failing to restore or contain internal peace in war-torn societies.

THE CAPACITY OF THE UN TO MANAGE AND RESOLVE INTERNAL CONFLICTS

Of all the criticisms to be directed at the actors involved in Rwanda, the UN has reaped a considerable amount of blame. But can the United Nations act alone to undertake Rwanda-style operations? To date, the most critical response has come from a five-volume detailed series commissioned by a host of humanitarian organisations (Steering Committee of the Joint Evaluation of Emergency Assistance to Rwanda, 1996). The findings explicitly criticise the United Nations for taking no immediate action in response to the genocide and human suffering witnessed in Rwanda. However, Josh Arnold-Forster asserts that this report does not scrutinise the actions of member states in the same detail or depth as it does the UN.[6] It is primarily for this reason that there needs to be some reconsideration of the events that transpired within the United Nations prior to, and in the immediate aftermath of, the crisis in Rwanda.

At the outset of the conflict in April 1994, the Secretary-General presented the Security Council with three options: to reinforce the United Nations Assistance Mission in Rwanda (UNAMIR) with additional resources and a new mandate; to leave the original mandate as it was; or to reduce the troops to the level of 240 to 270, (*UN Doc. S/1994/470*, 20 April 1994). It was the member states of the Security Council, and not the UN Secretary-General, which gave the formal decision to reduce UNAMIR's strength from 2500 to 270 (*Security Council Resolution 912*, 21 April 1994). It was not until 17 May that the Security Council revoked its earlier resolution with the decision to increase UNAMIR to 5500 (*Security Council Resolution 918*). This was later followed by the launch of Opération

Turquoise, a French unilateral operation from June to August, and the US humanitarian initiative, Operation Support Hope, from August to October 1994.[7] Despite these reactive policies by members of the Security Council, Shashi Tharoor, Special Assistant to the UN Under-Secretary-General for Peacekeeping Operations, argues as follows:

> Had the UN's General Roméo Dallaire had 5000 reinforcements within days of the shooting down of the Presidential aircraft that unleashed the carnage in Rwanda, he might have been able to save more than 500 000 lives; but none was forthcoming, and when the Security Council finally approved an enhancement of his Force, Dallaire had to wait more than three months for governments to make them available to the UN.
>
> (Tharoor, 1996:24)

This comment not only illustrates the dilemmas which confront the United Nations, but also what should by now be an all too apparent point: 'the UN can only be as good as it is allowed to be' (Tharoor, 1996:31). However, as Connaughton states, 'this assertion must not go unchallenged' (Connaughton, 1996:67).

The position of the United Nations has been called into question over the last few years and significantly over Rwanda, where it has faced serious allegations about its conduct prior to the 6 April 1994 massacre. The most prominent allegation is that the Secretariat failed to pass on relevant information to the Security Council, which could have prevented the massacre in Rwanda (Connaughton, 1996:67; Africa Rights, 1994:664–715). Study 2 of the Steering Committee of the Joint Evaluation of Emergency Assistance to Rwanda quotes a cable sent to the Department of Peacekeeping Operations (DPKO) on 11 January 1994 by Major-General Roméo Dallaire, the UNAMIR Force Commander, as evidence of the Secretariat's knowledge of the impending situation in Rwanda: '[a] "very important government official" turned informer had told him that "hostilities may commence again if political deadlock *ends*" '.[8] (Steering Committee, *Study 2: Early Warning and Conflict Management*, 1996:37). The study goes on to state that additional information exists to support their allegations of UN incompetence and suggests that 'the UN Secretariat had a propensity to discount the information and warnings received from within its own system while paying inordinate attention to media analysis' (ibid. 68). In defence of the UN's position in Rwanda, Sylvana Foa, the spokeswoman for the

UN Secretary-General, stated that the 'assertions did not reflect reality'. She then went on to explain the actions taken in reference to Dallaire's cable to DPKO:

> On 11 January 1994, there was an exchange of cables. Four communications were exchanged between the force commander in Kigali and the Department of Peace-Keeping Operations which basically resulted in the force commander being given permission on an ad hoc basis to assist the Government in securing areas so that illegal arms could be seized. This responded to the part of the report (in Study 2) which said that his communications were ignored and put in a black file.
>
> (UN Daily Press Briefing, 11 March 1996)

The charges against the UN need to be taken seriously. However, until more detailed analysis is undertaken fully to explain the nature of information available at the Secretariat, we are unable to support explicit suggestions that the UN could have prevented the massacre that took place within Rwanda. Needless to say that the role of the United Nations in conflicts like Rwanda does need more careful analysis. Further work needs to address the organisation's capacity to deal with internal conflicts and develop appropriate structures to manage humanitarian disasters. These issues were prominent in Somalia and are still being tackled in Bosnia.

Several reforms, ranging from better preventative and preparedness measures, to designing an effective information network to generate up to date analysis and coordination of humanitarian activities on the ground, are already taking shape within the Organisation. There is, however, the question of how the Organisation can best influence and generate support from within the domestic policy-making units of governments to undertake collective intervention in what are at best distant conflicts. This is the most crucial and complex issue confronting the UN. If it cannot devise ways in which to influence domestic policy, then the prognosis is not very good for the future of UN humanitarian operations. In a response to the Steering Committee's evaluation on Rwanda, the UN Department of Humanitarian Affairs (DHA) recognised the need for the UN to institute mechanisms to strengthen its capacity to respond to future crises, stating that more early warning and contingency planning is a fundamental prerequisite (DHA, 12 March 1996). There are other areas in which the UN has attempted to improve itself, especially within the context of peacekeeping and the management and resolution of conflicts. Notable among these, according to Tharoor, is the creation of:

[a] 24-hour-a-day-7-day-a-week Situation Centre to maintain constant communication with, and instant responsiveness to, the field; the creation of new units for planning, training, and logistics support; the merger into the DPKO of the former Field Operations Division of the Department of Administration and Management…; and a number of management improvements which have enhanced our ability to mount and manage operations, including the appointment of a new, independent Inspector-General reporting to the General Assembly.

(Tharoor, 1996:30)[9]

Of all the proposals to date on reforming the UN's role in maintaining peace and security, the most significant has been the call for an effective rapid reaction capacity within the organisation to respond quickly to crises. Certainly the genocidal crisis within Rwanda has eloquently shown that the organisation lacks the resources, both financial and military, to mount large-scale operations quickly. As a consequence of Rwanda the debate on a military force for the UN has intensified.

Senior officials working within the organisation recognise the need to improve its capacity to counteract the widespread intra-state aggression that has become a feature of the post-Cold War. It is largely due to this institutional weakness that some practitioners, both within and outside the organisation, again call for either the creation of a volunteer force or a rapid response capacity within the organisation (Urquhart, 1993; Boutros-Ghali, 1995; Qureshi and von Weizsäcker, 1995; and Tharoor, 1996). Tharoor argues that '[t]he future of UN peacekeeping demands a rapid response capacity'. While he notes that the 'Secretariat is largely agnostic as to how it acquires this', he goes on to testify that the UN cannot wait around for states to decide what actions they wish to pursue. Rwanda again bears witness to this: 'when the UN needed 5500 soldiers…, it turned to 19 governments which at the time had pledged a total of 31 000 troops for future UN peacekeeping operations; all declined to participate' (Tharoor, 1996:24). Tharoor's demand for a rapid reaction force complements previous remarks made by the Secretary-General in *An Agenda for Peace* and its supplement which argue that some form of international brigade should be at the disposal of the UN. However, ongoing work within a number of governments and various international organisations has illustrated the complex nature of instituting such a force.[10] More important, and contrary to Tharoor's assertions, they question whether the presence of such a force would avert tragedies like Rwanda. In a working paper that seeks to address 'Some of the Implications of the Current Debate', Josh Arnold-Forster asks whether, in the absence of a comprehensive political strategy designed to address the causes of the conflict, 'an expanded UN military presence [would] have promoted political stability and provided reassurance to those in Rwanda who were trying to prevent the conflict from escalating' (Arnold-Forster, 1995:5). Any consideration, however, for a force capacity for the UN, as Tharoor and Arnold-Forster state, is fraught with complex political sensitivities: first, there is the unlikely prospect of a consensus from within the Security Council to support what is essentially a 'supranational military entity under the command of the (UN) Secretary-General' (Tharoor, 1996:25), and secondly, there is the possible 'hostility' from among member states of the South who are not only cautious of the 'growing tendency of the UN to intervene in internal affairs of states, but who are also inadequately represented with the Security Council' (Arnold-Forster, 1995:6).

Rwanda has amply demonstrated the need for, and importance attached to, the idea of a rapid response capacity for the United Nations. In the absence of immediate political commitment, the UN needs to institute its own strategic planning to avert conflicts like Rwanda. However, while creating some form of military capacity for the UN, other areas within the framework of managing complex humanitarian crisis need more careful planning and coordination. One area that has been singled out over the last few years is the relationship between humanitarian NGOs and the military.

THE HUMANITARIAN AND MILITARY INTERFACE

The presence of a large international relief system working within a complex military operation like Rwanda has led to some reconsideration of the relationship between NGOs and the military. This debate has been set within the context of cooperation and coordination. While cases like Bosnia and Somalia have highlighted the need for closer coordination between NGOs and the military, Rwanda demonstrates that strategies need to be adopted to ensure the safe delivery of humanitarian assistance to those caught in civil wars.

The difficulties surrounding the planning and coordination of work with the military were among the critical comments raised in Study 3, *Humanitarian Aid and Effects*, by the Steering Committee of the Joint Evaluation of Emergency Assistance to Rwanda. The report raised questions about the predictability, effectiveness, costs and ability of the military to participate collaboratively in humanitarian operations (pp. 57–62). Important issues are being addressed on how to exchange information, coordinate activities, develop comprehensive strategic planning, and an agreed upon modus operandi (Mackinlay, 1995:65). However, the awkwardness and mistrust surrounding the agenda of the military still exists within the humanitarian relief community (Steering Committee of the Joint Evaluation of Emergency Assistance to Rwanda, *Study 3*, 1996:62). While the military has extended its role to providing innoculations and other emergency medical services, its agenda reflects the policy of its national governments, thus ensuring that NGOs are more sceptical about the military's role in providing humanitarian assistance. However, military presence is paramount in responding to complex humanitarian emergencies. As Lieutenant-General Sir Michael Rose notes, many of these humanitarian operations require a vast military back-up, thus this 'negative' effect can have no place in 'war-torn' countries (Rose, 1995:150). Despite the sensitivities towards the military, Connaughton suggests that:

> Rwanda witnessed a quantum leap in understanding and harmony developing between the humanitarian organisations and the military. Neither is monolithic: the constituents all have their foibles and differences. What Rwanda has revealed to the humanitarians was the resources, organisation and levels of protection the military can introduce in order to facilitate their work.
>
> (Connaughton, 1996:70)

However, as the military's involvement in humanitarian activities intensifies, new procedures and training are required. In their recent book on *Soldiers to the Rescue*, Larry Minear and Philippe Guillot state that '[w]e need to address the issue of whether the performance of the military will and should expand or constrict its role as a major actor in future humanitarian emergencies' (Minear and Guillot, 1996:1). In this respect, the US military has developed a manual on *Multi-Services Procedures for Humanitarian Assistance*

Operations to reflect its increasing participation in 'situations other than war' (Shiras, 1996:108).

The performance of NGOs in launching a humanitarian operation also needs to be considered. The crisis in Rwanda stretched the NGOs, both in terms of finance and resources available to them to coordinate themselves on the ground. It has also led to intense scrutiny of their capacity to deal with complex emergencies. As Jon Bennett states:

> For all their laudable successes, some NGOs have been guilty of poor practice, wastage and a lack of professionalism which to a large extent has gone unchecked…Critics of NGOs have highlighted the lack of accountability, mutual competitiveness and poor coordination as perhaps the most serious charges levelled at the so-called Third Sector.
>
> (Bennett, 1996:137)

As a consequence of Rwanda, and past conflict situations, a set of standards is being established to supplement the Code of Conduct developed by the International Committee of the Red Cross, the International Federation of Red Cross and Red Crescent Societies and associations of humanitarian NGOs.[11] Two options are available to the NGOs: (1) self-managed regulation; NGOs 'could be assisted in acquiring greater capacity to monitor member compliance with the Code and standards' and (2) an international accreditation system by both official agencies and NGOs to develop core criteria. However, '[t]hese would need to be adapted and supplemented for a specific complex emergency' (Steering Committee of the Joint Evaluation of Emergency Assistance to Rwanda, *Study 3*, 1996:161–2). Despite the criticisms levelled at the NGOs, their presence in conflict situations has been of benefit to the military. Many NGOs are usually present in countries before the military. Some already have historical knowledge and understanding of the cultural make-up of the societies involved in conflicts. Hence, Dallaire, the Force Commander to Rwanda in 1994, acknowledges that 'UNAMIR as a whole learnt much from the various Agencies and NGOs' presence':

> These providers of humanitarian assistance tended to have unmatched access to refugees and displaced persons, and some had a long-standing relationship with the local people and thorough knowledge of the local culture, including the local language

– kuyarwanda. They also helped UNAMIR understand the movement of internally-displaced persons, land-mine risks, local areas of potential conflict and provided reports on human rights abuse.

(Dallaire, 1996:214)

CONCLUSION

We have briefly sketched out some of the issues that have been raised within the context of Rwanda. They are not entirely new concerns. Both the ongoing conflicts in Bosnia and Somalia generated much debate on the perennial problem of intervening in internal conflicts. What Rwanda has done is to heighten and raise the stakes surrounding the possibilities and limits facing international actors in dealing with what are essentially violent and confused internal conflicts in which no legitimate authority structure exists. It is of course difficult to find an appropriate way in which to conclude on the question of what the various international actors ought to do in the face of human tragedy. Of all the three areas that we have tackled here, the most complex as we have already suggested, is that of state behaviour, or the political will of member states of the UN. Humanitarian and military intervention is not enough to resolve internal conflicts or to institute a viable peace; only political resolutions and diplomatic initiatives. Whether political opinion can will itself to respond to the widespread internal conflicts which generate large-scale human suffering that is not in its own backyard, is something this chapter has been unable to answer adequately. All we have done here is to highlight the politics of the debate and from there to consider complex issues and dilemmas facing the United Nations and the international relief system.

NOTES

1. See also Hoffmann (1995) who also considered the first and second of these areas within the context of the politics and ethics of collective action.
2. For a contrary view on the effects US casualties had on domestic support for US military operations, see the RAND report. This report rejects 'the

simplistic view that the public is unwilling to accept casualties under any circumstances' (Larson, 1995:50). Rather, it suggests that any understanding of public opinion has to be linked to the merits of each operation itself and the perceived cost and benefits for undertaking such an operation. So for example, whereas a majority of the public 'viewed important principles and interest to be at stake and showed a commensurably higher willingness to tolerate casualties than most realize' in the Gulf War (p.50), in Somalia, there were no perceived 'benefits or prospects to justify much loss of life' (p.50).

3. The two other defence roles are, (1) 'to ensure the protection and security of the United Kingdom and [its] Dependent Territories, even where there is no major external threat', and (2) 'to insure against a major external threat to the United Kingdom and (its) allies' (p.27).

4. For an analysis of the role of the media coverage in Rwanda see *Early Warning and Conflict Management* (Steering Committee of the Joint Evaluation of Emergency Assistance to Rwanda, *Study 2*, 1996:46–8).

5. Emphasis in the original.

6. Discussion with authors.

7. For a comprehensive analysis of Operation Support Hope, see Connaughton, 1996:56–66. In line with *PDD 25*, which sought to keep a clear separation of American force command structure from other parties, in particular, the UN Operation Restore Hope was strictly a humanitarian operation with no peacekeeping capacity.

8. Emphasis in the original.

9. For more detailed analysis on recent reforms in the UN along with future recommendations, see *Supplement to An Agenda for Peace* (Boutros-Ghali (d), 1995).

10. There is not enough space for us to discuss the complex technical and operational issues that surround the creation of a UN Force. For a clarification of the debate see the Report of the Government of Canada 1995; the Netherlands Non-Paper 1995 and Conetta and Knight, 1995. For an extensive review of these various proposals see Arnold-Forster, 1995.

11. See Overseas Development Institute, 1994.

BIBLIOGRAPHY

Africa Rights, *Rwanda: Death, Despair and Defiance*, Africa Rights: London, 1994.

Arnold-Forster, J., 'UN Rapid Reaction Forces: Some Implications of the Current Debate', draft discussion paper presented at United Nations Workshop, British International Studies Association Conference, University of Southampton, 18–20 December 1995, 1–17.

Bennett, J., 'Coordination, Control and Competition: NGOs on the Frontline', in: Whitman and Pocock (eds.), 1996, 136–45.

Boutros-Ghali, B., (a) *An Agenda for Peace*, June 1992, UN DPI/1247, New York: United Nations, 1992.

Boutros-Ghali, B., (b) 'The Situation in Somalia: Report of the Secretary-General', UN Security Council Documents: S/23693, 11 March 1992.

Boutros-Ghali, B., (c) 'Letter to the President of the Security Council', UN Security Council Document: S/24868, 30 November 1992.

Boutros-Ghali, (d) *An Agenda for Peace*, second edition with the new supplement and related UN documents, New York: United Nations, 1995.

Chopra, J. and Weiss, T., 'Sovereignty Is no Longer Sacrosanct: Codifying Humanitarian Intervention', *Ethics and International Affairs*, Vol. 6, 1992, 95–117.

Conetta, C. and Knight, C., *Vital Force*, Project of the Defense Alternatives, Cambridge MA: Commonwealth Institute, 1995.

Connaughton, R., 'Military Support and Protection for Humanitarian Assistance: Rwanda April–December 1994', *The Occasional*, No. 18, Strategic and Combat Studies Institute, 1996, 4–80.

Dallaire, R., 'The Changing Role of UN Peacekeeping Forces: The Relationship between UN Peacekeepers and NGOs in Rwanda', in: Whitman and Pocock (eds.), 1996, 205–18.

Destexhe, A., (a) *Rwanda and Genocide in the Twentieth Century*, London: Pluto Press, 1994.

Destexhe, A., (b) 'The Third Genocide'. *Foreign Policy*, No. 97, 1994, 3–17.

Fawn, R. and Larkins, J. (eds.), *International Society after the Cold War: Anarchy and Order Reconsidered*, London: Macmillan, 1996.

Gowing, N., *Real-Time Television Coverage of Armed Conflicts and Diplomatic Crises: Does it Pressure or Distort Foreign Policy Decisions?* Working Paper 94–1, Cambridge MA: The Joan Sorenstein Barone Center, John F. Kennedy School of Government, Harvard University, 1994.

Hoffmann, S., 'The Politics and Ethics of Military Intervention', *Survival*, Vol. 37, No. 4, 1995–96, 29–51.

Jones, B., 'Intervention without Borders: Humanitarian Intervention in Rwanda, 1990–94', *Millennium*, Vol. 24, No. 2, 1995, 225–49.

Larson, E., *Casualties and Consensus: The Historical Role of Casualties in Domestic Support for U.S. Military Operations*, Santa Monica, CA: Rand, 1995.

Mackinlay, J., 'Military Responses to Complex Emergencies', in: Weiss, T. (ed.), 1995, 51–67.

Minear, L., 'The Humanitarian and Military Interface: Reflections on the Rwanda Experience', 1996, 1–6. (Summary from the Humanitarian and War Project at Brown University.) This article appeared in a summer 1996 special issue on Rwanda, *Hunger Notes*, a publication of the World Hunger Education Service, Washington DC.

Minear, L. and Guillot, P., *Soldiers to the Rescue: Humanitarian Lessons from Rwanda*, Paris: OECD, 1996.

Netherlands Non-Paper, *A UN Rapid Deployment Brigade. 'A Preliminary Study'*, UN Docs.: A/49/886–S/1995/276, 10 April 1995.

Overseas Development Institute, 'Code of Conduct for the International Red Cross and Red Crescent Movement and NGOs', *Disaster, Relief and Rehabilitation Network Paper*, Working Paper No. 7, London, 1994.

Prunier, G., *The Rwanda Crisis 1959–1994: History of a Genocide*, London: Hurst and Company, 1995.

Qureshi, M. and von Weizsäcker, R., 'The United Nations in its Second Half-century'. *Report of the Independent Working Group on the Future of the United Nations*, Ford Foundation: Yale University Press, 1995.

Report of the Government of Canada, *Towards a Rapid Reaction Capability for the United Nations*, 26 September 1995.

Rose, M., 'Field Coordination of UN Humanitarian Assistance', in: Whitman and Pocock (eds.), 1996, 149–60.

Shiras, P., 'Humanitarian Emergencies and the Role of NGOs,' in: Whitman and Pocock (eds.), 1996, 106–17.

Statement on the Defence Estimates 1995, *Stable Forces in a Strong Britain*. Presented to Parliament by the Secretary of State for Defence by Command of Her Majesty, May 1995, London: HMSO, 1995.

Steering Committee of the Joint Evaluation of Emergency Assistance to Rwanda, *The International Response to Conflict and Genocide: Lessons from the Rwanda Experience*, Copenhagen: Steering Committee, 1996.

—— *Synthesis Report.*

—— *Study 1: Historical Perspectives: Some explanatory factors.*

—— *Study 2: Early Warning and Conflict Management.*

—— *Study 3: Humanitarian Aid and Effects.*

—— *Study 4: Rebuilding Post-War Rwanda.*

Tharoor, S., 'The Future of Peacekeeping', in: Whitman and Pocock (eds.), 1996, 19–34.

Urquhart, B., 'For a UN Volunteer Military Force', *New York Times Review*, 10 June 1993, 3–4.

Vassall-Adams, G., *Rwanda: An Agenda for International Action*, Oxford: Oxfam, 1994.

Weiss, T. (ed.), (a) *The UN and Civil Wars*. Boulder CO: Lynne Rienner, 1995.

Weiss, T., (b) 'Overcoming the Somalia Syndrome – "Operation Rekindle Hope?"' *Global Governance*, Vol. 1, No. 2, 1995, 171–87.

Wheeler, N. and Morris, J., 'Humanitarian Intervention and State Practice at the End of the Cold War', in: Fawn and Larkins (eds.), 1996, 135–71.

Whitman, J. and Pocock, D. (eds.), *After Rwanda: The Coordination of United Nations Humanitarian Assistance*, London: Macmillan, 1996.

Part VI
Intervention by Western Powers: Getting in and Getting out

In the sixth part of the book, the authors explore national attitudes to intervention in the main industrial powers. *Hugh Beach* sketches these different national cultures for assessing whether and when to intervene in *'Causes, Aims and Means of Intervention'*.

John Roper undertakes a similar task in *'The Foreign Policy of Western Countries: the Problem of Intervention'* and develops a number of conclusions from recent examples of intervention.

Clearly, American attitudes, which have oscillated in the twentieth century between isolationism and intervention, are essential. *John Langan, SJ* explains approaches to this issue in the sole remaining superpower in his chapter *'The Past and the Future of Intervention: a View from the United States'*.

16 Causes, Aims and Means of Intervention

Hugh Beach

Now war is exclusively an occupation for the poor alone. There are, the commentators tell us, thirty wars in progress in the world. They are taking place – where? In the world's remote, resourceless, unproductive places: in Bosnia, the poorest part of Europe, in the Caucasus, the poorest part of the old Soviet Union, in Cambodia, one of the poorest parts of Asia, in Angola, Mozambique, Somalia, Rwanda, some of the poorest parts of a Continent by definition poor. War, once a struggle over riches, or the proud vocation of the rich themselves, is now the calling of the wretched of the earth.

John Keegan, Lecture at Southampton University, Fall 1994

SELF-DETERMINATION AND THE NATION STATE

Around the second half of the eighteenth century there were about 35 empires, kingdoms, countries and states in the world. That figure roughly doubled, to 70, by the 1930s and almost doubled again, to 130, by the 1960s. Today over 190 entities are generally recognised as sovereign states and it has been predicted that by early in the next century the number may double again to around 400. What has been going on? In short the old dynastic system has broken down. Monarchies in Europe used to rule over different peoples and religions – what we would now call nations. Political unrest and rebellion came from many causes but not because rulers belonged to a different race or nation. That was taken for granted, the nation had almost no connection with the state. Britain, France, Germany, Spain are all mixtures of many different ethnic stocks. The Prussians are not Germans at all but Balts. The Anglo-Saxons are German but have been overlaid in England by the Normans who were Frenchmen of Viking origin. The Enlightenment regarded national sentiment as primitive. But the liberals who launched the revolutions of 1848 dreamed about realising liberties though new nation states. Herder, a Latvian pastor living in Weimar, reacting in part to the excesses of Napoleon, affirmed the primacy of the *Volksgeist*, the spirit which is embodied in the culture of a people. What the Enlightenment had dismissed as outworn superstition was seen, on the contrary, as the very substance of a nation's life. Nations, he thought, are not humanly contrived associations based on the rational decisions of individuals, but spiritual realities by which the individual is sustained. Men and women became convinced that they should fight not only for political and religious liberty but also against being ruled by foreigners. As Lord Acton put it: 'protest against the domination of race over race grew into a condemnation of every state that included different races, and finally became the complete and consistent theory that state and nation must be co-extensive'. He viewed this as a retrograde step. But John Stuart Mill, who approved of the idea, wrote: 'it is in general a necessary condition of free institutions that the boundaries of governments should coincide with those of nationalities'.

National self-determination received great impetus at the Conference of Versailles, which sought to make sense of the break-up of the Ottoman and Austro-Hungarian empires after the First World War. But since the Second World War international organisations have set great store by holding countries together within their existing borders. One of the great principles of the Helsinki Declaration (1973) was the inviolability of frontiers, meaning that they may not be altered by force. Nor in customary international law does there exist any right to secession. Yet the right of the Palestinians to self-determination has long been recognised by the UN. Slovakia has separated from the Czech republic. In Yugoslavia the arbitration commission of the European Union, finding the country in dissolution, decided that the frontiers of the constituent republics deserved protection in international law. Given the ethnic map of those countries, this was simply to push the problem one level down.

Morally it can be argued that secession from an existing state can be justified when certain conditions are met. These would no doubt include instances where:

- the group in the seceding territory has consistently suffered infringement of its rights or its culture;
- there is no practical way, short of secession, by which those rights or that culture can be preserved;

- the seceding group is able to compensate innocent third parties;
- the effect of the secession is not simply to establish an illiberal state provoking fresh injustices;
- the sum of the injustices avoided, and the rights protected and advanced, is politically significant enough to grant title to territory.

But in general the international community remains very reluctant to sacrifice the principle of territorial integrity to the notion of self-determination. Dr Boutros-Ghali speaking in Moldova in 1995 said that the international community should repel separatism.

The main problem with almost all nation states is that they have been founded on principles of exclusion, based upon such features as nationality, religion, culture or language. Most have arguably been a curse, as Acton anticipated, both to their own people, particularly to minorities, and to one another; oppressing their own citizens and preying on their neighbours. Certainly they have proved to be no more peaceful. The main reason seems to be that in playing up to the principle of nationality leaders deliberately re-awaken old fears and ancient feuds. Take the example of the former Yugoslavia. Svetlana Slapsak, herself a Serb, writing in the *International Herald Tribune* (*IHT*, 27 May 1993), was convinced that the bestialities of war in what used to be Yugoslavia were triggered by *words* – clichés put forward by intellectuals and taken over by politicians:

> To nationalist Serbian writers Albanians were 'bestial', Croats 'genocidal', Croats and Slovenes 'Machiavellian', Slovenes 'slavish'. Slovenian and Croat prose called Serbs 'Barbaric', 'Balkan' and 'Byzantine'.

These writings were soon recycled by journalists. Conscript soldiers were sent off to be killed with words of hatred ringing in their ears. The Serbian Academy of Arts and Sciences made a notable contribution in 1987 with a secret memorandum which made a paranoid case for Serbian nationalism, based on historic injustices done to Serbs in Kosovo. Yet in the former Yugoslavia there is no ethnic issue. All these people are southern Slavs, speaking the same language, genetically indistinguishable, separated only by the area in which they live, their religion (Catholic, Orthodox, Muslim), and a bloodstained history. If war, as Keegan says, is now the prerogative of the 'wretched of the earth', it has not been not so much poverty and backwardness but the bigotry of the articulate that has fuelled the flames.

WAYS AND MEANS

If we move on now to the question of ways and means it is clear that there are two quite different concepts according to which interventions can be organised. On the one hand there is the method derived from United Nations-style peacekeeping, as it has developed during the past 40 years. Although there is no reference to it in the Charter, and it has had to be invented on the hoof, what it consists of is now widely understood. A recent description suggests that the defining features are:

- operations established by the United Nations,
- with the consent of the parties concerned,
- to help control and resolve conflicts between them,
- under United Nations command and control,
- at the expense collectively of the member states, and with military and other personnel and equipment provided voluntarily by them,
- acting impartially between the parties,
- and using force to the minimum extent necessary.

(Goulding, 1993:455)

These are, in essence, the ingredients of classical or first generation peacekeeping: methods which have undoubtedly scored some notable successes in such places as Central America, Eritrea, Cambodia, Namibia and Mozambique. But during the past five years, as we have seen, the UN has undertaken, or subsequently blessed, a number of operations in which important features of classical peacekeeping have been abridged or totally overridden. Under the rubric of 'humanitarian intervention' operations have taken place in countries where the ingredient of consent has sometimes been lacking and where impartiality and minimum force have been compromised.

A quite different model of intervention exists in the form of operations which countries carry out unilaterally, normally in their own backyard (widely defined), in which the classical UN peacekeeping principles of consent, impartiality and minimum force are not merely abridged, with all the straining of language and ambiguity that this implies, but simply treated as inapplicable. This might be called the policing model, though it is important not to be prejudiced by overtones of oppression and arbitrary power. What is at issue here is the most economical method of controlling ethnic strife in terms of ending the killing as quickly as possible with the least loss of life. It can be argued that police-type operations, judged by this simple criterion, sometimes work better than peace-keeping. Obvious examples are operations carried out in the past 30 years by France, Britain and the USA, three states notoriously prone to interfere in the internal disputes of other lands.

The *French* make no bones about it. Their most recent *Loi-de-Programme* sets out a five-year rolling programme which seeks to make the French armed forces more mobile, improving power-projection and sizing them to undertake three types of operation simultaneously: a regional conflict as part of a coalition, intervention in an overseas low-intensity conflict and limited UN peacekeeping operations. They are moving to end conscription in favour of a professional force. It is to France's credit that she has come second only to Pakistan in the number of troops committed to UN activities, and her share of the peacekeeping budget is also high. Besides sending the largest contingent to Yugoslavia for several years, France also sent some 1500 men each to Somalia and Cambodia. But France's actions on a national basis have been equally notable. Everyone knows that in the 1940s and 1950s there were disastrous campaigns in Indo-China and Algeria. Less well remembered is the fact that since 1962, when French troops were sent to Dakar to help President Léopold Sédar Senghor of Senegal maintain order after a coup attempt, France has engaged in some 35 gendarme interventions in Africa including forays into Gabon, Chad, Zaire, Central African Republic, Togo and Comoros. Most were aimed at keeping in power leaders friendly to Paris. Sometimes it was to evacuate Europeans from danger as when French and Belgian parachutists intervened in 1978 in Shaba Province of Zaire. Sometimes it was to remove a ruler, like Jean Bedel Bokassa of the Central African Republic, whose excesses had made him too much of a liability. France carries off these man-oeuvres with élan: no apologies, no qualms over sovereignty, the helicopters swoop in as though by right. France's prestige among African nations rises. While in Paris there is a growing 'pragmatic' faction which sees sub-Saharan Africa as a burden France can no longer afford, under Chirac the 'traditionalists' still have influence and power. During his first year in office the French intervened both in the Comoros (October 1995) and in the Central African Republic (May 1996). Strong links still endure between France and its former colonies. John Darnton, reflecting on this in the New York Times (reprinted in *IHT*, 27 June 1994) says that France, and the large area of Africa which has twice as many French speakers as France itself, are held together by ties of language, love of French culture and the conviction that Paris is the 'centre of the Universe'. It is a Faustian bargain. Let in French technocrats to run state enterprises, trade mainly with the mother country, sign a military assistance pact and you will be looked after. France will prop up your economy by giving you the African franc (supported by the French treasury) and rush its army to your side if trouble comes. When killing erupted in Rwanda in April 1994 other governments quickly pulled out the 5500 UN troops serving there. The French then sent a sizeable force of soldiers to establish a safe area for refugees in the south west of the country. It may have been for the wrong reasons but it undoubtedly saved many lives.

The *British* also have laid great stress, in the reorganisation of their armed forces, on rapid reaction and the ability to despatch forces overseas. In terms of personnel contributions to the UN Britain came fourth in the league in May 1994, lagging behind only Pakistan, France and India. But the British act quite differently from the French in dealing with ex-colonies. Once they have handed over power their military involvement is confined to providing advisers and training teams, sending troops on exercises (often with a civil relations slant), and sales of military equipment. And yet, in the process of decolonisation, the British had as much experience of dealing with civil conflict as any nation. Looking back over 50 years, and disregarding the four actual wars – Korea, Suez, Falklands and the Gulf – what the British have actually been doing is coping continuously with ethnic, tribal or religious struggle; only in 1968 were no British troops killed in action anywhere. Sometimes they have attempted to cope according to a peacekeeping mode, receiving brickbats from both sides. Very often, as in the cases of Palestine and Aden, they left without finding any lasting resolution to the underlying conflicts, which persist to this day. Elsewhere their role was quite different, defeating rebellions against the colonial authority: the Mau Mau in Kenya, a communist-led insurgency in Malaya and revolt in the Oman. This led the British to develop very sophisticated and well tried doctrines, equipment and training to deal with low intensity operations. Tragically one of the longest running instances has been in Northern Ireland.

America is now regarded as the world's natural hegemon: only where it leads will the world follow – so it is said. The Gulf War of 1990–1 is the classic instance. But we are talking here of interventions in the internal affairs of strife-torn states, particularly in America's backyard. In theory the USA renounced any right of unilateral intervention in the Western hemisphere by the 1947 Rio Pact: armed attack on any American nation should be met by collective action. But in practice the Americans have continued to intervene on their own when they see fit. In October 1983 the USA occupied Grenada (thought until then to be a British sphere of influence) losing some 19 personnel. In December 1989 they invaded Panama to oust the dictator Noriega, and lost 23. The invasion of Haiti in September 1994 went off peacefully but in this case the Americans had the backing of a UN resolution and other nations' forces soon replaced a large part of theirs.

Outside their own backyard the Americans have never found their stride. Vietnam was, of course, the great defining trauma. The Lebanon was another expensive failure. The reasons for going into Somalia in December 1992 were wholly humanitarian – people were dying in hundreds from hunger and banditry – and to begin with much good was done, food convoys got through, lives were saved. The idea was to go on from saving lives to reconstructing the country and soon the American troops became subsumed in a UN operation. In this phase the Americans threw prudence to the winds, demonised one faction in the contest and went all out to 'get' General Aideed. Predictably this failed; 18 Americans died in a raid and Congress called a halt. It is important to recognise what went wrong. It was not simply that the abandonment of impartiality fitted ill within a UN-led operation. The crucial point was the failure of the Americans to apply the principles of low intensity operations. Notable among these are a clear political objective, an efficient intelligence network, the closest coordination between civil, military and police authorities and weaning the 'hearts and minds' of the population away from the insurgents in favour of the legitimate authorities. Little of this happened in Mogadishu, where forces (rangers, gunships) were used indiscriminately and in such a way as to subvert the purposes of the operation as a whole.

Trying to make sense of it all the Americans have come up with *Presidential Decision Directive No. 25*, based on the two premises that the UN is an inadequate instrument of peacekeeping and is costing the US too much. In fact the US share of UN peacekeeping costs is extremely high at 31 per cent, although they are about $1bn in arrears. But their contribution to UN operations has always been thin and reluctant: mainly to UNPROFOR but with a handful of observers in Angola and West Sahara. The criteria for taking part are set out in the PDD in the form of the following questions:

- Would UN involvement advance US interests?
- Is there a condition of international aggression, humanitarian disaster, disruption of 'established democracy' or gross violation of human rights?
- Are the objectives and mission clearly defined in scope and duration?
- Are realistic criteria in place for ending the operation?
- Is inaction considered unacceptable? (a good double negative!) and if the answers are 'yes', a further list of considerations comes into play:
  - What is the risk to US personnel?
  - Is their participation essential to success?
  - Are the command and control arrangements acceptable?
  - Is there a prospect of public and congressional support?
  - Is there a plan, a strategy that integrates political and military goals, sufficient resources, a commitment to a decisive outcome?

Decisions, they say, will rest on the cumulative weight of all these factors. This is sensible, but what it means in practice is that, where ethnic and tribal conflicts are concerned, outside their own backyard, American strategy is required to be as far as possible risk-free.

After the war against Iraq, George Bush triumphantly declared that America had finally kicked the 'Vietnam syndrome'. One can see what he meant. Unfortunately it has been replaced by the 'Gulf War syndrome'. This could be parodied as saying that the US will take part in military operations only if the fighting can be guaranteed to take place in a desert; to last for no more than five days; if casualties can be counted on one hand; if both oil and nuclear weapons are at stake; if the enemy is a monomaniac who will accept no compromise and if the whole operation will be paid for by Germany and Japan. This rather limits the field. It has led Bob Dole, for instance, to dismiss multilateralism as 'utopian'. 'Subcontracting American foreign policy and subordinating American sovereignty encourage and strengthen isolationist forces at home — and embolden our adversaries abroad' (*IHT*, 6 March 1995). Decoded this means that America should no longer be prepared to work with other countries, especially in military and peacekeeping interventions, unless it is simply commanding them, Schwarzkopf-style. In Bob Dole's view soliciting and bargaining for cooperation derogates from America's leadership, vitiates American interests, endangers American lives. Hence the move in the US to cut down on the finance for United Nations operations to the point where the whole exercise might come to a standstill.

PEACEKEEPING AND ENFORCEMENT

It has been the burden of this chapter that, setting aside the political background of the old imperial nations, some of the principles they developed for dealing with internal conflicts — under the rubric of 'low intensity operations' — may better serve the ends of humanity than the methods presently being attempted by the international community in the form of 'wider peacekeeping'. But at this point a further crucial question has to be confronted. It is an issue of principle which has underlain much of the discussion about the former Yugoslavia. Should the UN, in its conflict-resolution role, be prepared sometimes to support one side or the other rather than remain scrupulously impartial? This in turn raises other questions. Might it be right to support the stronger side on the grounds that this will enable the war to be brought to an end as cheaply in human lives and as quickly as possible? Or should the UN espouse the weaker side, on the principle of solidarity with the victims? The latter approach might well seem to have justice on its side — to be the more 'Christian' way of setting about things. But it might make for a longer war. And intervention on either side would be an overtly political act. Would the UN be prepared to take this path given its dependence on donor nations to provide troops and resources, tolerance by 'host' governments and favourable publicity? Bosnia has provided a particularly difficult case because of Russia's historic and emotional links with the Serbs, Germany's with the Croats and almost the whole Islamic world with the Bosnian government. It can be argued that no international body (be it the United Nations, the Organisation for Security and Cooperation in Europe, the European Union, or whatever) could agree to support one side against the others in a conflict of this kind. From here it is a short step to arguing that if one is not prepared to take tough decisions of this sort it is better not to intervene at all, but rather to rely on various non-military mechanisms. But when all these have already been tried and failed, or not even tried, where killing is in progress and genocide is both flagrant and continuing, to rule out a military response a priori is a counsel of despair.

The crucial distinction lies between peacekeeping and enforcement. Peacekeeping implies the use of force only in self-defence and proceeds on the basis of impartiality and consent. Enforcement implies absence of consent and some degree of partiality. Various aspects of recent UN mandates have required enforcement. These include the protection of humanitarian operations or of civilians in 'safe areas' and pressing parties to accept reconciliation at a pace faster than they were willing to accept. The former Secretary-General of the UN saw himself as acting on the basis of the 'conscience of the world'. This sits ill with an active role in killing or oppression. For this reason and because of obvious practical limitations the United Nations is ill equipped for enforcement action, Chapter VII of the Charter notwithstanding. In his January 1995 *Supplement to an Agenda for Peace* Dr Boutros Boutros-Ghali stated bluntly that neither the Security Council nor the Secretary-General has the capacity to deploy, direct, or command and control such operations, save on the smallest scale. To become itself a combatant is for the UN to compromise morality. The solution is to subcontract enforcement tasks to one or more member states.

In other words the answer is for the UN to rely upon a 'coalition of the willing', probably led by one at least of the habitual intervenors. On this basis it might be possible to take the necessary tough and early decisions, to intervene decisively in an internal conflict where the Security Council is powerless to act, or to act quickly or decisively enough. This suggestion in turn raises further problems:

- How much regard should be paid to legality? In some cases there might be a request for help from an established government (for example Bosnia) but obviously not always.
- How many of the 'willing' will there be?
- What happens if they intervene on the 'wrong' side (as arguably the French in Rwanda)?
- What if two lots of the 'willing' intervene on opposite sides (*vide* the Cold War)?

- What happens if the intervention fails to achieve the quick and decisive results hoped for? This is a predictable, indeed normal outcome. Should the intervening forces 'declare success and leave' or should they reinforce failure thus entering the quagmire (Vietnam syndrome)?
- Given early success in the sense of disarming the trouble-makers and suppressing any who fail to cooperate (as in Haiti), what should follow? There may then be a need to set up an interim administration, organise elections and generally engage in 'nation-building'. Faced with a possible long haul of this kind how many will be 'willing' to begin? It was notable that when in May 1994 the Security Council decided to expand the UN Assistance Mission for Rwanda (UNAMIR) not one of the 19 governments that at that time had undertaken to have troops on standby agreed to contribute.

These questions lead on to another. Is it proper to insist that, in order to justify intervention, some national interest must be at stake? If you think not then how do you, as a politician, justify sending young British men and women to suffer and to die where no British interest is involved? And when things get rough, how highly do you rate your chances of sweating it out: an essential consideration? Do you argue that, if hardline nationalists get away with murder in Bosnia, it will be the turn of Kosovo next followed by Macedonia and then perhaps a wider Balkan war; or at least the encouragement of villains in other places from which in the end Britain will suffer? This used to be a popular view known as 'domino theory', now largely discredited. Action should always address, as already argued, the here-and-now; not what may be possible elsewhere in the future. Or do you contend, following Donne, that 'no man is an island'? One person's death diminishes us all. In Henry Kissinger's words: 'humanitarian intervention asserts that moral and humane concerns are so much a part of American life that not only treasure but lives must be risked to vindicate them: in their absence American life would have lost some meaning' (*IHT*, 14 December 1992). He adds that no other nation has ever put forward such a set of propositions. Remembering Rome, this last point is doubtful. But the main trouble with this argument is that it proves too much. Why, on this basis, should the international community not intervene in Afghanistan, East Timor or a score of other wars? Will it do, morally, to say that these are not on our doorstep or, more to the point, our television screens? Or is Joe Nye nearer the mark when he says (*IHT,* 16 December 1992): 'a foreign policy of armed multilateral intervention to right all such wrongs would be another source of enormous disorder'? He is almost certainly right.

If so, it is a question of every instance on its merits. The answer, so far as Bosnia is concerned, is that, despite many misgivings and after long hesitations, NATO finally agreed to act as a 'coalition of the willing' in forcing all sides to accede to the Dayton accords and overseeing its outcome. It is remarkable that the Americans committed themselves so deeply. And the NATO operation in Bosnia is far reaching. The tasks given to the Implementation Force (IFOR) included such things as ensuring the free movement and resettlement of refugees, aiding humanitarian workers, resolving boundary disputes, creating secure conditions for free elections and responding to violence against civilians. IFOR could claim the right to complete and unimpeded freedom of movement by ground, air and water. It had the power to regulate all communications and all military and civilian use of airspace, ports and certain strategic corridors. IFOR was held harmless in the accord for any damage to property caused by combat or combat-related activities. The warring parties were under notice to withdraw from a score of two-mile-wide zones of separation within a month and leave areas agreed for swapping within 45 days. They were to remove landmines from these areas and within four months move all heavy weapons into designated places. This was very muscular stuff.

It is too early to draw up a balance sheet of success and failures. By December 1996 the country had enjoyed a full year of comparative peace and basic services were steadily being restored. Families were being reunited and some refugees slowly making their way back, though freedom of movement was very far from complete. National elections were duly held but certainly not 'free and fair'. The way was opened to allow some of the structures of a unified Bosnian state to come to life. It remains to be seen what use will be made of them, other than to entrench the separatism now deeply ingrained in the three communities. The successor force to IFOR, albeit much smaller, will be needed for at least two more years.

It is not at all obvious in what way subcontracting the hard work of enforcement to a subgroup of the willing is a more 'moral' way for the UN to set about this sort of action than carrying it out for itself. But as matters stand it is the only realistic way. NATO by its agreement in Berlin in June 1996 has for the first time created an expressly designed capacity for force projection and crisis management. Furthermore, it has agreed that such force can be used to defend its interests outside the NATO area: a further complete reversal of previously accepted principle.

The United Nations is determined to profit from past experience. Within the Department of Peacekeeping Operations a 'Lessons Learned' unit has carried out detailed analyses of operations in Somalia, Haiti, Angola and Rwanda. These clearly recognise some well tried principles. Most obvious is the need for a single unified authority to oversee all the agencies involved, normally in the person of the Special Representative of the Secretary-General, in British terms a 'Supremo'. Another great step forward lies in acknowledging the need for a comprehensive intelligence management plan. Until recently the very word 'intelligence' has been taboo within the United Nations because of its supposedly grubby military connotations. In this and similar ways the principles of low intensity operations are being re-learned and re-applied to the new circumstances and in this way credibility and effectiveness are steadily being restored.

RETURNING TO FIRST PRINCIPLES

Summing up on the rules governing intervention with force, the American Catholic bishops conclude that the criteria of just war *taken as a whole* must be satisfied in order to override the strong presumption against the use of force. And they put a useful and much needed gloss on the whole attempt to apply Christian moral principles to the messy business of conflict. They say:

> We also recognise that the application of these principles requires the exercise of the virtue of prudence; people of good will may differ on specific conclusions. The just-war tradition is not a weapon to be used to justify a political conclusion or a set of mechanical criteria that automatically yields a simple answer, but a way of moral reasoning to discern the ethical limits of action. Policy-makers, advocates and opponents of the use of force need to be careful not to apply the tradition selectively to justify their own positions.
>
> (US Bishops, 1993:454)

It is hoped that both this chapter and my previous attempt (Chapter 6) to apply the just war principles to the issues of intervention have lived up to the high standard of moral objectivity rightly prescribed by the bishops, but not so successfully as to obscure the author's own prejudices completely!

BIBLIOGRAPHY

Goulding, M. 'The Evolution of United Nations Peacekeeping', *International Affairs*, Vol. 69, No. 3, July 1993, pp.451–64.
US Bishops, 'The Harvest of Justice is Sown in Peace', in: *Origins*, 9 Dec. 1993, Vol. 23, No. 26, 449–60.

17 The Foreign Policy of Western Countries: the Problem of Intervention

John Roper

The end of the Cold War and the development of a 'hot peace' have created a situation in which intervention presents a series of problems to policy-makers and, in particular, for that section of informed opinion which is concerned about morality and international relations. In this chapter the problem will be considered under two headings, although this division is not intended to suggest that the two aspects are not related. The first examines the way in which international law and institutions have evolved in their approach to intervention, and the specific case of humanitarian intervention. The second section will look at the political operational experience, examining some general problems as well as briefly surveying the post-Cold War experience.

By way of introduction it may be useful to look at some of the definitions of 'intervention' which have been recently used in the debate. As scholars such as Christopher Greenwood (1993) and Mark Trachtenberg (1993) have argued, the discussion of whether or not there is a right of humanitarian intervention has been a long one going back several centuries.

Intervention in its broadest sense means interference by force or the threat of force in the internal affairs of another country. It presumably includes any use of force other than that of repelling overt aggression by one state against another. Trachtenberg (1993:16–24) argues that there were different traditions justifying intervention. The first of these was when in Europe interventions were justified in order to maintain a balance of power. In some cases such rights of intervention were embodied in treaties, as for example in the Treaty of Utrecht in 1713 forbidding Spain and France to unite or the 1839 Treaty of London which guaranteed the neutrality of Belgium. While these sorts of intervention are now relatively rare, contemporary arms control practice could be seen in some circumstances to be a form of justification for intervention of this sort. In the last resort, if a party to an arms control treaty continued to infringe its provisions would the other powers signatory have a right to intervene? This particular problem becomes most acute in the case of the non-proliferation of nuclear weapons. Do the international community collectively or individual states have the right to act to pre-empt proliferation? Some of the recent discussion of counter-proliferation policy implicitly raises these issues.

A second historical motivation for intervention in the internal affairs of a State was because one did not like the behaviour of its rulers. Not necessarily because of any external policy they were undertaking but because their system of government might prove infectious. The classic example of this was the 'Concert' of the European powers in the period after 1815 when, at the Congress of Aix-la-Chapelle, Tsar Alexander I proposed that an international army be created in order to protect the existing political status quo, and after the Congress of Troppau in December 1820 the Austrian, Prussian and Russian rulers claimed for themselves an unrestricted right to intervene to suppress revolution to check 'according to their means the evils resulting from the violation of all the principles of order and morality' (Trachtenberg, 1993:21). The position of the other European powers was resisted by Lord Castlereagh who set out his views in his state paper of 5 May 1820. In this he made it clear that there was no absolute right of national sovereignty that took precedence over other issues, indeed 'the principle of one State interfering by force in the internal affairs of another, in order to enforce obedience to the governing authority, is always a question of the greatest possible moral as well as political delicacy'. He did, however, resist the idea of there being any organised international structure to do this and made it clear that the alliance which had brought down Napoleon was not 'intended as an Union for the Government of the World, or for the super-intendence of the internal affairs of other states'. That having been said, the view that states might intervene in this way was a matter of continued dispute throughout the nineteenth century; and indeed American intervention in Panama or Grenada or Russian intervention in Afghanistan can be seen as recent examples of the use of military force to change a ruler whom one did not like. Already in the nineteenth century there were often mixed motives – national interests were combined with wishes to improve the condition of the inhabitants of the country concerned. An example of this can be found in the arguments President McKinley gave in 1898 for his intervention in Cuba. He talked first of the needs 'to put an end to the barbarities, bloodshed, starvation and horrible miseries now existing there and which the parties to the conflict are either unable or unwilling to stop or mitigate' but went on to say that 'the right to intervene may be justified by the very serious injury to the commerce, trade and business of our people'. The mixture of motives which we will see still plays a part was therefore already apparent in the nineteenth century. The other development in that century was a trend to restrain intervention in the domestic affairs of European countries, combined within readiness to intervene in the case of other countries who were considered to be failing to comply with European norms. This practice of double standards towards the rest of the world by the European powers (with which the United States became associated) has clearly left a memory in much of the Third World which continues to this day.

A third motive for intervention was that of protection of one's own citizens. This has been seen to continue in the twentieth century, particularly as far as their evacuation in situations of local crises is concerned. It may of course increase in importance with the attitudes adopted by Russia to people of Russian origins in the former Soviet Union outside Russia. On the whole intervention to evacuate one's nationals has been widely accepted, but intervention of a more permanent kind would clearly create considerable problems.

As has been seen, the concept of humanitarian intervention was already present as part of the justification for military action in the nineteenth century. It has become much more apparent in the present situation when intervention is formally excluded by international law. Christopher Greenwood defines 'humanitarian intervention' as:

> ... cases in which a substantial part of the population of a state is threatened with death or suffering on a grand scale, either because of the actions of the government of that state or because of the state's slide into anarchy. The situation in the Kurdish and Shiite areas of Iraq following the Kuwait conflict falls into the first category, while Liberia and Somalia are examples of the second. In each case, however, the avowed purpose of intervention in the state concerned was the protection of the citizens of that state.
>
> (Greenwood, 1993:24)

The use of military force in intervention for humanitarian objectives is therefore defined as being an altruistic one, that is an intervention which is undertaken not because of the interests of the country intervening but in the interests of the population, or parts of the population, of the country in which the intervention takes place. It will be necessary to examine how far all actions which receive the label 'humanitarian intervention' are undertaken for such straightforward altruistic motives or whether 'humanitarian intervention' does not run the risk of being used by states which wish to have moral and legal cover for action undertaken at least in part because of their own interests.

THE DEVELOPMENT OF INTERNATIONAL LAW AND INTERNATIONAL INSTITUTIONS

The development of international law in this area can be seen as beginning with the formulation by Hugo Grotius in 1625: 'no other just cause for undertaking war can there be excepting injury received'. This led to the formulation in Article 2(4) of the United Nations Charter whereby no state may use or threaten to use armed force against the territorial integrity or political independence of another country. The Charter not only forbade such action by the UN member states but also in Article 2(7) imposed upon the UN itself a restriction in agreeing that:

> ...nothing contained in the present Charter shall authorize the United Nations to intervene in matters which are essentially within the jurisdiction of any state or shall require the Members to submit such matters to settlement under the present Charter: but this principle shall not prejudice the application of enforcement measures under Chapter VII.

The reference to Chapter VII enables the Security Council to act in spite of this constraint on those occasions when, as set out in Article 39, international peace and security are challenged.

The question is raised whether military intervention becomes legitimate when it is in response to an invitation from the country concerned. The problem here is that an unpopular ruler or government can invite a country or an international organisation to intervene militarily to support them against their own people, and this in itself is not necessarily legitimate. As Edward Mortimer (1995) has pointed out; 'it assumes the sovereignty of a state is the exclusive property of its government, or rather of whatever body is recognized as being its government by another state which is willing to render military "assistance" '. As John Stuart Mill wrote in 1859 'a government which needs foreign support to enforce obedience from its own citizens, is one which ought not to exist; and the assistance given to it by foreigners is hardly ever anything but the sympathy of one despotism with another'. The cases of Hungary in 1956 and Czechoslovakia in 1968 exemplify this problem.

As has been suggested recently by Lori Fisler Damrosch (1993) there has been 'a shift from international law as a system of constraints on *unilateral* state action to international law as a system aimed at channelling the *collective* efforts of the international community'. She examines the cases when the Security Council has taken an 'inclusive view of the concept of "threat to peace" with respect to situations whose impact was largely confined within a single territory'. The first examples she gives were the cases concerning Southern Rhodesia and South Africa dating from the 1960s in which binding economic sanctions were imposed under the UN Security Council's enforcement authority, and in the case of Southern Rhodesia, resolutions called upon the UK to put down the rebellion using all 'appropriate measures which would prove effective'. The role of the United Nations in the Congo in 1960–4 is an example where UN force was used without reference at least in the early resolutions to any 'threat to international peace'. Similarly the United Nations was asked in Nicaragua (ONUVEN), El Salvador (ONUSAL), and Cambodia (UNTAC) to undertake actions which went far beyond peacekeeping or matters of peace and security but included the monitoring and organisation of elections. In the post-Cold War period the UN was also involved in Iraq, Somalia, Bosnia, Haiti, Georgia and Rwanda in situations which were on the margin between 'threats to peace' and domestic problems. Operation Provide Comfort undertaken by a small group of member states in northern Iraq to provide an area in which the Kurds of Iraq could be protected from repressive activities of their government was a military intervention in a domestic crisis. The basis of this intervention was the Security Council Resolution 688 which called on Iraq to cease its oppression and 'insisted' that humanitarian relief efforts have access. While there was a reference to the Kurdish refugee crisis as a 'threat to international peace and security' there was no explicit authority to carry out enforcement action within that resolution and the powers concerned used the earlier resolution of the Security Council (678) to have authority to undertake it. Similarly the initial resolution adopted on 23 January 1992 on Somalia found a 'threat to international peace and security' in very general terms. The introduction to the resolution states that the Security Council is *'gravely alarmed* at the rapid deterioration of the situation in Somalia and the heavy loss of human life and widespread material damage resulting from the conflict in the country and aware of its consequences on the stability and peace in the region...'. The action which was taken was 'perhaps the most purely humanitarian military intervention ever undertaken or authorized by the United Nations, in the sense that it is very hard to discern any broader political objective other than relief of suffering within Somalia' (Mortimer, 1995).

In 1994 the situations in Haiti and Georgia were both recognised as 'threats to the peace'. They are, however, in both cases rather unclear. In the case of Haiti it would appear that the problem posed to the United States by the flow of Haitian refugees was the most important factor leading to the decision, and in the case of Georgia the resolution of the Security Council of August 1994 was a legitimation of the presence of Russian forces. In the view of some this was seen as a reciprocal recognition by the world community that the United States and Russia have 'spheres of influence' in their immediate neighbourhoods.

The case of Rwanda and the failure of the members of the United Nations to provide forces after the Security Council had passed its resolution on 17 May 1994 suggest that the level of atrocities is not in itself a criterion in determining whether members of the 'international community' will provide military forces to assist the United Nations collectively to respond to a humanitarian disaster. The Secretary-General of the United Nations subsequently pointed out 'that not one of the nineteen governments that at the time had undertaken to have troops on stand by agreed to contribute'. This failure of the international community to respond led to the French proposal of June 1994 to send their forces and to occupy the south-west of the country. This action was not fully supported by France's European partners and indicates the problem of providing coherent responses to humanitarian problems.

While international law seems to have developed in such a way that the Security Council is now more ready to provide a legitimacy for collective or, as in the case of France, individual action to respond to humanitarian crises, there is still an absence of effective collective mechanisms to provide military forces to undertake these missions.

The development of international law and practice can perhaps be summarised in Christopher Greenwood's conclusions:

> The law on humanitarian intervention has changed both for the United Nations and for individual states. It is no longer tenable to assert whenever a government massacres its own people or a state collapses into anarchy that international law forbids military intervention altogether.
>
> (Greenwood, 1993:40)

At the same time the concept of humanitarian intervention has perhaps also developed as suggested by Adam Roberts (1993):

> The term 'humanitarian intervention' has subtly changed its meaning. It is still military intervention in another country, with limited or no agreement with the authorities there, to prevent widespread suffering and death among the population. However, whereas previously the term 'humanitarian' applied largely to the ultimate rationale of the operation (including in some cases the end goal of replacing dictatorship with democracy) it now relates more to the type of activity with which it is conspicuously associated throughout, including the provision of food, medicine, and shelter; and it now seems often to imply limited, short-term goals.

THE POLITICAL OPERATIONAL EXPERIENCE OF RECENT INTERVENTIONS

Recent experience of international military intervention for humanitarian ends as well as for such 'nation building' ends as occurred in Namibia, Mozambique and Cambodia shows rather mixed results. The situation existing before 1995 with the UNPROFOR deployment in the former Yugoslavia (not discussed in detail here) also shows the practically impossible dilemma when the United Nations is asked to undertake tasks which are contradictory.

There are a number of points which require consideration in the light of our experience of this group of operations.

(1) Most of the countries in Western Europe have had very limited practical military experience in the post-war period. They

have been preparing on the one hand for the major collective self-defence operation which was central to NATO's tasks and on the other for the relatively straightforward classical peacekeeping functions under the United Nations. The present tasks of military intervention come somewhere between these two and they are tasks with which relatively few countries have had experience.

(2) There is a problem in finding sufficient military personnel for these operations, particularly for those countries which rely on conscripts for the bulk of their armed forces. In many countries it is assumed that conscripts can only be used for territorial defence purposes and in any case their period of service is normally too short to permit a spell in a UN operation. The solution found in the Nordic countries whereby former conscripts re-engage for UN peace support operations therefore requires further examination.

(3) In the post-Cold-War world there has been an understandable wish in a number of countries, including in particular the United States, to find military solutions which minimise casualties on one's own side. This is sometimes referred to in a simplified form as a 'zero death' strategy. This presents problems especially for the deployment of ground forces, if humanitarian interventions for altruistic reasons are going to mean that young people of one's armed forces are being placed in 'harm's way'. Most ministers will be reluctant to put their armed forces at risk unless essential national interests are involved.

(4) Although 'humanitarian interventions' have been described as being undertaken for altruistic motives, in fact a variety of motives are likely to influence decision-making. As Adam Roberts has said: 'interest, prudence and political opportunism remain key-factors in state behaviour, and have powerfully influenced decisions favouring actions in some situations and opposing it in others' (Roberts, 1993:446).

(5) The problem of building a consensus either within the European Union, within the Atlantic Alliance, or within the United Nations to decide when 'humanitarian intervention' should be undertaken and when not is likely to prove difficult. Such consensus building is unfortunately all too likely to lead to minimalist solutions. In some circumstances such minimalist solutions are also the least satisfactory solutions and are likely to reduce the credibility and effectiveness of the missions decided upon.

(6) There is a risk that humanitarian intervention will be chosen rather than other more substantial action to deal with particular

crises as countries are not prepared to invest sufficient blood or treasure to deal adequately with the problems facing them.

(7) There is a need for more analysis of what actions can and should be taken to deal with 'failed states', that is countries who no longer have a mechanism to govern themselves. Can one conceive of a United Nations 'guardianship system' which would provide over a long term the development of a viable national structure? Attempting to combine such 'nation building' with other forms of UN action has not always proved satisfactory. Somalia is perhaps the best instance of this.

(8) In one way 'humanitarian interventions' may be linked with the classical UN view of its forces being impartial in a situation. Nonetheless, even if this is the intention of the UN the perceptions on the ground may be different. Can impartiality be compatible with siege breaking? It is certainly far from clear that those who are attempting to maintain the siege will see the siege breakers as impartial.

(9) There is a problem with multilateral interventions of 'mission creep' and something which has been established as an impartial mission being expected to move into an 'enforcement' role. This has been described in the British literature as 'crossing the Mogadishu line'; it is difficult to go from peacekeeping to peace enforcement but excessively difficult to return from peace enforcement to peace-keeping.

(10) There are a number of problems arising from the way in which relatively sophisticated military equipment is now widely diffused. One example of this was the way that the Bosnian Serb air defence required the French authorities to request in July 1995 the provision of US Apache helicopters to transport a thousand men the relatively short distance from Sarajevo to the UN safe area of Gorazde. It is significant that Western European armed forces do not at the moment have the capability to undertake a mission of this sort.

(11) There has been more than one American attempt to establish criteria for the use of military forces in different situations. President Bush in the last weeks of his presidency set out five requirements for military intervention:

Using military force makes sense as a policy where the stakes warrant, where and when force can be effective, where no other policies are likely to prove effective, where applications can be limited in scope and time, and where the potential benefits justify the potential costs and sacrifice.

(Speech to the United States Military Academy, West Point, 5 January 1993, quoted in Haass, 1994)

(12) Subsequently in May 1994 the United States issued a policy statement on 'Multilateral Peace Operations' which set out eight criteria which ought to be met or considered in the case of UN operations for which the United States was asked to vote, 14 criteria if the US was expected to participate in such operations, and 17 if US participation was likely to involve combat. This proliferation of criteria, linked to the negative attitude shown by the Republican majority in the Congress to UN peace support operations, suggests that it will be difficult to find both the resources and contributions from the US for such operations in future.

(13) The experience of the last five years suggests that large countries and organisations developed primarily for collective self-defence may not necessarily be the easiest to involve in multilateral peacekeeping operations. They have a sense of their own credibility being at stake if a particular operation is not 'successful'. Unfortunately the experience of multilateral interventions is that success cannot always be achieved or judged in the short term.

(14) In examining the desirability of changing the restrictive conditions on military intervention in order to carry out missions which Western countries consider desirable we must always bear in mind the precedents that such reductions in the protective norms of 'non-intervention' will create if others with different motives wish in turn to carry out their own operations. It may be that the Commonwealth of Independent States will be able to develop effective mechanisms for peacekeeping within its borders but given the dominant size of the Russian Federation it is not clear that actions in the other republics will always be perceived both there and externally in this way.

BIBLIOGRAPHY

Fisher, D., 'The Ethics of Intervention', *Survival*, Vol. 36, No. 1, Spring 1994, 51–9.
Fisler Damrosch, L.,'Changing Conceptions of Intervention in International Law', in: Reed and Kaysen (eds.), 1993, 91–114.
Greenwood, C., 'Is There a Right of Humanitarian Intervention?', *The World Today*, February 1993, 34–40.

Haass, R.N., *Intervention*, Carnegie Endowment for International Peace, 1994.

Mill, J.S., *On Liberty*, 1859.

Mortimer, E., 'Under What Circumstances Should the UN Intervene Militarily in a "Domestic" Crisis?', unpublished paper for Vienna International Peace Academy, 25th Seminar, 1995.

Reed, L.W. and Kaysen, K. (eds.), *Emerging Norms of Justified Intervention*, American Academy of Arts and Sciences, 1993.

Roberts, A., 'Humanitarian War: Military Intervention and Human Rights', *International Affairs*, Vol. 69, No. 3, July 1993.

Trachtenberg, M., 'Intervention in Historical Perspective', in: Reed and Kaysen (eds.), 1993.

18 The Past and the Future of Intervention: a View from the United States[1]

John Langan, SJ

INTERVENTION – VARIATIONS ON A TWENTIETH CENTURY FOREIGN POLICY THEME

Increasing life expectancy in developed societies has made it not at all uncommon for people to live well beyond the biblical three score and ten. When Cardinal Bernardin, the Archbishop of Chicago, died recently of cancer at the age of 68, most people regarded his death as untimely; this would not have been the case even a generation ago. But if we shift from thinking of the lifespan of a single individual to considering the transformation of societies, 75 years comes close to being the limit on what we can imagine and conceive as one historical unit. Moving back 75 to 80 years takes us to the period from 1917 to 1923, when the First World War was coming to an end and when the bases for a new order of things in Europe were being established. Of course, as we know, the European and world situation of 1997 is enormously different from the European and world situation of 1919. Power, wealth, and knowledge are more broadly diffused; horrors have been perpetrated and threatened which make the trench warfare of 1914–18 seem comparatively civilised and humane. The world is more complex, more interdependent, more aware of its vulnerabilities; the West is less confident, less militant, less religious, less imperial. But we need to take up some more specific points of comparison which bear on the problem of intervention today.

(1) The principle of national self-determination and the right of peoples to form states according to ethnic and linguistic identities were vigorously affirmed in both periods despite enormous political and theoretical difficulties. Nationalistic political movements were powerful engines of both destruction and creation in both periods.

(2) By 1991 all the major European states had lost their empires, those collections of peoples and territories which had been built up

during the long period of European expansion that ran from the Crusades and the *reconquista* through the conquest of Peru and Mexico and the imposition of the Raj and the partition of Africa to the Soviet invasion of Afghanistan.

(3) Whereas in 1919 the grand scheme for the revolutionary egalitarian transformation of economic society which we commonly call Marxist communism had vaulted from the barricades of the streets to the corridors of power; in 1994, with the exceptions of East Asia and Cuba, such overt communists as were still to be found were either in Western academic settings or in opposition political parties in a democratic context.

(4) There is the fact of the enormous and much envied success of the European Economic Community (now the European Union), which has transformed the basis of relations among its members from competition to cooperation (although competition re-emerges as a secondary and controlled element).

(5) The process of global diffusion of Western forms of knowledge, power and organisation, which was signalled in 1919 by the newly prominent roles of Japan and the United States, has been carried much further so that European predominance in international political and economic affairs is a matter of the past.

(6) The place of war in the political and diplomatic system of the West has been decisively altered, and with it the nature and scope of threats to national security. In 1919, it was manifest to the great majority of Europeans that war had ceased to be a desirable activity for states to engage in. It could still be justifiable and necessary. But there was no prospect that a total war for supremacy along the lines of the First World War could be seen as contributing to national growth and fulfilment or as manifesting the excellence and glory of the nation. One could make the regressive move of attempting to transform the tactics of war in the hope of avoiding the enormous attrition of the Western front (as Hitler did by turning to the *Blitzkrieg*), or one could attempt to prevent the outbreak of war by defensive barriers and pre-emptive concessions (as Britain and France did). But no one of sound mind desired a repetition of 1914–18. After the use of nuclear weapons at the end of the Second World War and the development of the arsenals of deterrence, no one could regard an extended and unlimited war between major powers as either rational or moral. Threats had to be made, and they brought security of a kind. But states had to abstain from a wide range of military and diplomatic behaviour that would in the

eighteenth and nineteenth centuries have been accepted as a normal part of the pursuit of national interest. The Soviet failure to observe this restraint around Berlin in 1948 and in the late 1950s and in Cuba produced the most serious crises of the Cold War. Intervention across the great divide, at least overt, military intervention, was unacceptable even to vigorously anti-Soviet leaders, as Budapest in 1956 and Prague in 1968 made very clear.

INTERVENTION IN TWO WORLD WARS AND VIETNAM

The contrast that I have been drawing between 1919 and the 1990s is intended to provide a context for what I will be saying about the lessons of intervention – as seen from a US perspective. Here a brief reflection on the term itself will be useful. On one level, we can think about intervention as a 'coming between', a stepping into a quarrel initiated by others and driven by their conceptions of their interests and their security needs. The intervening power is seen and is inclined to see itself as less fundamentally affected by the conflict; entering into the conflict is optional, a matter for debate and decision, something it could stay out of. To a very large extent this is the way Americans understood our participation in the First World War. Intervention may well have been in our national interest; but there was not a clear or strong consensus on this point. Revulsion against Germany's unrestricted submarine warfare and anger at Germany's clumsy efforts to involve Mexico in the war provided visible foci for interventionist agitation. The greater strength of cultural and linguistic ties with Britain, especially among Eastern elites, and the superior propaganda skills of the British combined with the distrust of Germany produced by the invasion of Belgium ensured that the debate was always about intervention on the side of the British and the French. But large numbers of German-Americans and Irish-Americans and Middle Westerners of all stocks were never fully convinced of the interventionist case. Suspicions that the US had been duped into rescuing the British Empire persisted until Pearl Harbour ended the second great debate on US intervention in overseas conflict, the debate that raged in the late 1930s and early 1940s.

In the debates leading up to America's participation in the two World Wars, two other themes were powerful, themes that continue to be important for understanding American attitudes. One is the deeply rooted sense of American exceptionalism, of America as 'the city set on the hill', as the new Israel, as the *novus ordo saeculorum*, as the new, undefiled, virginal land, as the refuge of the poor and oppressed, as the last, best hope of humanity. This sense can be found on the right and on the left of American politics; it can be found in pacifist and militant versions; and it can be propounded in religious or secularist terms. The second major theme was the belief, strongly held in some business and Protestant church circles, that the true future of the United States lay in its relations across the Pacific with the great societies of Asia with their rich history and their enormous economic potential. This, of course, is a view that need not be isolationist or pacifist; in fact it was held by those men who constructed a considerable American empire in the Pacific by acquiring Hawaii and defeating Spain in 1898. It does, however, go well with views of Europe as old, sophisticated, rich, decadent, self-destructive, effete, manipulative, and in sum comprehensively wicked. This way of thinking about Europe lost plausibility after 1945, when so much of Europe was devastated and impoverished and when both the evil deeds and the sufferings of the old continent were seen to have been more profound than the older negative stereotype suggested. The understanding of intervention as an optional entering into other people's quarrels had lost its point even before that, at the time of Pearl Harbour. But, given the vast oceans which continue to surround the United States, it remains as a continuing possibility, at least when the participants in a local conflict lack intercontinental missiles. It is actively present in many of the questions that are raised by conservative sceptics about current proposals for US intervention on humanitarian grounds. These questions commonly take the form of asking how this admittedly troubled and pathetic situation, for example, in Bosnia or Somalia or Haiti or Rwanda, actually affects US security and American interests. In the absence of strong and clear answers to these questions, why should Americans insert themselves into other people's quarrels?

The First World War was fought by two coalitions of states, in which the key states (with the exception of Austria-Hungary) were built around a national nucleus but which also had a more or less large imperial range. In 1917 the US intervened in an ongoing conflict between states with well-defined boundaries, rather than within states. This was also the case in the Second World War, although then the Japanese and the Germans took the final decision about US involvement.

But the most controversial interventions of the US government since 1945 have not fitted this pattern. They were not acts marking the entry of the United States into an ongoing war among sovereign states. Rather, they fit within the context of an ongoing confrontation with the forces of Marxist or Marxist-inspired or Marxist-supported revolution. This confrontation – the 'Cold War' – was ominous, brutal, direct, and comprehensive; but it involved the actual use of force only at the edges of communist expansion or in areas where dependence on or alliance with the West was repudiated by a local faction ready to use force.

The unhappy outcome of the very large and controversial intervention in Vietnam had very little impact on the broad lines of US international policy and even less on the ultimate outcome of the Cold War. Beyond Laos and Cambodia, the dominoes did not fall. Key allies did not realign themselves in search of protection from the risks of American inconstancy. Neither the Soviet Union nor China achieved a significant augmentation of power. The United States did suffer the loss of that easy and overwhelming preponderance of power which it had enjoyed since 1945. (This was a preponderance which for economic reasons, if no other, it was bound to lose in the course of events as its share of global economic activity diminished.) This was signalled by the economic crisis of 1971, when President Nixon dropped the convertability of the dollar to gold. After Vietnam, it could no longer be assumed that US intervention in a local conflict would be effective in ending local resistance or that it would enjoy continuing political support at home.

The impact of the failure of the Vietnam intervention was greatest in two closely related areas. One was the attitude of the general public to proposed interventions. Criticism, especially on the left, became routine and often shrill. There was more caution on the part of political leaders. Here one may compare the somewhat favourable attitude of the Nixon administration towards the possibility of intervention in Chile in 1970 to prevent Allende's coming to power with the more reserved attitude it adopted to the coup of September 1973, which actually overthrew him. Of course, by then, Nixon had other threats to worry about, much closer to home. The kinds of destabilising initiatives aimed at removing unfriendly governments which the US was able to carry out in Iran and Guatemala in the 1950s were subject to much more hostile scrutiny in the 1970s. When interventions were completely non-military and were kept reasonably covert, criticism was minimal both before and after Vietnam. This was particularly true if the interventions were aimed at preserving democratic regimes in what looked to be temporarily trying circumstances, for example Italy in 1948 and Portugal after 1973. There was also very little dissent about providing weapons and training for Afghan rebels after the Soviet intervention in late 1979. The US government was willing to intervene more vigorously in what it took to be its backyard, that is, the Caribbean and Central America. The fact that such interventions took place against Marxist or criminal regimes ensured that they would enjoy solid support from the political right and that critics on the left would have to work very hard to distance themselves from unsavoury and unpopular characters, of whom Fidel Castro is the most remarkable and the longest surviving. The most complex cases in this regard are Nicaragua and El Salvador. There was always considerable resistance within the United States to a straightforward policy of military intervention. This was strongly present not merely on the political left, but also in the Catholic hierarchy and in Congress. The Reagan administration in particular was eager to supply weapons and funds to the Contras in Nicaragua and to the government in El Salvador. The sacrilegious barbarism of the army and its political allies in El Salvador and the wariness of the Sandinistas in Nicaragua ensured that the Reagan administration did not have a simple or compelling case to put before the American public and that it had to pursue the goals of an interventionist policy in ways that were stealthy and illegal.

The other area where the failure of the Vietnam intervention had its greatest impact was the US military. The unpopularity of the prior US involvement in Korea, which was presented as a police action against the aggressor communist regime in North Korea and which had active participation from many members of the United Nations, had worked against the Democrats in 1952. But it had not affected the military as an institution or the broad cultural equilibrium of the country as the Vietnam War did. The negative effects of the Vietnam conflict on internal morale and discipline in the Army, and on the credibility and public reputation of the military leadership induced a caution in the middle and upper reaches of the military which lasts to this day. The facts that the war became the central object of fear and loathing for an entire generation of American young people, that its burdens were borne disproportionately by blacks and the poor, that drugs were widely available in the war zone, that the combined horrors of jungle warfare and sophisticated military technology were shared on a nightly basis with the folks at home watching the evening news, that prisoners could not be rescued or have their lot alleviated, that civilians were both avoidably and unavoidably the frequent objects of fire from US forces, and that the entire business was conducted in a country whose cultural and political life was opaque to the soldiers on the ground as well as to the 'experts' flown in by the Pentagon combined to make this intervention a period of intense personal and national suffering for an end which was no longer intelligible or plausible. The massacre at My Lai was both tragic and inexcusable; in the context of the war, however, it should not have been surprising. In the aftermath of this terrible experience, the US military has quietly but firmly opposed proposals to commit US forces in interventions which have no definite term, which lack strong popular and congressional support, which are likely to involve high levels of US casualties, and which do not have a manifest connection with US national security interests. This produces a stance which does not directly challenge the principle of civilian control of the military (than which few things are more sacred and more reliable in American public life) but which does put a powerful brake on any tendency to commit US forces without meeting a demanding series of moral, practical, and political tests. It is a stance which combines intra-group loyalty with professional and institutional self-interest; and it is not likely to change anytime soon. It continues in the Pentagon under the Clinton administration even as it did under the Reagan and Bush administrations.

INTERVENTION: FUTURE THEMES

What are the implications of this sketchy overview of US attitudes to intervention? What conclusions can we draw about future reactions of the United States to crises beyond its borders, especially to crises in the Eastern hemisphere? My presentation has, I realise, been weighted in a way that emphasises the long-standing reluctance of the United States to engage itself in overseas entanglements and the more recent reinforcement which the Vietnam experience gave to this tendency. Against this, one could develop an alternative interpretation in which the United States, admittedly with some hesitations and reversals, moves from isolated self-absorption to a position of world hegemony, in which the United States responds to the realities of world conflict and mutual interdependence in a variety of ways that range from unilateral initiatives through bilateral and multilateral alliances to operations of the United Nations. This movement out into the larger world can be welcomed and celebrated or regretted and denounced. It is important to note that these opposing reactions can come from either the right or the left.

Now it is my own conviction that this second interpretation is broader and more correct, and it is more likely to give us a comprehensive understanding of the progress of the United States of America through this troubled century and into the next. Prediction is always hazardous; let me nonetheless venture the following set of propositions.

(1) Given the disappearance of the Soviet threat, the preoccupation of China with economic development and political succession, and the defeat of Saddam Hussein, it is possible for the United States to defend an extensive but well defined set of interests and alliances at lower cost and risk than before. This set includes NATO and the EC; Japan and South Korea and Taiwan; Australia and New Zealand; Israel and its potentially peaceful neighbours; Saudi Arabia and other oil-producing states in the Gulf area. It would be comparatively easy to establish a public consensus for military action and, in the case of Israel and its neighbours, for continuing foreign aid, in order to protect the stability and the pro-Western orientation of these areas both against external aggression and against internal collapse. Our commitments to these parts of the world have been internalised both on a psychological level (the commitments are familiar and well accepted and are perceived as ours), and on a political level (the commitments enjoy the vigorous support of particular interest groups such as business associates or immigrants or co-religionists, who are ready to exert themselves within the American political process).

(2) There is a group of states which would strongly like to be included within this set of alliances and interests and more specifically within NATO and the EC. Some of them (Poland, the Czech and Slovak republics, Hungary, the Baltic states) also have the ability to gather support within the American political process. They are not concerned about an immediate threat from the East; but they do want reassurance, a reassurance which the United States and NATO have been reluctant to give for fear of producing negative outcomes within the Russian political system. The

reassurance might make the threat more rather than less likely. But, despite this present reluctance, it is likely that if a threat became urgent the West would move to protect these states.

(3) Within the area covered by this set of alliances and interests, the likelihood of violent conflict arising from internal disagreements is very low – at least if we except the Middle East. Forces will need to be kept in readiness to respond to possible dangers arising from Russia, China, and dissatisfied states in the Islamic world. But no one expects either Western Europe or the Western Pacific to fragment in bloody internecine struggles. Should a prosperous Russia become integrated in a larger version of Europe, and if China should develop into a prosperous democracy, we are likely to see the emergence of a sizeable body of opinion calling for drastic reductions in the military and security apparatus which the US with its European allies developed in response to the Soviet threat. After all, it can then be argued, the only way that less developed countries can harm the United States is by way of terrorist attacks, which are very unlikely to inflict harm that is politically or economically decisive.

(4) Both the United States and the EU/EC, while now more secure than at any previous time since 1914, have in their neighbourhood states which are not particularly anxious to be incorporated in the Western security system but which, by reason of their internal conflicts, can have a disruptive effect on their more prosperous neighbours. Here one need think only of the former Yugoslavia, Algeria, Haiti, Cuba and the Dominican Republic. Each of these states has the potential for developing civil war, bloody anarchy, brutally repressive dictatorship, aggressively militant popular movements or nasty combinations of these – a potential which has come close to full realisation in the Bosnian conflict. Each of them can send forth streams of refugees, can be a base of operations for terrorist activities, can damage economic interests of their wealthier neighbours. None of them poses a security threat in the sense of being able to win a military conflict directly against an economically advanced country; but actions within their boundaries are likely to provoke calls for humanitarian intervention when the level of bloodshed gets to be intolerably high, for partisan support and intervention when one side in the local conflict has a significant body of supporters or sympathisers (immigrants, business colleagues) in the wealthier countries, and for vigorous preventive and self-protective measures which will prevent the trouble from spreading.

(5) Conflicts within the territory of the former Soviet Union are unlikely to produce much in the way of sustained or effective calls for intervention. Russia is likely to maintain a monopoly on interventions in 'the near abroad'. The two exceptions to this point are Ukraine and Armenia. Because of Ukraine's size and economic potential, its cultural and religious links with the West, and (not least) its onetime possession of nuclear weapons, the Western powers will be actively concerned to support its independence but will not be willing to intervene forcefully in conflicts that may develop. Armenia, because of its tragic history and its large and successful emigrant population, will be able to get its grievances heard, even though its location and the hostility of its neighbours may make help virtually impossible to deliver.

(6) Interventions in the broader reaches of the Third World, that is those countries not affecting the Western democracies at close range or not affecting the security and stability of the Middle East, will not be justifiable for reasons of national security or the security of allies. They will have to be justified on humanitarian grounds, if they are to be justified at all.

The multiplicity of crises unfortunately does not seem to be merely a temporary bad patch that we are passing through. One need not elevate it to the status of being an inescapable feature of the human condition. We should probably think about it as we think about most medium-term problems, that is a conjunction of factors which will not vanish quickly but which is not likely to become permanent. Briefly, these factors are: the problems of the dissolution of empire in Eastern Europe with the resulting opportunities for separatist nationalism, not merely in the limits of the erstwhile empire itself but also in neighbouring states (Yugoslavia, Turkey); the unresolved task of achieving political maturity and stability in the Islamic lands with their distinctive religious heritage and their normative dissonance with the West in both its Christian and secular phases; the conflicts arising from profound poverty and ethnic hostility in Africa and that continent's failure to find the bases for a secure and reliable internal development of civil life and economic institutions; the unresolved conflicts affecting the poorest parts of the Western hemisphere in which revolutionary Marxism still retains considerable popular appeal and therefore the ability to provoke civil war.

The fact of multiplicity remains extremely important for both practical and logical reasons. For it ensures that the limited resources available for humanitarian intervention, whether by the United States, the West more generally, or by the United Nations, will be severely strained and hotly argued over. Among these limited resources we have to count not merely military personnel and finances but also public attention and political leadership, all of which are needed to sustain humanitarian intervention. The scarcity of these resources is not simply a given but is open to moral challenge both as regards its extent and as regards the decisions which determine its precise level. Multiplicity also ensures that in the public forum analogies and arguments will be offered which call for greater consistency in the way cases are handled. These arguments will always have the attraction of offering a 'better' solution to the crisis for at least one of the parties; but they bring to the surface a profound tension in the Western ethical tradition. On the one hand, there are strong elements in our ethical, legal, and religious traditions which stress equality and universality in applying our values to decisions; against this, we have to set the Aristotelian and Thomistic understanding of prudence which allows for considerable variation in the treatment of complex cases. This view of prudence is a flexible instrument which is enormously useful for those who wish to think seriously about the moral dilemmas of diplomacy and statecraft and specifically about the problems of intervention; at the same time it is a ready tool for rationalisation by those who wish to avoid hard decisions. The most important consequence of the fact of multiplicity is that in the present stage of international organisation and cooperation it will not be possible to respond in a humane and effective fashion to all the crises. This outcome may push us toward increasing the level of public expenditures and the commitment of military and civilian personnel to projects of intervention and pacification, and toward expanding the powers of international organisations.

(7) Humanitarian intervention, as contrasted with intervention for the sake of national security, will find its main constituency in American politics and, I suspect, elsewhere on the moderate left. National security interventions or interventions presented as such drew most of their support from the right, although they got significant support from the anticommunists of the left (Jackson and Humphrey Democrats) until the Vietnam War. The American left will be uncomfortable with the military character of intervention; but many will endorse it if the cause seems just, as one can gather from the interventionist views of the Congressional Black

Caucus on Haiti. This shift in the political base of support for intervention will produce many paradoxical reversals of arguments and alliances. Republicans, who applauded the clumsy and dubiously legal invasion of Grenada in order to overthrow a group of Marxists recoil in dismay from the shedding of the blood of American soldiers in Somalia. Democrats struggle to overcome the anxieties which they felt about US policy in Latin America to argue for humanitarian rescue missions in Africa. Intervention as a broad category is not likely to be attractive to the American people; it will have to be justified on a case-by-case basis by a national leadership that can interpret the crisis in a prudent way and that has the courage to adhere to its conclusions when intervention is seen to be more complex and more perilous than a parade down Pennsylvania Avenue or the Champs-Elysées.

NOTE

1. This chapter was originally a paper presented at the international meeting of the Council on Christian Approaches to Defence and Disarmament, Keble College, Oxford, September 1994 and revised for subsequent publication.

Part VII
Interim Evaluation

Rather than claiming to provide conclusions, the final section of the book draws together some key themes. Public opinion increases or limits the scope of governments for intervention, but can also be manufactured, or at least influenced. *Brian Beedham* therefore looks at the key role of well-informed and independent journalists in informing public perceptions of internal wars in other parts of the world. His piece is entitled ***'Sword and Pen: Journalists and the Wars of the Future'***.

In one of the last pieces which he wrote, *Anthony Parsons* drew on his long diplomatic experience to review the first 50 years of United Nations' activity in a chapter headed ***'The UN – Peace and Security: a Balance Sheet'***.

Finally, formulating some questions for further work, *Roger Williamson* poses the issue ***'An Ethical Framework – Or Just Intervention?'*** The just war theory provides a framework for ethical evaluation, but can also be misused to justify wars which are only intervention rather than justified intervention. No easy conclusions are provided; the evaluation of future wars will require scrupulous application of the just war criteria.

19 Sword and Pen: Journalists and the Wars of the Future

Brian Beedham

It would nice to think that the wars of the coming period will be fought, by the blessing of information technology, under the careful inspection of a public opinion which knows what is happening, and why, and what can be done about it. That is how war might at last be brought under responsible democratic supervision. It is, alas, probably not going to happen, because even the revolutionary changes in the way that news is gathered and distributed in the modern world may not be enough to cope with the equally radical change in the sort of war the news-gatherers will be reporting.

Wars of intervention – probably the most common sort of war in the next 20 or 30 years – are in one important respect different from most of the big wars of the past couple of centuries; because of this, they present a new challenge to the people who set out to describe what these new wars are about. At the same time, the transformation that has been taking place in the communications industry in recent decades (a transformation still not complete), though it is in some ways a huge improvement on the past, is in other ways not very good at peering into the complexities of this new kind of war. Add the fact that, for the time being at least, public opinion in most of the Western world is highly ambivalent about the waging of war – hot for action at one moment, flinching from the reality of the battlefield at the next – and it is clear that the relationship between war and the media is going to be more complicated than the optimists had thought. Take the three points in turn.

For the 40-odd years of the Cold War, the most important thing to know about that eerie confrontation was what was going on in the minds of the great powers whose disagreement had caused the Cold War. It was necessary to understand the political calculations and the military capabilities of the United States and the Soviet Union, of their main allies in Europe, and for a time of China too. If you could do this, you could make an intelligent guess about the next stage of the proceedings. It was much less important to know about the local politics of the places where the great rivals fought out their competition, either in head-on battles like the Korean War or in conflicts-by-proxy like those in the Africa of the 1970s. To be sure, it helped to know where the sort of things were happening that would tempt a big power to stick a finger in. But the big power's decision would depend largely on its calculation of how its big power rivals would react. It was not the local details that would decide the issue; the last word lay in Moscow or Washington or Beijing.

Of course, it was not easy to peer into the minds of the governments of the great powers. But at least the journalists' targets did not change: they were watching the same countries for over 40 years. The foreign policy newspaper columnist or the television specialist could gradually build up a body of knowledge about each of the major actors in the Cold War. Admittedly, it was done with more difficulty in Russia than in America, and with even more in China. Despite the varying shades of obscurity, however, the intentions of the cold warriors slowly became clearer. Their changes of policy could sometimes be detected in advance. The size and efficiency of their armed forces could be measured with a certain degree of accuracy. The possibility of being taken by surprise diminished. It would be an exaggeration to say that the media grew scientific about the Cold War; but quite a lot of journalists accumulated a fair amount of expertise about it, and could follow its twists and turns with reasonable confidence.

Contrast that with the task which journalists face when it comes to wars of intervention. The central issues of these wars are, by definition, strictly local. The outside powers send their soldiers and airforce personnel into action not primarily in pursuit of their own interests but in order to protect a small country from the neighbourhood bully, or to stop particularly vicious dictators doing dreadful things to their own people, or to provide emergency repairs for a country that has collapsed into anarchy. In the nature of things, many of these events will happen in remote parts of the world outside the usual range of the majority of European and American journalists. They will therefore come as a surprise to most outsiders, if not to the unfortunate people who live on the spot. And, since public opinion in America and Europe is likely to insist that such wars be as brief as possible, there will not be much time for journalists to fill their notebooks. A depressing amount of the media's coverage will depend on quick impressions, generalisations and guesswork.

It is not just the Cold War period from which this new sort of warfare differs. It is unlike much of the experience of the past 200 years. To understand what led up to the start of the Second World War in 1939, it was not necessary to be an expert about Czechoslovakia or Poland; what chiefly mattered was what Hitler wanted, and what the governments of Britain and France were prepared to do about it. The political-military history of the nineteenth century, up to the outbreak of the First World War in 1914, is a study in the balance of power manoeuvrings of the five strongest European countries of the time. Ever since foreign policy journalism seriously started, you might say, war has been chiefly a consequence of the conflicting wills of great powers.

That old pattern may reassert itself when China becomes a global power, 15 or 20 years from now, and if Russia re-emerges as a power in the world, and if some new Muslim coalition appears upon the scene. But until and unless that happens, Europe and America, freed for the moment from the great-power preoccupations of the past, will face a new military agenda dictated as much by conscience as by self-interest. That is the nature of wars of intervention.

Ah, some people will say, but what about the Vietnam War: surely that did not fit into the old patterns? No, it did not, and that was why it was so widely misunderstood. The Vietnam conflict, though its combatants were communists and anti-communists, was not like most of the rest of the Cold War. It was not chiefly a result of the manoeuvrings of the great powers. Its causes lay largely inside Vietnam itself, in the clash between a communist minority seeking to control the whole country and the reluctance of other Vietnamese to accept that control. The tragedy was that the outside world – including many of the journalists who went to Vietnam to cover the war – gave too much attention to its Cold War appearance and too little to its internal reality. Until the great exodus of the boat people, after the American defeat, not many outsiders had realised the full extent of Vietnamese opposition to the communists. The Vietnam War, which most people still think of as a Cold War horror, was in fact an early example of the war of intervention; and the fact that the intervention failed has lessons, in the coming period, for the journalist as well as the politician.

Can the media not do better in helping people to understand future wars of intervention? Yes, of course they can: up to a point. The information industry has much more technology at its disposal now than it had in Vietnam a quarter of a century ago. Newspaper reporters and television people can usually find their way to even the most remote and unexpected crisis within a day or two, and can at once start to tell huge numbers of viewers and readers the basic elements of what they discover there. The television screen, in particular, conveys to people back home with great clarity the horror involved in a civil war, a political mass extermination, the slow death of a starving community. The value of such reporting, in a world wondering if it can help to alleviate the distant horrors, should not be underestimated. Public opinion in America and Europe, the main sources of potential help, is being told: 'Look, terrible things are happening; something has to be done'.

Yet there are limits on what this quick response reporting can achieve. The full story of what led to the massacre or the insurrection or the outbreak of starvation, or whatever is being reported, is complicated and obscure, filled with unfamiliar names and the baffling contortions of local history. Just arrived reporters cannot do more than grasp a handful of the most vivid things that come to their attention, and hope they are the important ones. They will learn more if they stay longer; but that may not be possible if, as was said earlier, the countries that undertake wars of intervention understandably seek to keep their interventions pretty brisk.

The images on the television screen, in particular, though they attack the emotions of the distant watcher (as they ought to), do not provide a great deal of information to the reasoning part of the mind. They can make a small tragedy appear large, or a large one small; they seldom offer more than a rudimentary explanation of how matters reached the point now being illustrated; they by no means always make it clear who is really to blame. Television is a medium of the feelings rather than of analytic examination. An hour on the screen, though it can properly make the viewers cry out in dismay, probably gives them no more facts than a couple of columns of print in a good newspaper – and the newspaper is more easily available for re-examination and rereading if dismay leads to a demand for action.

Moreover, the growing strength of television has had its effect on written journalism. To keep up their circulation against the competition of TV, most newspapers have to some extent had to imitate the qualities of television. They have sharpened their visual impact, by more use of colour and illustrations; they tend to write less about the sort of subject, including many aspects of the world abroad, which they fear might lead the bored reader to switch over to the latest TV sit-com; and their style of writing has in many cases become less factual and analytic, more essay-like and emotion-plucking.

There are still large differences between countries in this matter. Switzerland, for instance, has preserved the old journalistic standards better than most; Britain is near the other end of the scale. But as a general proposition it is fair to say that, compared with 40 years ago, a much larger proportion of the total number of newspapers now sold in Europe and America is concerned more with entertainment than with conventional news reporting, and that even among the minority of real newspapers not more than one or two in each country provide a reasonably thorough and detailed coverage of foreign affairs. In short, the competition from television has made the written press less good at doing what television itself does least well.

Nor is it clear that the newest addition to information technology, the Internet, will do all that much to help. So far, at least, the two chief characteristics of the Internet are that it makes instantly available a stupendous range of existing writings – a global reference library in every user's home – and that it offers lobbyists an excellent new means of attracting people's attention to the ideas the lobbyists want to propagate. Both of these things are valuable. The first accelerates the circulation of existing knowledge; the second helps to make people sit up and think. But neither is a substitute for what good journalism can do in telling people about a sudden change in the existing situation: in 'breaking the news'. Neither of them combines a reasonable degree of objectivity with possession of at least some of the latest information. Good journalists, whether they are using television, radio or the printed word, can in principle be a jump ahead of the Internet.

But the good journalist, in this new sort of war, will not find it easy to make that jump. Imagine a possible future war of intervention. Things go badly wrong in some troubled corner of Asia or Africa. The governments of several of the Atlantic democracies decide that this is a case for intervention. The journalists, few of them with much previous knowledge of the area, scramble to catch up. The intervention force arrives on the scene, accompanied by the journalists. The situation, as usual, turns out to be more complicated than had been expected. The journalists start to adjust their description of the matter. The intervention force meanwhile proceeds with the military operation, under pressure from the governments back home to get it over as quickly as possible. By the time the journalists have put together a fully coherent story, the whole thing may be over. The television viewers and newspaper readers will then be able to pass judgement on what has already been accomplished. But they are unlikely to have been able to give a considered opinion about what should be done, before it happens.

Then there is the third factor, the one referred to in the previous paragraph when it was said that wars of intervention generally need to be short wars. To the change in the sort of war being fought, and the change in the characteristics of the media, has to be added yet another change. Almost everywhere in Europe and America, people are now much more volatile than they used to be about the wars their countries fight. Their compassion can still be aroused by descriptions of pain and injustice in foreign places: indeed, television has found new ways of touching the distant imagination, of increasing the 'something-must-be-done' response. But at the same time Europeans and Americans have suddenly become far more reluctant to see any significant number of their young men and women die in order to stop that pain and injustice.

This is a very recent change. After the 1914–18 war it was said that the people of the democracies would not endure a repetition of the carnage of that conflict. The allies of the Second World War therefore shaped their strategy so as to limit the number of casualties they would suffer; even so, their 1939–45 losses were large, yet their people's nerve did not break. Much the same was true of the Korean War of 1950–3. The potential casualties of a nuclear exchange during the Cold War with the Soviet Union were vast, and yet the 'better-red-than-dead' argument never came close to capturing the support of a majority of people in the West. It is only in the past few years that there has been a precipitous drop in the military price the democracies seem willing to pay to win a war. Before the Gulf War, it was argued that American opinion would not stand a casualty list that would have been a great deal smaller than that of the Korean War. One moderately bloody fight was enough to push the American army out of Somalia. In Bosnia, even a few dozen casualties for a time seemed enough to dictate the policies of the governments of Britain and France.

It is a radical change, and it has already had a powerful effect on the military planning of the democracies (not least in spurring their pursuit of new technologies which can find a target and smother it with explosives from a relatively safe distance). Some of the consequences of the need to minimise casualties are going to affect the media's coverage of wars of intervention. The attempt to keep such wars as brief as possible gives the journalists little time to find out what is happening, unless the intervening army's deployment is a prolonged business, as it was in the Gulf War. The generals will probably try to keep journalists out of the fighting zone most of the time, in order to limit the number of horror stories that public opinion has to endure. Sensitivity about casualties may also be one of the reasons why many NATO countries now prefer professional armies to conscript ones, on the theory that public opinion minds volunteers getting killed less than it minds conscripts. (But the theory may not hold water, if the recent experience of the American and British armies, both all-volunteer, is anything to go by.)

Much depends on how long-lived this reluctance to pay in blood for the sort of world one believes in proves to be. It may turn out to be a fairly brief interlude, a temporary product of America's reaction to its defeat in Vietnam plus a wider American and European desire to believe that after the Cold War the democracies of the West have earned a period of relaxation. If that is so, the democracies will eventually rub their eyes and remember that there is no such thing as a price-free foreign policy. They will realise that they still have a job to do. That will, among other things, liberate the journalists to tell the story of the next century's wars as truthfully as they wish.

But it is also possible that the Atlantic democracies are going through the change of life that comes, sooner or later, to all civilisations. These countries, after all, played the leading role in the twentieth century, a century which saw two world wars, a Cold War that could have been worse than either of the hot ones, and various other conflicts which, in total, killed far more people than any previous century. At the approach of the twenty-first century, the Atlantic democracies are being told by critics in the Muslim and Confucian worlds that the ideas they believe in are of no interest to other people. Because of these things, it is possible that they no longer have the will to argue that their dream of universal democracy is of universal validity. They may be slowly withdrawing from the world. If they are, it is not only the armies of the Western world that will lose their wars-of-intervention work. So will the West's journalists.

If all this sounds rather austere, it is because in the immediate aftermath of communism's collapse it was too easy to have rosy expectations. Smaller wars, a bigger information industry, computer-carrying journalists: such a combination, it was tempting to think, would naturally be able to give the world a swifter and clearer picture of the coming generation's military conflicts. The obscurity and complexity of many of the issues that would lead to these conflicts were not properly foreseen; nor was the fact that, for all the recent growth in the efficiency of the media, there have also been changes in the structure of the media which work in the opposite direction.

Given these difficulties, the performance of the media in the past half-dozen years is better than might have been expected. The journalists of the Western world were on the whole quick to spot who was chiefly to blame for the disaster in ex-Yugoslavia – the Serbs – and the fact that NATO's eventual intervention came so disastrously late is the fault of Western governments, because they exaggerated the likely cost of intervention, rather than of the reporters on the spot. The journalists' coverage of the Gulf War was competent (partly because they had plenty of time to get ready for the fighting), despite the restrictions under which the allied armies made them work. But the media of the Atlantic world never really got to grips with the issues that led to the intervention in Somalia. They were, with a handful of exceptions, surprisingly woolly about Haiti. Their reporting of the UN operation in Cambodia was less than fully illuminating. And on what a workable intervention in Bosnia might actually consist of, as distinct from pointing a general finger of accusation at the Serbs, few of them had much of value to say.

It will be a pity if this performance does not improve. The next 20 or 30 years will be a most unusual period, in which there may take place a number of wars of justified intervention – 'justified' in the sense that they will demonstrably be undertaken for the benefit and with the approval of a majority of the people at the receiving end of the interventions, and that those against whom the military action is aimed will be by general consent aggressors and dictators. This unusual period of history is opening up because, for a time, the democracies of the Atlantic world do not have to worry about balance of power calculations. Russia is no longer in global competition with them; China is not yet a major projector of power; no other substantial adversary has emerged. So long as these things remain true, the democracies can afford a foreign policy based on moral calculation – what is good for others – as much as on self-interest.

The necessary conditions are that the democracies of Europe and America continue to see the world in much the same way as each other; that they preserve the machinery for taking joint foreign policy decisions; and that their peoples are in a position to pass judgement on what is being done in their name. It is that last condition which makes it essential for Western journalists to do a sound job when they cover wars of intervention.

20 The UN – Peace and Security: a Balance Sheet

Anthony Parsons[1]

THE YEARS OF PARALYSIS

It has become commonplace for writers on the UN to describe the Security Council as having been 'paralysed' during the Cold War decades. I read an article recently in a journal relegating the UN to a 'state of somnambulance' during the same period.

To anyone who worked in the UN between, say, 1950 (the onset of the Korean War) and 1987 (when the Permanent Members (P5) for the first time jointly drafted a resolution in the Security Council – No. 598 – designed to bring an end to seven years of war between Iran and Iraq, and President Gorbachev publicly adopted cooperation rather than competition as Soviet policy in the Security Council) these characterisations are nothing short of ludicrous.

Admittedly it was hard and protracted work, sometimes unrewarded, to secure positive results in a Security Council divided for most of the time into three parts – West, East, and Non-Aligned – and the threat or actuality of vetoes hung permanently over the proceedings. However, even the veto was less of a cause of paralysis than many commentators imagine. From its creation to mid-1996, 195 draft resolutions have been vetoed by one or more of the P5 (only three since 1990).[2] Of these, 57 were membership applications, reflecting to a great extent Cold War rivalry but scarcely a factor in the pursuit of international peace and security. In the early years, the US was able to muster enough negative votes or abstentions in the Security Council to block applications by Soviet protégés without having to resort to vetoes. The Soviet Union, lacking a blocking five votes in the pre-1963 11-member Council, had to exercise its veto repeatedly in order to reciprocate against Western sponsored membership applications. The majority of the 117 Western vetoes (against 115 by the USSR/Russian Federation) have been cast to protect negotiating positions on, for example, Southern Rhodesia and Namibia, to avoid measures being taken against South Africa or to ward off criticism by the Council of protégé states, particularly Israel in the case of the United States. These vetoes were mainly cast in the 15-member Council whose membership reflected mass decolonisation and in which the Soviet Union made a practice of following the lead of members of the Non-Aligned.

There are surprisingly few instances where a veto has made the difference between peace and war, and it should not be forgotten that the original reason for this weighted voting system was to prevent members of the P5 from ganging up, with or without non-permanent member support, against each other. I am not arguing that the P5 have not misused their special power, only that its negative impact has been less than many people think. After all, during the period 1945–87 the Security Council succeeded in adopting over 600 resolutions, many of which had a profoundly ameliorating effect on international crises, as I hope to demonstrate.

With hindsight, it is impossible to deny the contention that the existence of the veto saved the UN from disintegration or from degeneration into a clamorous but insignificant rump. Following the flood tide of decolonisation in the 1950s and 1960s, there would have been at any time the necessary nine positive votes in the 15-member Security Council for the imposition of, for example, comprehensive mandatory sanctions against Israel for failure to withdraw from the Arab territories occupied in 1967, or against South Africa for the crime of apartheid. These are two vivid examples and there are many more – demands on the US over Washington's policy towards Nicaragua under the Sandinistas in the 1980s or on the USSR over the invasion and occupation of Afghanistan in the same decade. If members of the P5 had been unable to block such propositions, would they have meekly complied with them? No. They would either have withdrawn from the UN – domestic pressure on Washington to do so over Israel would have been irresistible – or have ignored the strictures of the Council, thus reducing the enforcement provisions in Chapter VII of the Charter to a farce. This argument may not be edifying in terms of internationalist idealism but I maintain that the continuing existence of a UN constrained by the veto has been better for the world as a whole than the kind of incremental ebb-tide of leading members which drained the League of Nations in the 1930s.

Use of the veto was after all only a symptom of the termination of that brief habit of cooperation which characterised Soviet,

American and more generally, East–West relations between 1942 and 1945, the pillar on which the UN was created and which was under serious strain even before the Japanese surrender in August 1945. The core of the Charter was of course Chapter VII (Articles 39–51) dealing with threats to the peace, breaches of the peace and acts of aggression. The Charter was built on the fundamental premise that interstate war was to be outlawed as an instrument of policy (Article 2) except in self-defence (Article 51) and that military action against violators of Article 2 would be controlled by the Security Council (Article 42), with forces supplied by member states (Article 43) under the 'strategic direction' (Article 47) of the Military Staff Committee (the Chiefs of Staff of the P5). This enormous leap into an unforeseeable future – the League of Nations had explicitly recognised the right of member states to wage war – was destined for failure unless the wartime alliance continued into peacetime. It did not. Indeed, I often wonder whether the great military powers ever thought, when they first outlined Chapter VII in 1944, that the system could work. It was significant that, even as early as 1950, when the United Nations reacted to the North Korean invasion of South Korea, no attempt was made to activate the military articles of the Charter in spite of the fact that the Soviet Union was absent because of a refusal to sit down with the Nationalists representing China. The relevant Council resolution simply recommended that all military forces be put under a unified command led by the United States. Thereafter the Cold War precluded any UN authorised military enforcement action (with the still debated exception of the Congo from 1960–4) until 1990 following Saddam Hussein's seizure of Kuwait. Even in the post-Cold War euphoria a tentative attempt by the Soviet Union and Britain to invoke the military articles, or at least to activate the Military Staff Committee, was brushed aside, the United States insisting on effectively the same procedure as that adopted for Korea four decades previously, that is, Security Council authorisation of a military coalition led by the United States. The same modus operandi, with minor adaptations, was followed in Somalia (1992), Rwanda (1994) where France took the initiative, and Haiti (1995). Even in Bosnia, where an unsatisfactory 'dual key' arrangement was cobbled together between the UN and NATO, there was no mention of the Charter's potential military structure.

If the Great Powers are not prepared to try the military structure out in what must be the most favourable international atmosphere in this century, we must assume that it is for good and all a dead letter and that the principles on which it was based were, and still are, incompatible with an organisation whose bedrock was, and still is, the national sovereignty and independence of the member states: Security Council authorisation, yes: Security Council command and control, no.

This empty space at the heart of the Charter has left the Council with only one weapon of enforcement, namely mandatory economic sanctions imposed under Article 41. For reasons associated less with the Cold War than with patron/client relationships between members of the P5 and lesser powers, sanctions were very seldom applied during the first four decades, in fact only (at British initiative) against the illegal regime in Southern Rhodesia from 1966–79 plus an arms embargo against South Africa from 1977–94. In neither case were they effective. In regard to Southern Rhodesia, it is true that UN sanctions probably prevented creeping recognition of the Smith regime: they certainly did not bring about the changes of heart which led to the independence of Zimbabwe in 1980. In regard to South Africa, the arms embargo stimulated the indigenous arms industry to the extent that South Africa became a significant exporter of military equipment to states, not only Iraq, which were ready to do business with the apartheid regime.

Not surprisingly, the principal achievements of the Security Council during the decades of paralysis or somnambulance were in the domain of Chapter VI of the Charter, the 'pacific settlement of disputes', where the Council acts at best with the consent and cooperation of parties to a dispute or conflict, at worst with their minimal acquiescence. In this broad area, by far the most significant creation was 'non-threatening' military peacekeeping, a concept unforeseen by the drafters of the Charter. This began in 1948 and 1949 with unarmed observer missions to Palestine and Kashmir respectively (UNTSO and UNMOGIP) to monitor truces.[3] The first substantial armed force deployed under the peacekeeping rubric was UNEF I in Sinai which helped to maintain peace between Egypt and Israel from 1956 until the June War of 1967. The supreme irony was that UNEF I was created not by the Council but by the General Assembly since the Council was blocked by vetoes, not cast by the wicked Soviet Union which had already vetoed 76 times, but by Britain and France which were struggling to sustain their Suez Canal adventure. Other notable peacekeeping operations during the Cold War period were

ONUC in the Congo from 1960–4 which unquestionably preserved the integrity of the newly independent state which had collapsed into civil war fuelled by foreign backed separatist mercenaries. ONUC, although initially created on a 'non-threatening' basis, found itself with majority African support engaged in war fighting to suppress the civil war and to recreate the failed state. In the process, the force suffered about 250 casualties and the Secretary-General, Dag Hammarskjöld, was killed in a plane crash while visiting the operation. Notwithstanding six Soviet vetoes and much controversy amongst the Western membership, there can be no doubt that, without the intervention of the UN, today's state of Zaire would not exist. Whether or not this has been advantageous for the people inhabiting the region is not for me to say: the UN was mandated to do a job and it did it, albeit at heavy cost.

The four other major peacekeeping forces established between 1964 and 1978 were UNFICYP in Cyprus (1964), UNEF II in Sinai and UNDOF in the Golan Heights (1973 and 1974 respectively) and UNIFIL in Lebanon (1978). All except UNEF II are still in place. UNFICYP was unable to deter a full scale Turkish invasion in 1974 but its presence has tranquillised the dividing line between the two communities for over 30 years, while UNDOF has helped to maintain a Syrian/Israeli ceasefire for 22 years. UNEF II was perhaps the most spectacular peacekeeping deployment: its last minute creation at the end of the Yom Kippur War pre-empted the impending arrival on a live battlefield of American and Soviet forces on opposing sides, one of the rare occasions since 1945 when World War III seemed momentarily imminent. Thanks to the sporadic nature of the cooperation of the parties, the complexity of the internal situation in Lebanon, Israeli incursions and a major Israeli invasion in 1982, UNIFIL has been the least successful, although its presence has brought about a measure of reassurance for the unfortunate civilian population in South Lebanon.

Diplomatically, the Security Council's outstanding achievement was the unanimous adoption in 1967 of Resolution 242 on the Middle East. True, 29 years later, its provisions have been only partially implemented. But it remains the sole internationally accepted framework for a settlement of the Palestine problem and the Arab/Israeli dispute.

Perhaps the most crucial function of the UN in the Cold War era was its ability to act as a ladder down which Great Powers could climb when their national policies had led them into dangerously exposed positions. For example, in 1956, for domestic reasons, Britain and France could not have withdrawn unilaterally from the Suez Canal zone, allowing it to be reoccupied by Egypt. The deployment of UNEF I provided them with a pretext for withdrawal while maintaining a simulacrum of honour. When World War III threatened over the Cuban missile crisis of 1962, the Soviet climbdown was facilitated by an identical letter written to both heads of government by the UN Secretary-General. In 1973, the deployment of UNEF II enabled the superpowers to dismount from the high horses they were riding on behalf of their respective clients.

I could also rehearse several examples of the utility of the Secretary-General's 'good offices', the Security Council's confidential instrument of diplomacy, another Cold War invention complementing military peacekeeping: settlement of the historic Iranian claim to Bahrain in 1970 was the most striking instance.

It is true that the UN played little or no part in the 20 to 30 'liberation struggles' and post-independence civil wars (with the exception of the Congo) which accompanied decolonisation. Few of them lent themselves to international mediation or enforcement and it was easy to hide behind the Charter provision (Article 2(7)) which precludes involvement in the domestic affairs of states. On the interstate front, the most contemptible failure of the UN in my view was the supine, or rather pro-Iraqi, attitude of the Security Council over the Iran/Iraq war from 1980 to 1987. Because of Iran's international unpopularity, the Iraqi invasion was not condemned and withdrawal was called for only when Iranian counterattacks meant that it was Iranian not Iraqi withdrawal which was in question. It is not exaggerated cynicism to state that the Cold War rivals and their supporting casts were content to watch a generation of young men slaughtered and massive economic damage sustained so long as neither of two unpleasant regimes gained an outright victory.

All in all, considering that for a whole series of reasons the UN had no effective means of enforcement at its disposal; that the two most powerful countries in the world were locked in a global ideological struggle; and that massive and unanticipated decolonisation was producing fundamental change in the international configuration and the membership pattern of the organisation, the performance of the Security Council in the first four decades was remarkable for its achievements rather than its paralysis. Now that the Cold War has been over for almost a decade, it is possible to assess the consequences for the UN of the new dispensation.

THE UN IN THE 'NEW WORLD ORDER'

One of the most beneficial consequences of the end of the Cold War was the withdrawal by the Soviet Union and the United States of their unqualified support for opposing sides in so-called 'regional conflicts'. This obliged parties to review their positions and, in many cases, to demonstrate flexibility when they realised that recalcitrance would no longer be buttressed by a Great Power patron as part of a global ideological struggle. As a result, a number of hitherto intractable disputes began to unwind. South Africa ceased to obstruct Namibian independence and the procedure agreed in the Security Council in 1978 was implemented in 1990. In the same year, Nelson Mandela and his colleagues were released from prison and black political parties were unbanned. Apartheid formally died in 1994 with the first multiracial election ever to be held. In 1991, at American urging, the parties to the Arab/Israeli dispute met for the first time in Madrid in direct negotiations: halting progress towards peace continues at a snail's pace. The UN was enabled to mediate an end to bitter civil wars in El Salvador (1994), Cambodia (1993) and Mozambique (1994). None of these consummations would have come about if Soviet/American global competition had continued. It is perhaps significant that the parties in Cyprus, never an object of superpower rivalry, remain obdurate to this day.

The Security Council faced its first major post-Cold War test when Saddam Hussein invaded Kuwait in August 1990. This was a classic act of interstate aggression, precisely the type of situation for which Chapter VII of the Charter had been formulated. In previous instances, for example the many Arab/Israeli wars, India and Pakistan, the 'football war' between Honduras and El Salvador, even the Iraqi invasion of Iran in 1980 which followed Iranian subversion of southern Iraq, there had been some doubt as to who was the villain, who the victim. But here the world could witness a powerful, expansionist dictatorship invading and purporting to annex a weak, innocuous neighbour at a time when cooperation in the Security Council, not only amongst the P5, had reached a level unprecedented in the history of the UN.

The Council reacted quickly and decisively. Chapter VII was invoked, mandatory economic sanctions were buttressed by a naval and air blockade (although the actual word was not used). The stream of mandatory resolutions culminated in No. 678 of 30 November which authorised 'member states cooperating with the government of Kuwait', that is, the US and its coalition partners, to use 'all necessary means', that is, force, to 'restore international peace and security in the area', that is, liberate Kuwait. Of the P5 only China abstained, the rest voted in favour. By the end of February 1991, Operation Desert Storm was complete: Kuwait had been liberated.

The euphoria greeting this dynamic expression of international solidarity was short lived and a groundswell surged in UN circles that the US had 'hijacked' the Security Council by insisting on authorisation of the use of force, without allowing the Council to exercise any control over the coalition's military actions, even to be kept informed of the course of events until after the job was done.

However, two important precedents for the UN emerged from the Iraq/Kuwait crisis. First, the UN as an organisation, rather than member states, was put in charge of implementing the stringent sanctions regime imposed on Iraq under the ceasefire Resolution No. 687. UN teams are still working on the destruction of Saddam's aggressive military capability and other matters as he does his best to evade and to defy the constraints imposed on Iraq. Secondly, the Council adopted Resolution 688 in April 1991 (avoiding a Chinese veto by a whisker) which blew a formal hole in Charter Article 2(7) about non-involvement in domestic affairs. SCR 688, drafted in mandatory language, was the Council's reaction to Saddam's pursuit and massacre of his rebellious Kurdish subjects following Desert Storm. It condemned the repression, and demanded its cessation. It was in the spirit of this resolution, which was dressed up in transparently bogus 'international' clothes, that Iraqi Kurdistan has remained under the military protection of the US, France and Britain, with the acquiescence of the Turkish government, to the present day.

Since 1991, the Security Council, with Resolution 688 having shown the way, has moved into a zone previously alien to it (with the exception of the Congo 30 years previously), namely intervention in civil wars and the reconstruction of collapsed states, an activity in which the risk of failure is greater than in interstate conflict. Motives for this abandonment of the principle of non-intervention in domestic affairs have varied. Of the large-scale operations, an end to the civil war in El Salvador was mediated by the OAS and the UN at the insistence of the Presidents of the Central American states; Cambodia and Mozambique were rescued and rebuilt by the UN at the request of the parties; the UN/US intervention in Somalia was mainly humanitarian; Angola was (and still is) an attempt to settle unfinished Cold War business; Haiti was an American priority because of the flood of refugees arriving in Florida; the operation in the former Yugoslavia was partly humanitarian, partly strategic in motivation. In Rwanda the UN was present with a small, lightly armed peacekeeping force designed to buttress negotiations between the Rwandan government and the Uganda based Rwandese Patriotic Front before the tempest of genocide burst in the Spring of 1994.

A number of important lessons have been learnt from these experiences. Peace restoration and the rebuilding of a shattered state is a far more complex and costly business than deploying a thin blue line of lightly armed peacekeepers to separate combatants following a ceasefire in an interstate war. If the Security Council mandate is manageable on the ground, if the resources of money and manpower are adequate, if the UN has itself been involved in the formulation of a peace settlement, if, above all, the cooperation of all or most of the parties is assured, all can go well. In El Salvador, Mozambique, Cambodia (to a great extent) and Namibia, these desiderata were met and the UN operations succeeded. In Angola, in 1992, none of them had been met and the minuscule UN presence was unable to deter the loser of the elections, UNITA, from returning to the bush. In Bosnia and Somalia, the error was made of trying to combine impartial, 'non-threatening' peacekeeping and mediation with military enforcement which meant taking sides. The result in Somalia was fiasco and humiliating withdrawal in 1994 in the face of determined militia resistance; the situation in Bosnia had ultimately to be saved by vigorous American diplomacy and the interposition of a 60 000 strong NATO force in 1995. Rwanda was a disaster for the UN as the peacekeeping force withdrew and genocide followed. The thugs who had ousted the elected President of Haiti were toppled after the failure of an inadequate UN exercise and then only by an overwhelming show of American led, UN authorised force.

It has also been learnt that major military powers, in particular the United States, are reluctant to the point of refusal to commit their forces to situations where significant casualties and indefinite engagement are likely, unless there is a strong national interest (Middle East oil in the case of Desert Storm) or overwhelming public pressure (for example Somalia briefly in 1991–2 because of television reporting of the civil war induced famine). This factor militates strongly against intervention in militarily confused, politically intractable and emotionally charged civil wars.

Then there is expense. By the end of 1993, there were over 70 000 Blue Helmets and Blue Berets deployed worldwide at a cost of over \$3 billion a year, a bagatelle in relation to national defence budgets but enough to arouse the US Congress to a high temperature of denunciation.

With these factors in mind, the disposition of the Great Powers has set against further large-scale UN involvement in the types of conflict prevalent in today's world: straightforward interstate war has for the moment gone out of fashion. The tendency is to avoid intervention in civil conflict wherever possible (there are about 25 such wars going on today with UN involvement in only a handful) and to limit it to peripheral involvement with regional or subregional states being expected to do the hard work of armed peace-keeping or enforcement. This modus operandi has been adopted with the creation of small UN missions in Liberia and in certain of the former Soviet republics – Georgia and Tadjikistan – which erupted in civil conflict after the disintegration of the USSR in 1991. This tactic gives international validity and a measure of respectability to the so-called 'peacekeeping' of West African states in Liberia and of the Russian Federation in the southern republics.

The essence of the problem is as follows. Although, in the present international climate, the Council can pass far more resolutions and deploy far more blue-helmeted forces with far wider mandates than it could in the 'bad old days', the instruments at its disposal are no more effective than before. There is no sign of the UN developing into a global collective security institution: the membership is as nationally minded – perhaps more so with the decline of any sense of post-imperial responsibility – as ever and rich countries are mired in a quagmire of opposition to public expenditure on international causes. Persuasion (Chapter VI) has its limitations and, although continuing sanctions have neutralised Saddam Hussein's warlike proclivities, they have not in general proved much more effective than in the days of Southern Rhodesia and apartheid. Arms embargoes on Somalia, Liberia, UNITA in Angola and Haiti have done or did nothing to decrease levels of violence. In the former Yugoslavia, the arms embargo of 1991 handicapped the victim (the Bosnian Muslims) leaving the aggressor (the Bosnian Serbs) untouched. Sanctions may well have turned President Milosevic of Serbia from being the standard-bearer of Greater Serbia into a man of peace, but only after 200 000 deaths, 2 to 3 million people displaced and all the horrors of ethnic cleansing. Sanctions against Libya have not led to the handover to Scottish justice of the Lockerbie suspects.

As the millennium approaches I anticipate more of the same, notwithstanding the blizzard of reports and recommendations which accompanied the 50th anniversary of the organisation. If there is no change of heart in Washington, the largest contributor and debtor to the UN, financial stringency will combine with lack of political will to hamstring the launch of fresh operations except on a small scale on the lines of Liberia, Georgia and Tadjikistan. The UN will continue to be a unique asset which it comes to mediating disputes which the parties genuinely wish to settle but cannot if left to themselves. Perhaps the tendency of the Great Powers to which I have referred will serve to strengthen the mediating and, in the last resort, enforcement capabilities of regional and subregional organisations from the OAS across the globe to ASEAN. Even the Russians have allowed the OSCE a little latitude within the borders of the Russian Federation in Chechnya – something unthinkable under the USSR.[4]

This is part of a new trend which encourages me more than any other. In the Cold War days, the superpowers acted first and either ignored the UN or vetoed criticism – the USSR in Hungary in 1956, Czechoslovakia in 1968 and Afghanistan in 1979; the United States in Central America and the Caribbean (Guatemala in 1954, Nicaragua in the 1980s, Grenada in 1983, Panama in 1989). The Americans and their allies could have mounted Operation Desert Storm in 1990–1 on the simple basis of Kuwait's right of 'collective self-defence' under Charter Article 51, without reference to the Security Council. But great trouble was taken to construct an elaborate edifice of Security Council resolutions to validate every step taken. The same was true in Somalia, Haiti, Bosnia and all the other crisis areas which I have mentioned in this essay including the brief French intervention in Rwanda. A habit is growing which is bound to act as a restraining influence on states so powerful that they do not need international backing for their actions. This may seem a small step, but it is certainly one taken in the right direction.

NOTES

1. A fuller factual account of the disputes/conflicts mentioned in this chapter can be found in my book *From Cold War to Hot Peace* (Parsons, 1995). [This chapter was completed in August 1996 and is thus one of the last pieces of writing finalised by Sir Anthony Parsons – Ed.]
2. A summary of Security Council resolutions and a table of vetoed draft resolutions can be found in Foreign and Commonwealth Research and Analysis Department memoranda both dated January 1994.
3. UN peacekeeping forces:

UNEF	United Nations Emergency Force
ONUC	United Nations Operation in the Congo
UNTSO	United Nations Truce Supervision Organisation
UNMOGIP	UN Military Observer Group in India and Pakistan
UNFICYP	UN Peacekeeping Force in Cyprus
UNDOF	UN Disengagement Observer Force
UNIFIL	UN Interim Force in Lebanon

4.

OAS	Organisation of American States
OSEAN	Organisation of South East Asian Nations
OSCE	Organisation for Security and Cooperation in Europe

BIBLIOGRAPHY

Parsons, A., *From Cold War to Hot Peace*, London: Michael Joseph/Penguin, 1995.

21 An Ethical Framework — Or Just Intervention?

Roger Williamson

We live in a new situation following the end of the Cold War, characterised by the following elements. The threat of nuclear holocaust has receded (Mueller, 1995) but violence within societies takes many forms (Hoffman and McKendrick, 1990), including ethnic and religious forms (Williamson, 1990; 1991). Nearly all current major armed conflicts are internal conflicts of low intensity (van Creveld, 1996:91) – not the troops of country A fighting country B. This is borne out in the Yearbook of the Stockholm International Peace Research Institute (SIPRI) which – over the last ten years – has regularly documented about 30 current major armed conflicts (involving more than 1000 battle deaths in the duration of the conflict). With few exceptions these are internal conflicts. The UN is ill equipped by its member states to deal with internal conflicts, but will be blamed if it does not do so. Most of the killing is done with non-major, portable weapon systems, such as machine guns, sniper rifles, mortars and landmines. Yet arms control focuses primarily on major weapon systems. Indeed: 'something must be done'.

THE HUMANITARIAN DIMENSION

Relief agencies are not constrained as much as states, and much of the work of humanitarian relief – including cross-border humanitarian relief work – can better be done by those not constrained by the 'rules of the game' involved in being a nation state in the community of nation states. There is clearly a humanitarian imperative to try to help wherever this is possible. In recent years, one has the impression that the taboo on attacking and killing aid workers and Red Cross/Red Crescent personnel has not been as effective as previously. Total warfare has, in many situations, engulfed the humanitarian imperative. I have been deeply impressed by returning British army officers describing in detail the work with which they were involved in the former Yugoslavia in ensuring that aid was delivered. This indicates that, even if one speaks of military intervention, it is necessary to do so with precision. Talking aid convoys through the road blocks of different factions to reach starving people and preventing any attempt to loot the convoy is one thing, trying to hunt down Aideed in Somalia quite another. The dynamics of the relationship between humanitarian NGOs and armed intervention by the UN or individual governments is a complex area requiring further analysis.[1] One serious problem in effectively protecting the maximum number of lives, whether through humanitarian aid by NGOs, 'humanitarian intervention' by the international community, or by direct armed force to overthrow or repel armed forces (whether government or non-government) is that those with power always have a vested interest in how the history is written and assessed. Concluding his lengthy review of recent literature, Farrell says:

> At the end of the day, political will, not knowledge, is the main obstacle to learning from humanitarian intervention. The books reviewed..., and the work of area specialists elsewhere, contain within them sufficient knowledge about past failures to draw accurate and useful lessons for future interventions. But UN member states, and the UN Secretary-General [referring specifically to Boutros-Ghali's presentation of the Somalia situation], have political reasons for seeing things differently.
>
> (Farrell, 1997:163)

THEOLOGICAL INSIGHTS FOR THE ETHICS OF INTERVENTION

The book of Genesis reminds us that human history is the history of Cain, of brother killing brother. 'Brother killing...' is description rather than sexist language in this genocidal and fratricidal century. It is mainly men who are the soldiers. But brother killing brother is not accurate as a description of today's wars: it is overwhelmingly civilian women and children (cf. Machel, 1996) who are the casualties – either through death or injury, the use of rape as an instrument of war (Gnanadason, 1993), or eviction as with the more than 20 million who have crossed an internationally recognised boundary (according to the United Nations High

Commissioner for Refugees) or at least as many others who are internally displaced.

The most convincing basis for a theology of intervention has been provided by Fred van Iersel, a Roman Catholic military chaplain in the Netherlands (van Iersel, 1995). It centres around the concept of *Stellvertretung* (derived from Bonhoeffer's *Ethics*), meaning 'standing in' for others in a representative capacity (Bonhoeffer, 1965:224 ff.). I have developed the following summary from van Iersel's central insight. In this context the representative function can be described as follows. Under Article 51 of the UN Charter a state has a right to self-defence in the event of being attacked. In extreme circumstances, like military occupation, tyranny or genocide, a people is unable to exercise that right effectively. The international community then has a *duty* to ensure that they create conditions whereby reasonably good government can be restored. In situations of occupation, the occupiers should be removed. In situations of genocide, a government committing massive and systematic violation of human rights should be removed and deprived of the capacity to do it again. In Biblical terms – for example the story of the Good Samaritan – communal victims must be put back into a position where they 'look after themselves' or 'stand on their own two feet'. Unfortunately, this theological framework which I have sketched seems to create obligations and duties which go far beyond what is politically realistic. It could be more readily accepted as a framework of obligations for the Christian community to provide aid to far-off contexts of suffering, than as showing why a nation state has a duty to provide military intervention into a far-off country.

JUST INTERVENTION

In general terms, I suggest that the just war framework once again stands the test of time and changed circumstances. Like everything human, it is open to abuse and manipulation. One of the clearest systematic attempts to spell out the right or even duty of intervention in an authoritative way is the statement by the US Roman Catholic Bishops' Conference *The Harvest of Justice is Sown in Peace* (US Bishops, 1993). On the subject of humanitarian intervention they define and outline five concerns. The point of departure for these considerations is Pope John Paul II's statement urging that:

humanitarian intervention be obligatory where the survival of populations and entire ethnic groups is seriously compromised. This is a duty for nations and the international community.

(US Bishops, 1993:460)

The Pope has also stressed that states do not have 'a right to indifference'. The US Bishops then outline their five points:

1   First, human life, human rights and the welfare of the human community are at the center of Catholic moral reflection on the social and political order. Geography and political divisions do not alter the fact that we are all one human family, and indifference to the suffering of members of that family is not a moral option.
2   Second, sovereignty and nonintervention into the life of another state have long been sanctioned by Catholic social principles, but have never been seen as absolutes...
3   Third, nonmilitary forms of intervention should take priority over those requiring the use of force...
4   Fourth, military intervention may sometimes be justified to ensure that starving children can be fed or that whole populations will not be slaughtered.
5   Finally, a right to intervene must be judged in relation to the broader effort to strengthen international law and the international community.

(US Bishops, 1993:461)

SOME DIFFICULTIES IN APPLYING THE JUST WAR CRITERIA

I will conclude with some further ideas about which I want to reflect more deeply in trying to apply the just war criteria to just intervention. The application of the just war theory to armed intervention is a less ambitious programme than the attempt to formulate an ethical approach to international relations, and probably more likely to succeed.[2]

(1) *Last resort* is problematic. What does it mean? The best time to intervene militarily is early, not for example after sanctions have been tried for a considerable time and then adjudged to have failed. Military advice might be given: 'Put in a preventive peacekeeping force before the killing starts'. But how can you convince anyone

that it is necessary? No killing – no crisis, no crisis – no peace-keeping force. Is the term 'last resort' one of escalation of means or passage of time? Is *'ultima ratio'* (in Latin) about the *'äußerste Mittel'* or *'letzte Mittel'* (in German) – the most serious means or the last means in terms of time?

(2) *Proportionality*: We should be under no illusions, peace enforce-ment means *war*. The traditional understanding of peacekeeping requires the consent of the conflicting parties and creates a buffer keeping them apart. We need more study of the possibilities. There are coercive non-violent measures such as sanctions, diplomatic disapproval, non-supply of weapons. But these have consequences. There is no area of human life free from dilemmas. Sanctions can kill as well as bullets – but with less discrimination (as Oliver O'Donovan has shown in Chapter 7).

(3) *Right intention*: 'The path to hell is paved with good intentions.' Democracy is a good form of government, but, as we have been reminded, the popularity of a policy is no guarantee of its correct-ness. We should treat the saying *'vox populi, vox Dei'* with suspicion. The voice of the people – particularly when filtered through the mass media – is not the voice of God. But we should also be suspicious if we, as those who try to divine the voice of God, come up with policies which are so moral as to be impractical or involve other people making sacrifices for *our* ethical principles.

This raises questions about the media and the manufacture of public opinion and consent. There can be no doubt that TV helps to create and destroy the political possibilities for military interven-tion by democracies. This has good and bad effects and requires deeper understanding.

Intervention, if done, should be done because it is right not because it is popular. But if it is very unpopular, it cannot be done – at least by a democracy.

(4) *Legitimate authority*: I am unhappy at the selectivity with which UN Security Council resolutions are implemented. Palestinian friends, Christian and Muslim, argue as follows: Kuwait was occu-pied and within six months the world assembled a massive military force to expel Saddam Hussein. Palestinians wait for 25 years and more, but receive little help in ensuring that UN Security Council Resolution 242 is implemented. The arms supplies to Israel con-tinue. There has been little in the way of withdrawal even from the territory occupied after the 1967 war. For the UN to carry convic-tion as the 'legitimate authority' to authorise armed intervention –

and to carry conviction, above all in the Muslim world – it must be seen to be impartial and consistent in the application of international law.

Investigation of some of the complex facets of the possibility of 'just intervention' in a military sense has been the purpose of this book and an urgent task not exhausted by the contributions presented here.

NOTES

1. See the review by Theo Farrell (1997) of the following books:

    Whitman, J., and Pocock, D. (eds.), *After Rwanda: The Coordination of United Nations Humanitarian Assistance*, London: Macmillan, 1996.
    Ramsbotham, O. and Woodhouse, T., *Humanitarian Intervention in Contemporary Conflict*, Oxford: Polity, 1996.
    Mayall, J. (ed.), *The New Interventionism 1991–1994: United Nations Experience in Cambodia, Former Yugoslavia, and Somalia*, Cambridge: Cambridge University Press, 1996.
    Harriss, J., (ed.), *The Politics of Humanitarian Intervention*, London: Pinter, 1995.
    United Nations, *The United Nations and Somalia 1992–1996*, New York: United Nations, 1996.
    International Federation of Red Cross and Red Crescent Societies, *World Disasters Report*, Oxford: Oxford University Press, 1996.

    The review article is important for a number of its central contentions, particularly highlighting the problems associated with calling a military intervention a humanitarian intervention.
2. Mervyn Frost has made a serious attempt to outline an entire theory in *Ethics in International Relations* (Frost, 1996:104–36).

BIBLIOGRAPHY

Bonhoeffer, D., *Ethics*, New York: Macmillan, 1965.
Farrell, T., Review of *After Rwanda* (Whitman and Pocock, eds.) and five other books, in: *International Affairs*, Vol. 73, No. 1, January 1997, 161–3. (For full listing of books, see Note 1.)
Frost, M., *Ethics in International Relations: A Constitutive Theory*, Cambridge: Cambridge University Press, 1996.
Gnanadason, A., *No Longer a Secret: The Church and Violence against Women*, Geneva: World Council of Churches, 1993.
Hoffman, W. and McKendrick, B.W., 'The Nature of Violence', in: McKendrick and Hoffman, 1990: 2–35.

Machel, G., *Impact of Armed Conflict on Children: Report of the expert of the Secretary-General, Ms. Graça Machel*, submitted pursuant to General Assembly resolution 48/157, New York & Geneva: United Nations, A/51/306, 26 August 1996.

McKendrick, B. and Hoffmann, W., *People and Violence in South Africa*, Cape Town: Oxford University Press, 1990.

Mueller, J., *Quiet Cataclysm: Reflections on the Recent Transformation of World Politics*, New York: HarperCollins, 1995.

US Bishops, 'The Harvest of Justice is Sown in Peace', in: *Origins*, 9 Dec. 1993, Vol. 23, No. 26, 449–60.

Van Creveld, M., 'New Wars for Old', in: The Economist, *The World in 1997*, London: Economist, 1996, 91.

Van Iersel, F., 'Going beyond Victimisation: a Way out of the Dilemma between Justice and Peace?', in: Wicker and Van Iersel, 1995, 41–77.

Wicker, B. and Van Iersel, F. (eds.), *Humanitarian Intervention and the Pursuit of Justice: A Pax Christi Contribution to a Contemporary Debate*, Kok Pharos: Kampen, 1995.

Williamson, R., 'Why is Religion Still a Factor in Armed Conflict?' *Bulletin of Peace Proposals*, Vol. 21, No. 3, September 1990, 243–53.

Williamson, R. (ed.), *The Role of Religion in Conflict Situations*, Limassol, Cyprus: Middle East Council of Churches, 1991.

Index

Index of Bibilical References